Speaking
for the Oldie

Speaking for the Oldie

NAIM ATTALLAH

QUARTET BOOKS

First published by Quartet Books Limited 1994
A member of the Namara Group
27 Goodge Street
London W1P 1FD

Edited extracts of the interviews in this book first appeared in *The Oldie*

A catalogue record for this title is available from the British Library

ISBN 0 7043 7091 3

Typeset by Contour Typesetters, Southall, London
Printed and bound in Great Britain by
Bookcraft (Bath) Ltd, Avon

CONTENTS

PREFACE

Speaking for The Oldie speaks, as it were, for itself: a collection of some fifteen interviews which I conducted for the fortnightly magazine edited by Richard Ingrams. While some have yet to appear therein, all are published here in full and not in the necessarily abridged format seen in *The Oldie*.

The present volume, however, was very nearly a *memento mori*. A combination of critical circumstances all too common in the crowded market-place of magazine publishing almost led to *The Oldie's* closure. Inquests began, N.H.S. Thribb (aged 17½) bade it farewell in *Private Eye* and in certain trendy quarters there was a predictably unseemly enthusiasm for the wake. Nevertheless, at the eleventh hour an ingenious proposal of imaginative compromise served to guarantee the periodical's survival as a monthly pleasure, and *The Oldie* confounded its obituarists to the great relief and evident delight of its growing number of friends.

DIANA ATHILL

DIANA ATHILL

Diana Athill was born in 1917 and spent her childhood in Norfolk. She went to Oxford in 1936 to read English at Lady Margaret Hall and throughout the war was employed by the BBC in London. She was a founding member of André Deutsch Ltd and remained a director until she was seventy. She is the author of several books including two based on actual experience: *After a Funeral* and *Make Believe*, but she is best known for her essay in autobiography, *Instead of a Letter*, which was considered by the *Washington Post* to be among the 'few totally honest accounts of human life'.

You had a comfortable, privileged family background with which you have been uneasy for most of your life. When did you first start to question the notion of privilege and what you call your family's 'smug assumption of superiority'?

At school, where I had a splendid old headmistress of the liberal tradition. She was determined to make her girls think and she used to leave newspapers of every kind on the table in the hall, and we were very much encouraged to read them. I was a child at a time when it was very difficult not to question what was going on. It was a time of the most awful depression and unemployment, and if you had any intelligence at all you began to ask questions. I never really felt uneasy at home because I always loved my parents dearly but I knew that I didn't think the same way they did. I rather wish that I had rebelled, but in those days it was somehow unthinkable, so I just quietly slipped underground.

Your childhood memories are very rich and happy, and I have the impression from reading your autobiography that this derived at least in part from the comfort and security in which you grew up. Would you agree?

Yes, but I think that there were certain elements of insecurity. For example, my parents quarrelled a lot. Of course it would have been much worse if we had been living on top of each other in a very small house in some miserable place, but as it was we lived in the country with space round us, with nannies who were loving and comforting. When my brother and I were stressed a bit by my father and mother, I remember my governess telling us that our parents were both very nice people but they probably shouldn't have married each other. And we accepted that as a kind of formula which steered us into a calm way of thinking about the situation. Things improved between them towards the end of their marriage. My mother – who had fallen in love with someone else but had been unable to leave because of the children – gradually came to recognize that my father was an extraordinarily nice person, an honourable and good man who hadn't punished her for trying to bolt.

Your family displayed disdain and distrust of anyone who was not of their class, and you say how strange it was to be bound by ties of habit and love

3

to people who were like that. Do you think it is ever possible to untie the bonds, to remove the early influences entirely?

I'm not sure that I do. It would have been interesting if I had been more openly rebellious, if I had simply taken friends home in spite of my parents' disapproval on grounds of their colour, for example. But I used to think, what would be the point, because it would be horrible for everybody. It might have broken relations completely, but on the other hand it might have educated them into being less prejudiced than they were. I shall never know, but at the time I chose not to put too much strain on our relationship, because of my affection for them all.

You say that their attitude was at best comic, at worst repulsive. What effect did it all have on you in later life?

I suppose it gave me a prejudice in the opposite direction. As I grew up I automatically veered towards people who were of a quite different class and nationality. I have always got on better with people who are not Norfolk county.

Although you say you liked your father, it seems to have fallen short of love. Do you understand the reasons for this?

He was not a man who easily expressed emotion. He rarely hugged or kissed his children, and I think I picked up from my mother, without realizing it, her reservations about him. I remember once when he was getting quite old, and he was beginning to suspect that he had a bad heart, he spoke to me about my grandmother who was very ill at the time. He mentioned death, and I imagined we were going to talk intelligently and without restraint, so I answered him in a way that showed I was interested in the subject; and he just froze. He suddenly realized he was much too frightened to talk about death. In the same way he was too shy to talk about love.

Your parents seem to have been physically incompatible . . . your mother hated sleeping with him. You sided with your mother in this unhappy situation. Why did you not feel sorry for your father? After all it must have been difficult for him . . .

Because if one goes back to one's childhood one simply was at that time more instinctively on her side. I did come to feel very sorry for him, and after my mother's death, when I was reading some of his letters to her, I could have cried for him. He was so unquestioning, and he apologized to her for being unattractive to her, which was dreadful because he wasn't an unattractive man at all.

As you got older, you came to see your father as an intelligent and an agreeable man, and yet you never felt closely bound to him . . . why not, I wonder, and what effect did this have in your own adult relationships?

I honestly don't know why we weren't close, except that his work took him away a lot and we were more with our mother in our infancy. She was the physical presence, and in that sense easier to love. The obvious consequence was that if ever I fell in love it was always with someone as unlike him as possible; I never fell in love with anyone who had blue eyes, fair skin, fair hair, because I saw these features as unattractive. It was an instinctive thing, and it was a long time before I noticed it.

Sex was a distasteful subject in your family, and yet you seemed to have a strong interest in it. Do you think the two factors were related?

I don't think so. My parents were too reserved about sex to be repressive about it, so one was free to read and so on. Largely because they were so reserved they left the whole subject alone; one wasn't told it was revolting or anything like that, it was just something not talked about.

You seem not to have agonized much about giving up God and the Church. Why were they so easily dismissed, do you think?

Again because of the mildness of the background. It was the custom to go to church, and darling granny read us lovely bible stories which we enjoyed, but there was no great morality surrounding it. The chief thing one was told was that God loved everybody and understood everything, and whatever one thought, whatever one did, God understood it. I remember thinking, well if God understands, He can understand that I don't believe in Him. This nice kind English Christian God was not difficult to go against. Later on when I looked at the world and all the different stories people have told to try and explain themselves and life, each one struck me as more absurd than the last. Why should we, little grains of dust, know what is the truth? Why do we feel that we ought to know? How can we possibly believe that we are capable of knowing the meaning, whatever the meaning is, if indeed there is a meaning? It's extraordinary how religious people say to me, 'I don't understand how you can live without a faith, because then there's no meaning in life.' What meaning are they talking about? To me it seems that one simply cannot hope to know how this thing we belong to works, but I don't see why one should be depressed about that.

You went up to Oxford in 1936 and lived, in Stephen Spender's phrase, 'in the shadow of war'. How much did that occupy your mind?

You couldn't pretend that it wasn't going to happen. You could see it coming and we all went to meetings about it and thought about it. On the other hand university life carried on and we managed to have a lot of fun. My feeling was, get in as much good time as possible before it happens.

There is very little in your biography about what you thought about the war, how it affected you. Was that an accidental or deliberate omission?

For me the war was a period of great blankness; there wasn't really much to say about it except in a flat and miserable way. If one wasn't directly involved, one felt very dead about it. It would have been different if I'd been in the forces, but I was leading a quiet little civilian life in the BBC, knowing what was going on because I worked for the newsroom, but not influenced except by the dreariness.

You say that you owe to Oxford the fact that you were able to live through twenty years of unhappiness without coming to dislike life. What did Oxford give you to make that possible?

It gave me wonderful friends, it gave me an esteem and an understanding of achievement and intelligence. It gave me lots and lots of books, a good deal of self-confidence, but chiefly it gave me a comfortable sense that beauty existed in spite of everything.

In those days you were preoccupied by the thought of losing your virginity. Do you think that applied to most young women at Oxford in those days?

It certainly applied to most of my friends. The twenties had been the first sort of breaking loose period, and by the thirties we were able to have a love affair if we felt like it, instead of having to think about it.

But when the moment came it was a profound disappointment. Do you think that was inevitable in a sense?

It was not a profound disappointment, it was just not as good as I thought it would be; but I still knew it was going to be all right quite soon. 'Profound' makes it sound traumatic, but it was more a question of, oh yes, well never mind, we'll soon get this going all right. Much more practical.

Would you say that the greatest satisfaction and joy of sex come from experience of life and love rather than the vigour and energy of youth?

Yes, I think I would, though I'm not sure whether many men would agree. I think that tenderness becomes a very important element as one gets older, but it may well be that we comfort ourselves by thinking this is the case. When I was younger I had affairs because they provided good sex, and I enjoyed them for that reason, and they certainly weren't horrid because of that. But the times that I remember as important in my life are those when love was involved as well.

The person to whom you promised your love and your life was killed in the war, but before that he had broken off your engagement – something from which perhaps you never fully recovered. Do you still think of that time now?

Diana Athill

The fact that I wrote about Paul tidied up that time as far as I was concerned. I still regard it as the most important thing that happened to me, because it did dreadful damage to my self-confidence for a very long time, and to that extent it changed me quite fundamentally. But it doesn't occupy my mind any more . . . the writing was very therapeutic.

You described your unhappiness as a 'taint' as well as a misfortune – you were somehow 'diseased' in other people's eyes. That must have made things even harder to bear . . .

It was a horrible feeling – how much of it was subjective I don't know – but it was dreadful. I felt I had been written off by everyone as a failure, utterly useless.

Do you think you indulged your state of unhappiness, that you were prey to self-pity?

No, I don't. I think I did as much as I possibly could to pull myself out of it.

Do you think in cases of this kind the impact on women is much harder than it is on men?

I can't say, because I haven't known any man who has suffered a loss like that. Certainly in those days, marriage for a woman was equivalent to a job; it wasn't just a love affair, it settled your future, you were to be so and so's wife for the rest of your days. So when that fell away you had your future cut right off, as well as losing your man. No man would have been in that position.

Looking back, would you have preferred simply to have bounced back, or has the experience been, however painful, enriching in some ways?

Just bouncing back would have made it such a different experience. The fact was I had it, I survived it, and I feel lucky that not much harm was done to me in the long run.

How long was it before you stopped equating love with pain?

In the sense that I avoided falling in love, it was a very long time indeed. The next time that I was happy in a love affair was when I was in my early forties. I'd had affairs, but I had avoided commitments, and it wiped out marriage as far as I was concerned.

You say that for years and years the most intense emotion you experienced was pain. What would you say is the most intense emotion you experience now?

Now that I'm 76, I have rather got out of the way of having emotions. There are lots of very agreeable things, like learning to draw and going to life classes, and other activities which are tremendously interesting, but I wouldn't say I have intense emotions now. I'm contented in a quiet way rather than happy, but I did have about ten years of positive happiness, which is a long time in anybody's life.

After the break-up there followed a period of promiscuity when as a comfort you slept with just about any man who asked you to . . . how do you think it was possible to go against your background and upbringing so fundamentally?

I honestly don't know. All I can say is that I did, and I think a lot of people have done. Once you decide you don't believe in what has been preached at home, then you're free to do what you want to do. I don't think it's mystifying really. The world does seem to be divided into people who grow up following the patterns they are given, and people who grow up questioning them; and I was one of the latter.

Did the one night stand never lead to guilt, to feelings that one had behaved badly perhaps?

I suppose just occasionally, particularly if it was someone with whom it had been a great mistake. It's difficult to remember, but occasionally one got into a silly situation simply out of being polite, not wanting to say no, and then one would feel bad. But I never really had much time for guilt.

*You describe these brief affairs as 'threadbare rags against a cold wind'.
Were they really better than no rags at all?*

Oh yes, no question about it. When you're younger you need it. Now that
I'm 76 the sexual impulse is no longer there – in fact several things have
gone which before I couldn't have imagined doing without in my life. For
example, I can't drink coffee any more, or wine or whisky. Now that they
disagree with me I have not the slightest wish to drink, not even if I am
offered a beautiful malt whisky which was once my favourite tipple. And
sex is rather the same. Once you stop wanting something you don't mind
not having it, and life becomes very much simpler and easier. There was an
intervening time when I could see things falling away, and that was sad
because all this had meant so much to me and had been so lovely, but once I
was over the hump I felt free. If someone came along to make love to me
now, I'd say, please go away, it's not anything to do with me any more. It
is very peaceful.

But is it because the desire is no longer there?

Yes, and so you don't want it. I know one woman who was much older
than me and she used to say, oh what nonsense, one goes on having desire
forever. Well, perhaps she did, but I think that she imagined that she ought
to, whereas if you actually listen to your body, you just let it go . . .

When did your body tell you to stop?

It was a slowish process, but by the time I was at the end of my 60s I was
clear of it. I had an Indian summer during my 50s and early 60s, but once it
went, it went. I had a very attractive friend whom I loved dearly and hardly
ever saw, and whenever he came to England it was always a delight to go to
bed with him. And one time I thought, well, I don't actually want to do
this, that's it over. That was in my mid or late 60s.

*When you were 26 you met André Deutsch, a man who was to shape the
rest of your life. You left your job at the BBC to join him in publishing . . .
have you ever had cause to regret that decision?*

Never. It was easily the most interesting and agreeable career I could imagine, although when I finally left it I was thankful to get out. Our kind of publishing was having such a terribly hard time. It was being battered from all sides. André had got out smartly before I did, and I remember his saying, 'You know, it's not any fun any more.' I had to go on because I hadn't got any money, but in the years after André sold the firm it became worse and worse.

You were both very different in character, and yet you were strangely drawn to one another. Was this on the basis that opposites attract, do you think?

I suppose it was. We worked well together because we both had quite different aptitudes. And it became one of those curious relationships, rather like in a family, when we were both very aware of each other's shortcomings, but just accepted them.

You describe your intimacy as being more fraternal than anything else. Why do you think it did not develop in the normal way?

I really don't know. André was very romantic as a young man, and I was very down to earth and realistic; I was annoyed by his romanticism and he was annoyed with me being practical. We didn't fit in that way. Sexually we didn't gel at all.

In due course you won the Observer short story competition, which seemed to give you a much needed boost . . . or do you think it would have happened in any case with the passage of time?

I don't think it would have happened to quite the same extent. Winning that prize was a wonderful bonus. It really did give me such a push up.

As you recount it, as soon as you stopped actively searching for love, or expecting to be loved, you immediately fell in love and were loved in return. Was it really as simple as that?

It almost was. It wasn't like a love affair to begin with, it was just great affection and great interest, and a feeling of how nice it was to have found someone to be with and go to bed with. It was much happier than any of my earlier experiences, because I never ever believed it would end.

Your work in publishing allowed you to meet all kinds of people whom otherwise you would not have encountered. Were you always aware of the dangers of vicarious living?

Although my sexual self-confidence had been damaged, I think that at bottom the security that came from childhood was always there, so that I never really felt that anybody else's world was better than mine.

You became involved with an Egyptian writer who came to live with you and ended up some five years later committing suicide in your flat. Had your early painful experience with Paul equipped you in some measure to deal with the horror of that situation?

No, this was utterly different; it belonged to a separate part of my nature. During the time I knew Paul I would never have become involved with neurotic people – I would have been too frightened – whereas at a later stage I was definitely attracted to dangerous and damaged people. Twice I formed relationships with men who were a bit mad, and I found them extremely interesting. My own explanation of it is that some sort of frustrated maternal impulse was at work, and that made me want to take these people on and help them in some way.

You are known to believe that sex and the maternal impulse are very closely woven in childless women of middle age. Did you regard that as a weakness or did you feel that it opened up opportunities?

It opened up opportunities, but it certainly trapped me in some curious situations, though I don't think I minded much.

Your relationship with Hakim, the black American friend of Malcolm X, is described in terms of a kind of madness. Would you say that falling in love is always a kind of madness to some degree?

I was really half joking when I said that about Hakim – I wasn't enough in love with him for it to be a good example of madness. But I do think that falling in love tends to be neurotic, because it has very little to do with the person you're drawn to; it has more to do with your own needs, your own hang ups. I'm very disrespectful of the idea of falling in love. People get into terrible messes because they get married to a person they've invented and then they are furious when the man or woman turns out to be different.

Have you ever been able to pinpoint what has attracted you to a man?

No, I think it's entirely mysterious, and I'm very glad that there is still some mystery left in life. Apart from the fact that they've always been dark-eyed, dark-haired, sometimes dark-skinned, they've been very different people. When it clicks, one recognizes it at once.

You speak of the alarming power of beauty in relation to Hakim. In what sense was it alarming?

I meant that if one had felt it strongly and had fallen in love with this person because of his appearance, one would have been lost, so to speak, because he wasn't the person he looked. His looks would have led you into being obsessed with somebody who was not worth loving.

You were on the face of it an unlikely person to become involved in the turbulence and violence of other people's lives. Was it partly the attraction of the world outside the safety of the publishing house?

Yes, it was seeing another kind of world, rather like reading some fascinating book. I was experiencing vicariously a completely different way of living, which expanded my own sense of life. I thought it was rather a good thing.

Diana Athill

You have resisted the temptation to dress up the narrative in your books, even when it means you are placed in a less than flattering light. Why this break with convention?

If you're going to write about an actual experience, there's only one reason to do it, and that is to understand it as far as possible. If you're going to be honest about other people, the least you can do is to try to be equally honest about yourself. If I had whitewashed myself I would have produced a very peculiar artefact which would have been of no use to anybody. I was never tempted to censor anything because at the time of writing I did not imagine that either book would be published – indeed they both went into drawers for about twenty years. They were written as exercises to deal with a sadness; in the end they were terrible things to have seen, these tragedies, and they were haunting and worrying. They were written as therapy, and I have felt slightly embarrassed about both of them ever since because they were not intended for publication.

Did the therapy work?

It has worked for me, and I think this is why I'm not writing now, because I have nothing I want to cure myself of.

In Instead of a Letter *you describe the business of writing as 'hardly more than a private satisfaction'. That makes it sound like a self-indulgence. Is it, do you think?*

It is more something that I've been driven to. Self-indulgence sounds too much like fun, but it's not particularly fun. It's fascinating and totally absorbing, but I did it because I felt the need.

When one reads your books there is a element of shockingness about them . . . are you pleased with this effect?

I'm rather surprised by it . . . and yes, perhaps a little bit pleased.

Somehow your middle-class respectability, your quintessential Englishness

14

makes the candour and detail of the writing all the more outrageous. Was this something you were consciously aiming at?

No, I was aiming at writing accurately. The important thing always was to try and get it the way it really was.

Did you ever come to feel embarrassed by anything you've written?

Not nearly as much as you would expect. My dear relations and friends think I've written shockingly embarrassing books, which sometimes makes me feel a bit shy, but then I think, well to hell with it, what can I do about it? Whenever I've had a temptation to feel embarrassed I've said to myself, look, you wrote the damned thing, you'd better stick with it.

You are prompted to write by the desire to make sense of something which has happened to you. Do you believe that your writing is in any sense instructive, that others can learn from your experience?

I would not have thought so, but the fact remains that I still get letters about *Instead of a Letter* from people who nearly always say that what I describe is so like what happened to them. They then go on to describe situations which sound to me completely alien. Indeed the most extraordinary people have claimed that their experiences are the same. Years and years ago I had a letter from a lovely lesbian dentist who had hundreds of miserable affairs, and I remember thinking, what makes her believe her life is similar to mine? But the fact is she did.

What are your views on marriage? Do you regret not having married?

No, not at all now. I'm perfectly content and have been for many a long year. I know in my own family some very happy marriages, and I think that if you have the luck to get into that kind of relationship, it must be the best there is. But very few people do.

Writing in 1963 you said: 'It's unlikely that I shall ever have a child.'

15

That sounded like an anguished thought at the time. Has it been a major source of regret?

It was at one time quite a serious source of regret, yes. But that's died away. It's eased over the years, and I waste no time thinking about it now.

Later in life you seemed to suggest that the people you fell in love with were rather helpless and vulnerable and in that sense were perhaps the children you never had. Is that still a theory?

Yes, it was a black period in my life, and it was certainly true of that time. But it was of shortish duration, and only a part of life.

You had abortions at an early stage. As time has passed have you ever wondered about the children they might have become?

The only one that I have wondered about is the one I intended to have, and that was miscarried. There was a time in my life when I decided I was going to have a child, regardless. This is one of the reasons why André remains such a dear friend. I remember telling him that I was going to have a child and that I probably would have to give up work. He asked me how I thought I would support a child without a job, but I told him I was worried that if I stayed on I might perhaps embarrass people. He said, 'Anyone who is embarrassed can get out.' And for that I will always feel very affectionate towards André. Sadly, when I had made up my mind to have a child, I was prevented by nature, not by me doing anything about it. And I have certainly thought about that child. From time to time, I wonder how old he or she would be by now, and all that sort of thing . . . but not with any great intensity of pain, I have to say . . .

Most women are distressed in some measure by the experience of abortion. Why do you think you escaped the trauma?

I really don't know. The ones I did deliberately affected me not a bit; I was saddened only by the miscarriage. I think perhaps I'm a person without very strong maternal passions.

Diana Athill

You looked back on your life at the end of Instead of a Letter *and wrote, 'I have not been beautiful or intelligent, or good, or brave, or energetic.' Does that not strike you as extreme self-deprecation? Would you put things rather differently now?*

Certainly I've not been beautiful, or brave or energetic, but I probably have been more intelligent than I suggested there. What I was trying to get at was that there was nothing in my life that one would say gave the world anything important. It was just an ordinary life, and yet one wasn't disappointed in it. I was trying to get at what one likes about living, just living, as opposed to achievement. Usually we say, if one has achieved this, that and the other, life has been worth living. But I think life is worth living even when one hasn't achieved. I still find it a bit mysterious that I think so, but I do.

When your grandmother was dying she asked what life had been for . . . how would you answer her question in relation to your own life?

I would answer it very much as I answered it to her really: it has been for just what it was, worth something in itself, part of the process of being. I shan't ever think it was worth nothing.

SISTER WENDY BECKETT

SISTER WENDY BECKETT

Sister Wendy Beckett was born in Johannesburg in 1930 but spent five years of her childhood in Edinburgh. She left South Africa at the age of sixteen and joined the Notre Dame order of nuns in Sussex. After her novitiate she was sent by her order to St Anne's College, Oxford where she was awarded a congratulatory first in English. In 1954 she went back to South Africa to teach, returning to Britain in 1970 to live a fully contemplative life under the protection of a Carmelite monastery in Norfolk. Her books include *Contemporary Women Artists* (1986) and *Art and the Sacred*, and she is a regular contributor to art magazines. Her two highly successful television series, *Sister Wendy's Odyssey* (1992), and *Sister Wendy's Grand Tour* (1994), deal with British and European works of art and have also been published as BBC books.

Your family was extremely devout. Do you think in that sense it could be said you 'inherited' your faith, rather than came to it by a more personal route?

I would qualify 'extremely devout'. We were not a family who had prayers in common, for example. It was just obvious to me that my parents' faith mattered a lot to them by what they were, as opposed to what they said, and I'm sure that's how most children receive their religion, as opposed to their faith. They get their politics through their family, their religion through their family, but faith comes completely from your own depths and your own personal contact with God, and it is faith which fills out the bare bones of the religion. Faith is the spirit; religion is the body. I inherited my Catholicism, but the faith was a gift to me, direct from God. Does that make sense to you?

Yes. But would you not agree that your faith relied heavily on an accident of birth, and that if you had been born into an atheistic family, or perhaps a Moslem family, then things might have taken a very different course?

I would still have to distinguish between religion and faith. My religion certainly was an accident of birth, but my knowledge of God didn't come through the formats of the faith; it came directly. It's very hard to say what could have been if things had been different. I would like to say that if I had been born into another religion I would still have become a Catholic, but this may not be true; I may have found God equally well in whatever I had inherited. I think that has to be a question one can't answer.

You said that you realized at a very early age that if God was responsible for you, then you were responsible to Him. That seems a remarkably adult and philosophical idea for a child to articulate . . . was it really like that?

Those words come from adulthood, but the experience was in early childhood. Only later was I able to express it and make sense of it. I was born with an innate sense of God and I found it very hard when I was young to understand that everybody hadn't been shown God as I was shown. I thought they all saw God as the centre of everything, and I was very surprised when I grew up to find that this wasn't so.

21

Sister Wendy Beckett

How do you define God? Who is God?

God is mystery . . . we can't possibly know. The point about being a Christian is that we believe only one person ever was able to look deep into the mystery and turn round and say to us: 'It's Father . . .' Jesus saw that the infinite mystery was the Father, it was total supportive love, and we live in the strength of that. But we can never make a definition of God or have an idea of God, because then it is something limited. We can't define what by its essence is so infinitely beyond the concepts of our mind.

I know that you admired both your parents very much. What were the qualities you detected in them? And did you see them like that at the time or was it only in retrospect?

I don't think my parents would have believed that I thought they were wonderful people, because I was so rude and self-willed with them and far too proud to say what I thought. So all the actual understanding is in retrospect, but I knew consciously that I was very fortunate. I was absolutely certain that if there were needs to be considered, they would always put their children's first. And also, I didn't know that adults ever quarrelled or spoke sharply, because I had never seen it in my home. I thought only children did that, and I was looking forward to being grown up and being part of a world where nobody was ever unkind or impolite or spoke sharply. There were big shocks ahead for me.

I'm not really sure about your relationship to your order. Are you a nun in the same sense as your sisters? Are you subject to the same vows?

This is a tricky question and one really only a Catholic could understand. At age 16 I entered the teaching Sisters of Notre Dame and very soon realized that in fact I didn't want to teach. I wanted to pray, and I asked them if I could transfer to a contemplative order, but they said no. They believed God wanted me to be a teacher, because I had a good mind for teaching, and I thought – and I still think the same thing – that if you offer yourself to God and you have the vow of obedience, you don't take it back when you don't like what you're being asked to do. But from early 1947 till 1970, I kept asking if I could transfer and being told no, and accepting it as God's wish for me, until in 1970 they told me that they thought I had perhaps been right, that I did need more prayer, and that they were going to let me go. It's a complicated story, but to simplify it: the Carmelites said that they would allow me to live as a hermit in their grounds and the Notre Dame nuns said that I could live 'exclaustrated', a technical term meaning that you're living somewhere else but you still belong to your order. I said I didn't think that was honest, that since I wasn't going to teach I shouldn't be able to belong to my original order. In the end we got permission from Rome to transfer me to being a consecrated virgin and living under the authority of the Carmelite nuns with the vows intact, but not in their community. So I don't really belong to an order; I'm a kind of singleton nun, but the Carmelites act as my order and I obey the friaress. Whatever money I make goes to them. It's different only in the sense that I live alone, but it's not different in the sense of the obligations.

What exactly does 'consecrated virgin' mean?

It's a new thing in the Church, though it used to be an old thing. Before the Church had orders of women, it had single women who made a vow of virginity and worked for the Church; they were called consecrated virgins and the bishop was vaguely in charge of them. I would imagine that most of them were virgins in the physical sense too, but whether that was gone into, I don't know. Widows also became consecrated virgins and the vow of chastity takes no account of what has happened before. In the very early days of the Church when the Benedictine nuns – the oldest order – took their final vows, they each also took an extra vow as a consecrated virgin. I don't know whether this happens in all the Benedictine convents, but I know at least one where it has been dropped, because there are girls entering now who are not virgins, and they say that although they are going to live a virginal life, they don't feel happy about making this extra vow. They say it adds nothing because they are making a vow of chastity anyhow, so why add this bit which they feel verges on being untrue. It doesn't affect me, because I feel perfectly justified in accepting this term which the Church is now offering to women who don't live in convents. I am a consecrated virgin, and I am also a virgin, but that's just been my good luck, or bad luck. I don't actually believe the state of the hymen has very much to do with the holiness of the person. It's just a fact like whether you have all your teeth.

But in this regard you have more liberal views than do ordinary nuns . . .

I don't think you should be too quick to think that all nuns think this or that. Many nuns and many Catholics, many priests and many non-Catholics would feel that the Church has a lot of rethinking to do about the role and the definitions of sexuality. I would not like to go into that as I would not want to discuss those areas where I think the Church hasn't quite got it right. The Bishop of Durham, every one of whose views practically every thinking Christian would accept, has actually not helped the Church in this regard. It's rather like taking an image of art – obviously the best thing is to have the real work of art in front of you, but if you can't have that, you can have a coloured reproduction or even a black and white reproduction. Now you could say that a black and white reproduction is so far from the truth that it's better to have nothing, but this would be wrong. The best thing is to have the whole picture, but for people who haven't got that, a black and white reproduction can still give them an awful lot of pleasure and understanding. It is a question of half a loaf being better than no bread at all. A lot of the understanding of Christianity which goes on today is very inadequate. But if you take that away from people and tell them it isn't in the least true, you run the risk of leaving them no bread at all because they're not yet able to digest the whole loaf. It would damage people's faith, just as I think the dear Bishop of Durham has damaged the faith, although his intentions are of the highest. So with sexuality and the Church, we wait for the Church to grow in wisdom, as it will do, and until then we are obedient; but that doesn't mean we can't think it wrong. We may think the Church is mistaken; but we don't say so.

Why exactly is chastity so important? What has chastity to do with God? He has after all created our bodies which are designed to function in particular ways, including sexually. That must surely also be a gift from God.

I agree with you totally. God gave us these beautiful bodies, and He loves all parts of them. Anybody who feels that the vow of chastity involves pain and frustration should not take it, because God does not like us to suffer. He takes no pleasure out of people making themselves frustrated and unhappy. But we only have so much psychic energy, and for myself I know I could never have had a deep emotional relationship with anybody, let alone a sexual relationship – even on the emotional level I couldn't have done it. All my energies are utterly absorbed in loving God. This is not everyone's vocation; obviously most people's vocation is to come to God through loving somebody else. I don't compare myself to Jesus, but I'm sure he couldn't have had a sexual or emotional involvement at very great depth, because he was so totally taken up with his father.

Has chastity involved any degree of suffering for you?

No. I'm a totally fulfilled woman, and I don't miss a thing, but I recognize that it is not the normal way to God. The normal way is by receiving His gifts in gratitude and using them. But our vows are functional; they are meant actually to set you free for God. Obedience is to set you free from all the struggles of having a career and making your own decisions; poverty is to free you from all the hassles of earning and possessing; and chastity is to set you free from the psychic involvement with close friends and family. All your energies can then get out; if you're an active religious they go out to the world in service, if you're a contemplative religious they go out to the world in prayer.

Do you not need a remarkable number of dispensations to free you from your order to follow the profession of art critic and historian?

First of all, I don't follow the career of art critic and historian, and I won't let the BBC put on publicity that Sister Wendy is an art critic. Sister Wendy is a nun, and her profession is to pray. The other business is just a sideline which I hope will soon peter out. But if I were a true Carmelite I couldn't do it, because Carmelites never leave the enclosure. Of course I didn't realize this was what was going to happen when I came to live in solitude ... I expected I'd just be spending the rest of my life in prayer, but it so happened that I can come out without dispensations, because as a consecrated virgin living under their protection I simply have to ask them if this is all right, and they always trust me. No dispensation is necessary, and there is no profession, no career. Art isn't the centre; it is very much peripheral.

Have you ever been criticized for doing what you do?

I may well be, but I don't know. People write saying how they love it, but the world may be full of people saying they think it's shameful. There was someone who wrote a letter after I was on the *Terry Wogan Show*, saying she was very 'disedified' by seeing me showing off on the programme and telling dear Cliff Richard that he was mistaken in his Christian views, and she said that she looked for more humility in a nun. I wrote back to her and said I was very sorry I had disedified her and would she please pray for me to become humble.

How did it come about that you entered an order in Sussex, such a long way from South Africa?

The nuns with whom I was at school in South Africa were an international order in America, on the Continent, in England, in Africa and in Japan, but their novitiate was in Sussex which I entered 47 years ago on the 1st of February. I keep that day with great joy.

How aware were you of the political situation in South Africa while you were there? Was it possible for you to help in any way?

I was completely unaware. I only knew the servants in my parents' home. My grandmother was a great benefactress of the African schools, and I can remember her buying a huge box of sweets when I was about 9 and taking me with her to distribute them to the African children, and it never entered my head that this was all terribly wrong. It was only when I was an adult that it came as an awful shock to me to realize that in fact the only citizens of my country were white. It just shows that you can live in a situation that's crying out aloud to God for vengeance and never see it; rather like the American southerners who say all their black servants are so happy. It shocks me now to think that we were so fond of our servants and we did not see the injustice of it at all. I pray a lot, and I get very upset about South Africa, and although I tremble for them at the moment, there's no doubt whatever that it's got to be lived through.

At the age of 16 you were separated from your parents for years. How did you cope? Were you ever homesick?

It's a shocking thing, but no, I wasn't. I was so delighted to be a nun that I tripped off to the plains with a heart full of happiness and never thought of the grief, especially my father's. I entered the convent in 1947 and after the novitiate I was sent to Oxford, so I came back to South Africa only in 1954, and even then I was teaching, not living at home.

Did your father feel he had lost you to the Church?

He was thrilled by the idea of my becoming a nun, but he just wondered how this difficult, selfish teenager was going to cope – that was his problem. Also he had only been back from the army for about a year or so, and he thought he needed to get to know his children again, but by then I had left. It wasn't that he felt unhappy about losing me to the Church; in fact he had given me to the Church. Both my parents said to me that the only child you keep is the child who becomes a nun; she doesn't start a new family with other interests, she remains your child. My mother was certain that I idealized them both because I never had adult relationships with them. My brother and sister who grew up with my parents saw them in a much less glowing light than I did, because I had kept enshrined the child's view of wonderful parents.

I read somewhere that you were unable because of your vows to set foot in the Ashmolean while you were in Oxford. Did this not strike you as being an unnecessarily harsh and pointless restriction?

I went to St Anne's which allowed the nuns to live in the convent of Notre Dame. We had a new Reverend Mother who was worried about these young nuns going to the university, and she said to me, 'You must remember that the rule of silence holds. You mustn't talk to the students and you don't go anywhere but to your lectures or tutorials and back again.' So it wasn't the vows, because all the other nuns went everywhere – it had to do with this particular nervous young Reverend Mother. And I didn't mind particularly. It gave me a wonderful Oxford in fact, because since I didn't get to know people they all kept their glamour and stayed romantic to me. And in those days I'd never been to a museum or a gallery, so I didn't really know what I was missing. I only knew art books, so I didn't hanker after the Ashmolean. In the fullnes of time when I went to make a programme I got to drink deep at the cup of the Ashmolean. So it all came right in the end, and when it did I was so much more ready to understand.

When you are in your caravan do you talk to anybody?

No, I don't. I don't live with the other sisters. After morning prayers, the sister who looks after me brings me some coffee and sits down and tells me what's going on. Perhaps I'll say to her that I need a new pair of socks, or something like that, but I don't chat. As soon as Mass is over I take my basket of provisions and go back to the caravan and I stay there all day in complete silence.

But how is it possible to live in silence when you so obviously like people and enjoy talking?

This is going to sound very rude but I've never met anybody I'd rather talk to than be silent with God. That to me is the height of joy.

How did you reconcile your love for art, and its liberal expression, with the rather repressive teaching of the convent?

I was never taught repressively at a convent.

Would you dare in a convent, for example, to look at a painting of a nude and discuss pubic hair – as you have done in your books?

Yes, of course I would. I would expect all nuns to have reverence for the body God has given them. Anything else is narrow puritanism which has nothing to do with the faith. For some extraordinary reason this narrow puritanism seems to have taken over, but it's not Christian. Jesus speaks freely about excretion, for example, about faeces coming out, and He certainly didn't feel this wasn't quite nice. This fear of the body is a late development, and of course a lot of people have been taught it by the Irish, who have a real puritanical fear of the body. But I was lucky; I knew nothing of all this guilt that is supposed to cling to Catholicism. Guilt and sin were words never mentioned in my upbringing, and when I hear people talking like this I just feel very sad. If this is the way they think they've got the wrong end of the stick, they never have been Catholics, because this is not the teaching of the Church. It is a version of it that is unfortunately favoured by people who like the tyranny of puritanism. God doesn't live in blacks and whites; God lives in the lovely fluid greys of the world, and he asks us never to accept black and white from above, but to look into our own hearts and see what is true.

When you were obliged to teach you insisted that you were not unhappy . . . why then did you have a nervous breakdown?

The reason I was not unhappy was that I felt I was doing what God wanted me to do. However, it was at a tremendous cost. The price I was paying for doing what I believed God wanted me to do was evidently higher than my nervous system could take. And so – this is how I describe what happened – my body rescued me. I became so ill that my order, who were the kindest and dearest people imaginable, understood what the cost had been. Up to then I had not shown it, and because I had not shown it they thought it was just that I wanted to lead a life of prayer. The breakdown showed that I *needed* a life of prayer. And actually I think this will always happen: when God sees you've had enough, your body in itself will intervene.

What was it about teaching that distressed you so much?

I think it was this constant having to act a part. This is also why I don't like television. When I'm in the caravan there's simply God and me and I can be absolutely free, but when you're speaking to other people you have to be attentive to what they're asking you, you have to respond to them, you have to play the part that a social relationship requires. This isn't a bad thing in itself; there is no higher vocation than to be a teacher, but I wasn't big enough for it. I was too limited to be able to do it and live in freedom. It was an inadequacy in me.

Is the urge to live an entirely solitary life a strength or a weakness, do you think? Christ after all seems to have been rather a gregarious person . . .

I'm positive it's a weakness. It's a life only for the very weak who cannot stand the normal strains of life, perhaps the almost neurotically weak, who also have such a strong passion for God that they can impose upon their life the austerity that it demands.

Is there some connection between the contemplation of works of art and the spiritual life . . . is it an avenue to God?

For me it is, absolutely, and this is potentially what it is for everybody. Whenever you look at real art you're looking at something that's challenging you to be more wholly human, to enter more deeply into truth; and whenever you touch truth, you touch God. God is truth.

But I thought God was indefinable . . .

He is indefinable, but wherever there is beauty and truth, there is God. Yes, I put that badly, you're quite right to have corrected me. Truth and beauty don't encompass God but their presence shows us the presence of God, just as light shows us the presence of the sun.

You have spent more than 20 years living alone in the caravan. Does that preference not reflect a little on your sisters in the convent? I mean that you choose not to be with them.

Not at all. It's not because of their inadequacies, but because of mine. I lead a different life pattern from them. My day, for example, has seven hours' prayer and theirs has only two. By prayer I mean absolutely silent pure prayer. God made us to live in community with one another, He made us social animals, but occasionally you get the odd one who is inadequate. I remember when I was a very young nun another sister said of me that I was the only person she had ever known who didn't need other people. It's true, but it's not nice. I'm not sufficiently able to work with other people and to grow with other people, but we have to accept the poor selves that we are; this is what I am, so I try to rejoice in it rather than lament over it.

I think many people must be puzzled by your conscious wish to be a hermit

and your simultaneous exposure to many millions of people on television.
Are they compatible ideas?

No. At the moment I'm what I would call a hermit of interruptions . . .
that is, for most of the year I'm a hermit, but then for parts of the year I'm
on television. But they're not very big parts and they will diminish. I'm
hoping very soon they'll find somebody else who can do what I'm doing
and then I can withdraw completely.

But you seem to enjoy doing it . . .

Only relatively. Compared to being alone in the caravan anything else is
unenjoyable, but if I have to do this other business then I will enjoy it as
much as I can; but I wouldn't wish it.

But nobody forces you to do it.

My conscience forces me to do it, because I think there is a need for
somebody who can speak about art in a very simple way and make people
see that it's something of a potential enrichment. But it's a gap that I hope
will soon be filled by somebody else. It doesn't have to be filled by me.

'God is asking me to do this now', you said in an interview. How do you
know it is God?

You only know what God is asking of you through the circumstances of
your life. The context of your life tells you. The good Samaritan knew that
God was asking him to succour the man who had fallen among thieves
because he actually met the man. If he hadn't met the man, God wouldn't
have asked him; but that's the only way God does speak to people, through
the actual context of lives. Whom does God ask you to love? The people
you know, the people you live with. So we only have to look at our lives to
know what we're called upon to do.

You said once that you hated writing and you would not do it unless you
had to. Why then did you do it?

One of the reasons is that we have to earn our living in the convent, and this is the only way I can earn any money for the community. The second reason is that people tell me that they like what I write and find that it really is useful for understanding art.

You appear on television in the traditional habit of a nun. Was that a matter of course or something encouraged by the BBC?

This is what I wear – I'd never dream of wearing anything else. It's nothing to do with the BBC.

Are you not worried that you are perhaps being exploited by the image-makers – to put it bluntly, that a nun in a habit is a good gimmick?

Yes, I think that is probably true. I think that if I were just a little old lady from Norfolk, not too many people would have watched the programmes to begin with. It was probably the nun who got people watching, but I think they stayed watching because they liked it.

I don't wish to sound disagreeable, but do you think permission for a hermit nun to enter the world of television might have been prompted by the thought of the fees that would accrue to the order?

No, I'm sure not, because the sisters are extremely unworldly, and I don't think it entered into their heads. In fact they were happy to let me go ahead only because I thought it was right. They didn't know why I thought it was right until the BBC brought them down the films and showed them. Then they thought it was right too.

You have expressed some ideas which do not at first sight seem compatible with the faith. In what sense, for example, can homosexuality not matter, given the views expressed in the Bible and in the tradition of the Church?

This is one I would prefer not to answer, on the grounds of what I said about the Bishop of Durham, that half a loaf is better than no bread at all. Let me give you a parallel: the Church condemned Galileo for saying that the earth went round the sun, and not vice versa. Only when the man in the street understood, and it was common knowledge that the earth did indeed go round the sun, not the other way round, did the Church accept it. The fact that the Bible seemed to say the opposite was meant to be poetry. I don't believe the Church is the glorious unspotted leader, marching ahead of humanity; that's not the Church Jesus left us. The Church is a poor wounded creature and it's moved at the pace of the slowest. When the man in the street understands the full meaning of love, then the Church will understand it, and a lot of the present prohibitions will just dissolve. But they haven't dissolved yet, and I don't think it helps people for somebody who's totally committed to the faith as I am, to say the Church as yet hasn't fully understood. I'll say it to a friend, but I don't think it's wise to say it in public, because it doesn't help the Church.

I understand what you're saying, but do you ever conceive of a time when the Church will look upon homosexuality in a different way?

That's a completely acceptable way to put it, and my answer is a resounding yes. The Church in the fullness of time will come to accept women priests, homosexuality, and perhaps divorce. I am sure eventually these things will all change, but they haven't changed yet, and I wouldn't like people to have their faith in any way shaken, or their obedience and loyalty challenged; which is why I say, let's wait. This is what it means to belong to a church; you wait lovingly, you strive to make things different but you don't criticize the Church in public.

Are you not at odds with the Church too about the ordination of women? Would it not split the Church and forever prevent reconciliation with the Orthodox?

No, because the Orthodox too will eventually come to favour the ordination of women. Jesus ordained only Jewish males, so why should only one half of that, the male, count as standard and not the Jewishness? The Church ordains males who are not Jews, though Jesus didn't, so I think the Church will in time ordain females, but not now. The average man still does not think the average woman is fully human, though he thinks he does. We haven't in fact got equality, but when we get it, then it will be on all levels.

33

There will be many who see the campaign for the ordination of women as just another feminist effort directed by women with no interest in religion. Do you see it as principally a theological or a political matter?

I don't know very much about the ins and outs of it, but to me it's a completely theological matter, or perhaps I should say it's a matter of practical understanding of God's plans for His children, and in God's eyes gender is not very important. On a purely practical level it's a kind of lunatic arrangement in that you have a whole convent full of nuns, all of whom have deep theological understanding, any one of whom in theory could celebrate Mass, but the priest has to be imported at great expense to say Mass every morning. I don't think it's just a question of feminism. Men don't realize how terrible it's been for some women; the bright girl in the family who wasn't educated because her stupid brother had to get all the money; or the clever woman in a firm who could take reponsibility easily and is overlooked because the men get it and make a mess of things. There is a lot of buried frustration and it'll take a long time for this to work itself out, but I think we'll see light at the end of the tunnel. Think how recently women weren't allowed to go to the university, or to vote. We forget what enormous strides have been made to see women as fully human; there are more strides to be made still, but we are making progress.

Would you have wished to have been a priest had it been possible?

No. I don't think it would ever have been my vocation. If it were open to me now I wouldn't want it; I prefer to be alone with God. It wouldn't have entered ever into my desire. A priest has to be a servant of the people, and the only service I can give is the service of prayer.

You were reported as saying of sexual activity: 'There is not going to be a personal involvement, but I would cheer it on.' That seems a remarkably liberal view for a nun. What did you mean?

I don't remember saying it, but if I did say it I would have meant that for me there is no sexual involvement and never has been and never will be because God is complete fulfilment, but I'm delighted that the world is full of people who appreciate God's good gift to them. Of course sex is something to cheer on. Why did God invent it if He didn't want it to be something of a delight to people?

You speak of art as giving an insight into mysteries. Can you elaborate on that? What sort of mysteries are involved here, and what is it to have 'insight' into a mystery?

Art is working at a very profound level. It is almost by definition at the level of the mysterious . . . it is concerned with those deep things in us that are there but which we find it so hard to bring to the surface of our consciousness: the desire for goodness, the desire to be fully human, the desire for eternal life, the desire for happiness, the desire to make sense of suffering. A very great picture opens you up to a lot of these truths, perhaps not always consciously, but you're stirred at those depths, and if you have the kind of mind that wants to reflect upon what the experience has been, then you would have conscious insight into truths that perhaps you hadn't realized before you were faced with that great work of art. A work of art that leaves you untouched is not a great work of art, or you haven't opened yourself enough.

A great deal of fuss is made about 'originals' in the art world. Largely of course that's a commerical matter but you have been content for the most part with postcards and reproductions. Do you feel that you missed anything by being unfamiliar with paintings at first hand for so long?

I don't myself think I missed anything. When you look at your postcard you are looking at it in ideal circumstances, alone, sitting down, quietly contemplating. Think of walking round the V and A with lots of other people and noise and sore feet. Obviously the ideal would be every man his own Cézanne, every woman her own Leonardo, but I don't think we should ever let the ideal get in the way of enjoying what we do actually have.

How do you think the idea of art as beauty correlates with paintings whose subject matter is ugly? – of dead bodies, for example, or indeed of any picture in which the artist wishes to depict something ugly, like Goya's '3rd of May 1808'.

There is a beauty in ugliness, you know. Think of Rembrandt's old people, with gnarled features, but absolutely lit up with wisdom. Goya was indeed painting something very ugly but he was showing the human spirit grappling with it – that's the beauty. Beauty doesn't mean pretty; beauty means something of the spirit which can show itself in a misshapen form. Beauty is often horrible, terrifying, with nothing of the attractive or the gentle about it; but it is equally beautiful.

When one stands in front of a painting and contemplates it, what is it one should look for . . . perhaps 'should' is the wrong word . . . but what sort of satisfaction does one look for from an image?

If you're looking at all you're delimiting yourself. Let the work of art impress itself upon you, let it try and draw you into it, keep your options absolutely open, don't look for anything. Start with the things that start to come to you, and then receive them. The more intelligently passive you are the more you'll get.

Is there a distinction to be drawn between art appreciation and art criticism?

That's a good question. I know that in some circles I'm criticized for liking too much. I never write about or speak about art that I don't like. In other words I do try just to appreciate but I hope it is not an unintelligent appreciation. In that sense you can criticize appreciatively – it really means bringing your mind to bear on the work.

Speaking of Murillo at one point you say you wanted to make up your mind about his 'importance'. What does the word mean when applied to a painter . . . what makes one artist more important than another?

It is partly the consensus of the centuries, but it's also a personal thing. There are some artists who are very important to me, who are not considered among the very great artists. I was baffled by Murillo who at his time was considered possibly the greatest artist in the world, far greater than the other 17th-century artists. He was enormously successful, then he took a steep nose dive in popularity, and then people began to think

Murillo a very poor artist. Now he's slowly beginning to creep back again into critical acclaim and I wanted to discover why people loved him so much in his century, and why he was again beginning to be the subject of serious exhibitions. But I still haven't made up my mind. He is a most beautiful colourist, but I still find the images rather too saccharine.

You once said that words are a vulgarity. I can see that a hermit might have little use for them in one sense, but is it really possible to respond meaningfully without them? How do you even know what you feel without them? How can you know that ground of your admiration?

When I was doing English at Oxford I realized that what you had to do was to open yourself to the literature, experience its depth and dig out of yourself the experience and put it into words for your essay. Basically that's what I'm doing in my art appreciation. But the more you are exposed to great art the more you know that what you say is so inadequate; yet it's got to be said. It's again the half a loaf; it's better than nothing. I hardly ever include any landscapes in my programmes or books. It's not that I don't love landscapes – I do – but all you can say is, 'Look, isn't it absolutely beautiful . . .' which doesn't help anybody. Words are so inadequate, so vulgar compared to the depths to which you've been moved.

You admire the skill (which you say you yourself will never attain) of being able to use words so exactly that no one will misunderstand them. Would you agree that the language of faith is singularly imprecise, that it is impossible for one person to understand what another means by 'knowing God' for example?

Absolutely. I agree totally. Not only have you a language difficulty here, you have a moral difficulty in that we only know as much of God as we want to know. Psychologists say that if you're faced with an unbearable truth, you won't bear it; you'll just block it out. And I can understand this. In a way, the truth about God is unbearable because it is so enormously large, and it's easy to see that people may not want to hear it. With the real God you're completely out of control the minute you look at Him. So where there's a difficulty of language, there's a difficulty of desire. Oh yes, the language of religion is absolutely hopeless. Everybody has a different picture in mind, and some are horrible. That's why I say I love atheists, because they're people who've thrown out a false God. They were perfectly right to disown the kind of God they thought was God. The point is they haven't met the real God yet, because if you meet the real God you can't possibly not love Him. So hurrah for atheists.

You have more than once stressed the centrality of prayer, but what is it that one prays for? To put it bluntly, God surely does not change His mind?

What one is really praying for is the strength to cope with what happens. Let's say, for example, that you pray that your business venture will go well, but in fact it goes very badly. Your prayer is answered if you are helped to cope with that, to grow in human stature through disaster. God will always make us grow in this way if we let Him, and that's what prayer is always for. God won't come in and change the world. He's not a kind of little puppet God who'll stop the car from having an accident. No, no, what God will do is that when you have your accident He will be with you to make that accident fruitful.

Have you any ambition for the future?

Only to get back to solitude.

How can you be sure now that you have seen so much of the outside world that you will not miss it in isolation?

I don't think we can ever be certain of anything, because we can't put any trust in ourselves. I think it would be highly unlikely because nothing that I've ever seen or experienced has seemed preferable to getting back to the caravan.

What is your attitude towards death?

As a child I looked forward very much to dying. I thought how wonderful it would be to leap into the arms of God. Now I see it as the one chance to make a great act of faith, because we all go into the darkness in death. God says, 'Though he slay me, yet will I trust in him.' When God puts the knife to the throat, and I go into the darkness I will be able to make an act of faith that I've never made before, so in that sense I'll be very glad to die.

HUGH CALLAGHAN

HUGH CALLAGHAN

Hugh Callaghan was born in the Ardoyne in Belfast in 1930 where he spent an impoverished childhood. After the war he went in search of work to Birmingham where he married and settled down. After the Birmingham pub massacres in November 1974 he was arrested and charged as an IRA bomber along with five other men. Sixteen and a half years later the Birmingham Six were released from custody on 14 March 1991 after a successful appeal at the Old Bailey.

From reading your life story there was nothing in your childhood and early life to suggest that the future would be anything other than straightforward and uncomplicated. Did you yourself ever have a feeling that your life would take an extraordinary turn?

No, not at all. My book is called *Cruel Fate* and that is actually what it was. It hinged on deciding in just a couple of seconds to go somewhere with some people, no more than that.

Looking back, do you think the values you learned in your childhood in Belfast stood you in good stead for some of the difficulties which were to come?

Of course they did, because I had a very hard life in Belfast. If I had been spoilt in my childhood I would not have had the will to fight all the way against my conviction. My father was very dominating. He was an ex-army man and a real tyrant, mostly in drink, and some nights if he didn't have his own way it would be terrifying. He once gave my brother Tom such a terrible hiding for selling a little harmonica to get the money for a game of snooker. He took him upstairs and it just was awful what he did. My mother and I were helpless because we were so frightened of him. Another time he beat me up because I wore his shoes – mine were too small and had holes in them. So I was used to a hard life and people treating me badly. Going to prison and being shouted at by the prison officers reminded me of my young days. Not that I wasn't frightened. I was always a nervous individual and it didn't take much to break me down. I really couldn't stand violence.

You must have gone over in your mind a million times that fateful day, 21 November 1974, and how differently things might have turned out if only, if only . . . Have you ever been able to make sense of the series of events which led to your being arrested?

It is difficult to make sense of it because it was just a million to one chance that we met together that night. The only thing I had in common with those other fellows, apart from being Irish, is that we had never met together before. Certainly I went to the same pub and I'd seen them there before, but it wasn't them I went in to see, but a friend of mine, who is

43

Hugh Callaghan

now deceased, to talk about football. I think I may just have had a drink with one of the fellows, Paddy Hill, and that only once, but I had my own circle of friends in Birmingham, and they weren't part of it.

Had you or the others ever had any connection with the IRA?

I was never a member of the IRA. My family always voted Labour, and I still vote Labour up to the present day. I've never been a Republican. I wasn't close enough to the others to know their politics, but I would say that they were just ordinary nationalist people, that is to say, part of the Catholic community.

You were in a sense set aside from the other five [of the Birmingham Six], in that they had all left on the train for Belfast. You hadn't – you had merely seen them off. Did that seem to you at the time of arrest to be any sort of advantage?

Well, the solicitors always said to me that I was on the outskirts of it all, but I knew I was in an awful lot of trouble because I was at the railway station with the others; the only advantage I had was that they were arrested before me – I was arrested the next evening. I knew from Gerry Hunter's wife that they had been arrested and I was able to tell her that in my honest opinion, nothing had happened, but she said, 'They've been here and they've turned the place over. You'd better go.' That frightened me, not in a sense that I had done anything wrong but in the sense that they could be looking for me too. I told Sandra [Gerry Hunter's wife] that they would have to let them go, and if they didn't I would go and tell a solicitor that I had been with them that night and that they had done nothing. But as it was I was arrested on the Friday evening, so I didn't get a chance. Whether that would have made much difference or not, I don't know.

But did you at any point imagine that the other five could have been involved without your knowledge?

No. They couldn't have been, because they were with me all the time. The only time Gerry went out was to make a phone call to his uncle to say they were getting the train, but that was all. I knew quite well that those men did not plant the bombs. I didn't know them well, but I knew them well enough to know that they weren't IRA men. I could say without a fear of contradiction that they weren't bombers.

Under pressure and physical beatings, four confessions were extracted from the six who had been arrested. You yourself said that the others were all officers in the IRA. We all know now the circumstances under which you came to say this, but what I want to know is, what view did the others take of your saying this to police officers?

Well, I got a bit of stick, but they were quite good about it really. Sometimes they even made a joke of it and told me to address them as 'Captain', and so on. But it wasn't really funny at all. They knew that I was under a lot of pressure, and they were too. They also landed me in it, but there was never any animosity between us over that. It must be said too that I didn't give the police the actual ranks. They asked me what my rank was in the IRA, and I answered that I wasn't in the IRA. When the deposition papers came, we had all been given ranks, but it was the police who had done that, not me. It even came to light afterwards that there were no such ranks.

Did it take time for you to be able to forgive yourself for inventing these details and thus making the situation so much more complicated for everyone?

Well, I wanted to retract those things I said straightaway. I was conscious of what I had done, and when I was being taken by car to another police station I told the police that I wanted to retract everything. But they stopped the car and put a gun to my head and said they would throw me in the lake unless I stuck to what I'd said. It was really horrific. Remember, I had never had any dealings with the police, I had never been in a police station before in my life. And to be interrogated for such a terrible crime . . . it was very frightening. They were out to get people, and they didn't care which way they got them, what means they used.

Did you think at any time that the people who were interrogating you believed that you were guilty?

Hugh Callaghan

They still do today, not all of them of course, but most of the West Midlands police force still think we did it. Even if they were to get the people who did do it, they'd still say we were involved. That's how the police operate. That was the whole point of the *Sunday Telegraph* article – they're still trying to reconvict us. It's a sore point with them, especially because such a big case fell away for them – after all, they thought at the very beginning, 'This is it'. Deep down I expect some of them know we didn't do it, but they're not going to come out in public and say that; they're going to fight and fight to say we did do it, just like they maintain they did nothing to us. They will never never give in.

Has anybody from the police force ever apologized to you about anything?

No. Even the judges never said sorry. The only time they got close to it was when the Broadwater Farm people got released, and they said they were sorry that this had happened to other people in similar situations. But they did not mention names, and nobody has ever offered us an apology.

Your experience as a remand prisoner was savage and brutal, and you came to regard everyone in officialdom as the common enemy . . . doctors, warders, solicitors. Before that had you had a high regard for people in authority?

It was something I never thought about, people in authority, but I will say this: I never dreamed that the police would treat me in the way they did. I may have been naive about police, but I didn't think that they would actually lie. When I went to the magistrates' court, I remember seeing all the police smiling and I thought to myself, they will be smiling on the other sides of their faces when all our evidence comes out and we go to the proper court. But when I saw how it was handled and heard the lies that were told, I knew then why the police had been smiling. We were hated in that courtroom. The national feeling was so against us that nothing we said was believed. I recall looking over at the jury and seeing them look up at the ceiling whenever any good points came out about us – one of them was even sitting there biting his nails and spitting them out; but when the bad points were mentioned, when the police said all those things against us, the jury would turn towards us with sinister looks. We didn't have a dream of a chance.

You described the atmosphere in the courtroom as being very intimidating: 'I could almost touch the hatred I felt from all those present in the court – magistrates, the clerks, the general public.' At that point were you made to feel guilty simply by virtue of all being Irishmen in England?

Listen, I will tell you this. We were found guilty even before we went to court. That is my firm belief.

After the confessions were ruled admissible, your attitude became resigned and defeatist. Apart from your own self-belief was there anything else which saved you from the depths of despair?

I'm not a pessimist by nature, and during the trial I always firmly believed that something would show up, but as the trial went on, I could see how things were going. My wife said to me that if things went well she would see me in the square – that was in Morecambe – but I really knew by then it would have taken a miracle for us to get off. But I couldn't just tell her that – you know how it is, you always hope. I was really depressed after we were convicted, but by the time of the first prison visit from my wife and my daughter, I told them, 'Look, it's very, very bad, but I still believe that we will win this.'

After the trial, which was eight months after your arrest and lasted 45 days, you say that you still had faith in British justice. Was British justice ever something you had questioned before your own experience of it?

No. I was never involved much with the judiciary or justice, but I wasn't against British justice at all. I'm still not against it today, but the way I see it, it is very unfair to many, many people.

Do you think Irishmen are traditionally suspicious of British justice?

Irish trials are show trials. They are glamorized in the papers, and you haven't got a hope in hell if you're an Irishman up on terrorist charges. There is no British justice in Irish trials, but sometimes there's not much justice for other people either, Englishmen included.

Hugh Callaghan

But the police can't influence the jury, twelve good men and true . . .

But you must understand that the judge sums up in such a way as to put ideas in the jury's heads, and that's exactly what he did with us that day. That's the sort of thing that the Royal Commission is trying to put a stop to.

After you were convicted and sentenced to life, you say that there was no solace from the visits by the prison chaplain and you regarded him rather as a part of the prison establishment. Was that a huge disappointment for you?

Yes. I would have expected a man of the cloth to have sympathized with me, but that wasn't the case; he didn't. And he spoke to me in that tone of voice which suggested he thought I was guilty. I said to him, 'You realize we didn't do this?' and he said, 'Oh come, come, come'. I asked him what he meant by that, and it was obvious he thought we were guilty. I told him that if I couldn't get a man of my own religion to listen to what I had to say, then it didn't say much for the RC chaplaincy.

Are you a religious man?

No, but I'm not unreligious either. But when you are in the situation I was in and you can't get an RC priest to sympathize with you, it's bad.

You say at one point in the book that your faith in God declined rapidly and you didn't experience Christ's compassion in any Catholic chaplains you met around that time. Did you ever think that perhaps you were being tested by God?

No, I didn't. I know that some of the clergy treated me badly, but I wasn't against them particularly. If I didn't go to Mass on a Sunday in the prison, I just said Mass in my own cell, away from the people. And I still had faith in God.

But when you were under extreme pressure, did you appeal to God for help?

Of course I did, I often prayed in the cell. We all used to pray, especially at the beginning when we were going back and forward to Winson Green Prison for court appearances. We had to run the gauntlet each time between rows of policemen with guns, the crowd shouting abuse, 'Bastards! Murderers!' And there were Alsatian dogs which terrified me. And when we were beaten at Winson Green and I thought we were going to die, I prayed as I've never prayed before. Everyone wanted to unleash their anger on us, and I remember saying to Gerry that they might as well kill us outright, 'They're going to do it anyway.' We really thought we were going to get killed at Winson Green. After we were beaten we were put in a locked room and then we heard them call out, 'Send the filthy bastards up!' We were dragged one by one to the washroom, and I thought they were going to finish us off. By the time I was shoved into the bath it was full of blood and hair from the beaten bodies of the others. They dipped my head in the water and pulled it up again, and dipped it in again, then they dragged me out of the bath and kicked me on the floor.

Father Hugh Sinclair of Wormwood Scrubs was the only priest you established any real rapport with during your imprisonment. Was this less to do with the Church and more to do with his compassion as a human being?

More his compassion, I would say. In that respect he was completely different from the other RC priests that we met. All you want in prison is for somebody to talk nicely to you for a change and to help you, even if it's just to make a phone call for you, or get the papers. He was very good in that way and I found him a very sympathetic man. He didn't question my innocence the way the other chaplains did.

How important was it for you all to bring assault charges against the police in 1976 – what you called the screws' trial? Was there an element of revenge, or was it principally to make known the truth?

It wasn't revenge, that's the last thing we wanted. We just wanted the truth to come out, nothing else. Revenge and bitterness are like cancer –

they just eat away at you. At the very beginning, I was bitter, and that lasted for maybe three or four weeks, but I soon realized I would have to get a grip on myself. I settled down to trying to prove my innocence.

Even though a verdict of not guilty was passed, the judge agreed that someone had beaten you up. Did you take heart from the fact that it was now known that you had been assaulted in custody?

Not really, because the trial concentrated on who had beaten us first, the police or the prison warders. I gave evidence that we had been beaten at the police station and the subsequent beatings at Winson Green Prison were done to cover up the police beatings. But the judge in his summing up drew the juries' attention to the screws' long and outstanding service and to the 'class of men' making the accusations, and a verdict of not guilty was returned on all 14. I expected nothing else.

Your seven years in Albany Prison built up your resistance and gave you greater strength to deal with the difficult years ahead. Were you conscious of these changes in yourself or were they happening imperceptibly, as it were?

I don't know where I got the strength, maybe from God, but it gradually came and gave me the will to fight to clear my name. I was just hopeless at the beginning, I couldn't even make my bed up. But when I got to Albany, it was a better prison, there was plenty of exercise, plenty of fresh air, and when my family visited me for the first time there they saw a big improvement in me.

You wrote in your book: 'To be a sensitive soul in prison is hard enough, but to be an innocent and to have to endure every day the barbarity of prison life is pure hell.' You wrote these words of someone else, Michael Hickey, one of the Bridgewater men, but do you also think that applied to you? Were you a sensitive soul?

In prison you meet all sorts and you have to be as hard as possible – you cannot afford to be a softie. You put on a show, you joke and laugh with the rest, but when you get away from them, you say to yourself that you're not one of them. There were only a few people I could tell I was not a criminal. I couldn't say it to everyone, only those I could really trust. The others would have scoffed and said, 'Who do you think you are then? The bee's knees?' There are some very violent people in prison and there were times I was glad to get behind my door at night, just to get away from them. It's no good being a softie in prison, but deep down I was a softie.

Did you ever make genuine friendships in prison?

Oh yes. There was a Scots fellow, a nice fellow, and strangely enough a Protestant Orangeman into the bargain. We got on well together and it was great. It also proved that I wasn't a bigot – if the fellow was a good man I didn't care what he was, I talked to him and befriended him. But for the first three years I was on my own, nobody wanted to walk with me during exercise in the prison yard, partly because of what I was in for. They thought that if they were seen walking with me, they probably wouldn't get parole. Ironically enough, there were eventually two fellows who did walk with me occasionally, and they got a lot of parole, probably because I wasn't in any sense a troublemaker.

You said that you preferred solitude to the company of others in prison . . . and yet on the outside I have the impression that you were a gregarious person. One always imagines the loneliness of prison to be one of the worst aspects . . .

It is a very lonely business. A lot of people go to pieces in prison because of the loneliness, but you can't afford to get too emotional. I used to get very upset particularly after visits. When you go into the visiting room it's full of visitors, people from the outside world, and it's all very tense. It's really difficult when your family walk away and you have to go back to your cell. Especially when you haven't done anything, when you're an innocent person, it was heartbreaking. It took me years and years to get used to it.

Although it was undoubtedly hard for you in prison, you concede that it was much harder for your wife. But that in turn must have made it more difficult for you to bear, knowing what she was going through . . .

Hugh Callaghan

At least I only had the prison population to put up with, but she had the whole city of Birmingham, the whole wide world to put up with. I always worried that something would happen to her, that she would be treated badly, that somebody would throw a petrol bomb through her house. That's the sort of thing they said to me in the police cells would happen to her – they even said that my daughter had been killed in the bombings, and I didn't know whether or not it was true because I hadn't seen her. So you can imagine what sort of things went through my mind in prison.

Not all marriages survive prison and there were casualties among the Birmingham Six also. Your marriage did survive. Did you always feel it would?

Well, I did, yes. But if my wife had ever come to me and told me she couldn't handle any more and that we would have to separate, I wouldn't have stood in her way. I couldn't have blamed her, but I somehow always knew that she wouldn't do that. She is a very very strong woman. And a very brave one. She even went on to the streets to get signatures, and that meant facing the crowd and putting up with insults. I don't think I could have done it in her situation.

It would be naive to assume that the marriage could have remained the same over your 17 years in prison, or that you could have picked up where you left off with your wife. What changes did it undergo, what were the main differences?

Of course it's very difficult after 17 years. You just can't get together as man and wife and expect everything to be the same. We both realize that, and we've discussed it. We are very fair to one another, but it is difficult. I live in London now most of the time – I don't feel I could live in Birmingham any more, although I go up there to see my family. My wife has her house in Birmingham which is where she feels she wants to live, and she understands that it would not be easy for me to live up there on a regular basis. So there is a bit of estrangement, just as a result of the difference between years ago and today.

You never wanted to be considered for parole because you always wanted to establish your innocence through the courts, and parole, you felt, would have compromised your position. It must have been very difficult at times not to waver from this . . .

If I had accepted parole I would have been saying I was guilty. You don't get anything out of prison unless you show remorse for the crime you've committed, so how was I going to ask for parole when I hadn't done anything? I said quite categorically that I wasn't going to accept parole – I told the assistant governor and I said it on BBC television – and if they gave me parole nevertheless I told them they would have to carry me out of the prison gates. The assistant governor watched the programme with his wife and when he heard what I said he told her he thought I was a man of my word, because I had said the same to him.

Your first real break came in 1985 with the World in Action *programme. Were you amazed at the power and influence of television?*

I was really over the moon with that. The first thing I thought was that now perhaps they would get off my family's back. People would talk to them and be a bit more friendly. It was terrific, it gave me a new hope. I jumped for joy when that programme came out.

In 1987 the Home Secretary referred your case back to the Court of Appeal. What were your feelings when you heard that?

I knew then there was no going back. Even if we lost, there was no going back. It was a great feeling.

The psychiatrist's report on you before the appeal said that you were suggestible, submissive, timid and nervous. Did you have mixed feelings about the report, even though it was likely to help your case?

I had no mixed feelings about the report. It was a brilliant report, and completely accurate.

When the appeal was dismissed in January 1988 you said that the

53

humiliation was almost as bad as the rejection. What did you mean by that?

It was clear after a couple of days of the appeal hearing that we weren't going to get anywhere, you could just tell by the hostility of the judge and the way all the evidence put forward was just dismissed out of hand. It really was frustrating and humiliating, and for the first time I felt real pessimism. I thought, here we are, we've got great witnesses giving good evidence, and they're just throwing it all back. When we lost the appeal I remember Richard Ferguson, our QC, saying, 'I'm sorry.' But even though I felt down, I said to him, 'Don't be sorry, Richard, because we'll be back again.' And we were.

Lord Denning, the former Lord Chief Justice, spoke on television after your appeal, saying that the public confidence in the law was more important than one or two people being wrongfully convicted. How did that make you feel?

Well, I'll be honest with you, although it was the most outrageous statement, it probably helped us a good deal along the way. When people start saying it's better to keep innocent people in prison so as to keep the system in the right perspective, that can only help innocent people. He did us a favour.

He also said that Chris Mullin had done a great disservice to British justice. Do you think that Lord Denning ought to have been publicly condemned and brought to account for his part in it all?

Of course, but Lord Denning is known for making outrageous statements, so Chris Mullin wouldn't take a lot of notice of him anyway. Chris was a very brave man and he did a lot of brave work to get at the truth. Lord Denning would have been discredited by the people who knew Chris Mullin.

When you were in prison your daughter got married. How were you able to cope with not being able to attend the wedding?

Oh, I was very sad, very sad. I found it difficult to come to terms with that. I was looking forward to the day she got married, and the only consolation was that I got a video of it and saw it in prison, but even so . . .

Did her husband come and visit you?

Oh yes, and I liked him very much. He was a very special person who touched many people's hearts in his short lifetime. He was killed in a motorway pile-up in January 1992. There was a lorry on the hard shoulder, with smoke coming out of it – he went into the smoke, and all the vehicles behind pushed him straight into the lorry, so he was killed instantly. He was only 30 and his death totally devastated my daughter. She was left alone with a 14-month-old daughter and another on the way. It was a tragic death, and very sad for me, because I was up in Birmingham at that particular time, staying with her. On the evening in question I was in the shower when I heard screaming. I knew it wasn't the baby, and when I rushed out of the shower, my daughter was lying on the floor downstairs screaming, 'Arthur's been killed! Arthur's been killed!' The policeman who had broken the news was still in the room.

When you were waiting for the second appeal you had news of your brother Tom's death. Was that a very low point for you?

Yes, the lowest perhaps. We had been very close once and when we were young, Tom had been my hero. The governor of Long Lartin, Joe Whitty, was a very fair man – he did us a lot of good turns, getting us on TV, and that sort of thing. He told me he would give me parole to go to Tom's funeral, but he also said, 'Mr Callaghan,' – that was how he always addressed me, which was most unusual – 'I'll give you a bit of advice. I'll certainly give you parole, and I don't even have to ring up to ask the parole board, but you have to think what's going to happen if you go out there. The TV people will get to hear about it, the police will get to hear about it, and your brother's funeral will be turned into a charade.' He told me to go back and think about it and said I could make as many phone calls as I wanted. I went back and thought about it, and the next day I told him I wouldn't be going. I didn't want my whole family to be upset. Joe Whitty was the best governor I ever met.

In August 1990 you went back to the court for the third time. This time you won a small victory over what you called 'the spite and stupidity of the screws' who had wanted you to travel as top security Category A prisoners. Was that an important and symbolic victory for you?

Very important, and I say that without fear of contradiction. When you go in a Category A van you're in a big wagon escorted by police. Category B and C prisoners travel in ordinary vans. When we saw the Category A wagon Gerry Hunter and I refused to go, and we took our stuff back to the wing. We contacted our defence solicitor Gareth Peirce, and she got in touch with the Irish embassy and they talked it out. Eventually Gareth rang up and told us we would be going in an ordinary little van. We won a good victory and all the people in the prison were very pleased. The police were still trying to discredit us, but they failed.

Did you ever feel that in some curious way what happened to you was meant?

No, no, I never thought that. I just put it down as fate. Cruel fate.

Did anything good come out of your 16 years in prison?

Not really. Prison taught me not to trust people in general, and although I feel – without being big-headed about it – I'm still a good human being, I do think it's made me harder in my ways. I haven't got the patience with people I used to have.

You came across many bad, embittered, hard people, full of hatred, yet you also encountered many good people on the way. Do you believe in the end that good triumphs over evil, or is that just wishful thinking?

The only way I can answer you is to say that there are a lot of people who are so bad you cannot release them from prison, but there are also many good people in there, even though they may be guilty of terrible crimes. There are also loads of innocent people, people who are on their own, who haven't had the publicity we have had, who haven't had the campaigns we've had. We were very lucky in the people who took up our case, the type of campaigners we had, the support from all over the world. Some people, though innocent, aren't so lucky. As for good triumphing over evil, I still feel we haven't been fully vindicated in certain areas of the media, and that grieves me some. People will say we got off on a technicality, and so we have a battle on our hands all over again.

When you describe your moment of release, you said you wanted to hug everyone in the waiting crowd, and that you had not forgotten the faith of ordinary people like yourselves who had believed in you. Was it not a bitter thought that the faith of the ordinary people, no matter how sincere and well meaning, could do nothing to save you and have you released? That had to be left to people of power and influence like Chris Mullin and Ludovic Kennedy . . .

Well, it is a sobering thought. But I never forgot the many letters of support I had, not just from Irish people, but from others too. Of course a lot of people just hopped on the bandwagon when it became clear we were innocent, but I wouldn't have expected people years ago to believe in us. How could they in view of what the papers were saying? I had a famous radio announcer do an interview with me and he said to me beforehand that he was really sorry that he had done nothing to help me when I was in prison. My answer to that was that I didn't expect everybody to help me. After all, a lot of people just don't take any interest in things, and it's not everybody that starts fighting people's cases for them. But I thought it was a very nice thing for the fellow to say, and I feel the same about all those people amongst that crowd outside the Old Bailey.

Your freedom, although you craved it, must have been very difficult to come to terms with. Are you still adjusting?

In this situation you learn day by day. Some days you're OK and other days you're not. Believe me, it takes a long time to adjust after 16 and a half years, and I bet the other five men would say the same. I'm certainly not the same person that I used to be.

Do you wake up sometimes thinking you're still in prison?

Hugh Callaghan

Oh yes, I do. When I was in prison I sometimes used to think I was in my own bed at home, and now it's the other way round. And sometimes my wife has had to shake me because I have been having nightmares about the beatings at Winson Green. I have nightmares every other week.

Do you think you'll ever enjoy life as you used to do before you went to prison?

I don't expect I will, because I'm not the same person I was. I'm known as one of the Birmingham Six now, and that has changed everything. But I live in hope.

LORD CHALFONT

LORD CHALFONT

Lord Chalfont was born Alun Jones in 1919. He was commissioned into the South Wales Borderers in 1940 and served in Burma during the war. After a distinguished army career spanning the Malayan Campaign (1955–57) and the Cyprus Campaign (1958–59) he became defence correspondent for the *Times* in 1961. In 1964 he was appointed Minister of State for Foreign Affairs by Harold Wilson to deal mainly with disarmament. He held this post until 1970 when he became deputy chairman of the IBA. Since 1980 he has chaired the House of Lords All Party Defence Group, and since 1991 he has been chairman of the Radio Authority. He is author of several books including *Montgomery of Alamein* (1976) and *Defence of the Realm* (1987).

Most people describe you as a military man first and foremost. Is that a description you bear with pride?

Yes, it is. I've always regarded my principal profession as being that of a soldier. I joined the army when I was 19 years old and I didn't leave it again for nearly 25 years. I'm the kind of animal who likes to live in a structured environment; I don't like untidiness and lack of self-discipline. There was also an immense sense of common purpose which I've never found anywhere else outside the army.

You had a very distinguished army career ... was it very difficult to make the transition to civilian life?

I thought it was going to be, but I had the advantage of having a transitional period. I was invited by the editor of the *Times* to join the newspaper as military correspondent, a post which came to be known as defence correspondent. For the next three years I spent a lot of time with the armed forces, so I was able to make the change very gradually.

In what ways do you think your military career equipped you for life in the 'real' world, so to speak?

As part of my military career I had to pass through a series of educational establishments and staff colleges, and there one learned the art of organizing one's thoughts. I was under the supervision of soldiers of great distinction, carefully chosen for this job, and they would not allow second rate thinking. They demanded first rate answers to the problems, be they military, political or human, and this gave me the ability to approach every problem in a considered, organized way. I also served in five different military campaigns, mainly anti-terrorist campaigns, which helped condition my thinking, so all in all it was a very interesting and worthwhile training for the real world.

You spent a great deal of your life with men. Were you more at ease generally with men rather than women?

No. I've never found it difficult to communicate with women. If it's not

61

Lord Chalfont

politically incorrect these days to say it, I find women much more interesting intellectually than men. They have lively, flexible minds, and I prefer their company.

In 1961 when you became defence correspondent on the Times *you were widely considered to be the most influential journalist in that area. Were you conscious of the influence you had, and the responsibility it carried?*

Yes, largely because my editor at the time, Sir William Haley, had a very strong sense of the moral responsibility of a great newspaper, and he instilled a great deal of that into me. It was he who impressed upon me the importance of the job; he used to say that what I wrote in the *Times* would be noted by everybody in the government, especially the Ministry of Defence. I was the very first *Times* correspondent to be named. The editor broke the longstanding rule because he felt that what I was saying about the analysis of our defence policy and military strategy was important enough to broaden it out, and he also thought that some of the credit would rub off on the *Times*. So, yes, I was aware that I was having a good deal of influence.

You became Labour's disarmament minister under Harold Wilson. Were you surprised to be offered this post?

I was astonished. I knew that Harold Wilson was looking for someone to fill this post, but it never occurred to me that I would be offered it. I was sitting quietly having a drink one Friday when I got a message saying that the Prime Minister would like to see me in Downing Street. I thought that he wanted to discuss some article that I had written, but to my surprise I was conducted into the Cabinet Room where Harold was sitting, puffing his pipe. He simply said: 'I'd like to offer you the post of Minister of State for Foreign Affairs to deal mainly with questions of arms control and disarmament. Because of the nature of our majority I shall have to ask you to go into the House of Lords, and because of the nature of the information and intelligence with which you will be dealing I will have to ask you to be appointed to the Privy Council.' I said I would require a little time to think about it, that I would have to consult my wife and the editor of the *Times*. He said, 'Fine, there's a room next door with a telephone, why don't you go and do your consulting now and let me know your answer.' The whole

62

thing had to be decided there and then. I rang my wife who offered her support, and William Haley said that although he would be sorry to lose me it was a challenge I shouldn't refuse. With that encouragement, I went back and told Harold Wilson that I would be delighted to do it. We had a few words which I have never really revealed to anybody before regarding the fact that I had never belonged to a political party, and that there were many things about Labour Party policy with which I disagreed. But he fully understood and said that I would not be required to support all the party policies.

Did having to join the Labour Party not go against the grain?

Yes. I have to confess that I'm not at home in ordinary political life; I'm only interested in foreign and defence policy, not domestic policy. In fact to some extent I am repelled by the internal workings of party politics. So it was a bit of a wrench at the time, but it did mean that I could carry out an exciting assignment which would involve negotiating with the Russians on nuclear weapons, and that was very worthwhile.

Your conversion to socialism was seen as your Road to Damascus, and this has perhaps made you slightly suspect in political terms, certainly inconsistent. Do you think that in those terms the appointment did you some harm?

No. It's had nothing but good consequences. I know some people feel there has been political inconsistency, but it wasn't a Road to Damascus, because I didn't *become* a socialist; I joined the Labour Party purely for politically expedient reasons. What led a lot of people to be embittered and to accuse me of political expediency of the worst kind was not when I joined the Labour government, but when I left the Labour Party in the 1970s. But all I was doing then was reverting to my old political beliefs.

After Labour lost office you gradually lost faith before resigning the Labour Whip. How did this disillusionment come about?

There were two principal areas. The trades unions were having much too much influence on the policy of the Labour Party and I felt that this was dangerous but what was really decisive was their attitude towards Europe in the 1970s. They refused to take part in the European parliament, and I was then a very strong pro-European. I believed in the Common Market and in the good sense of our attempt to get into the Common Market. I found the Labour Party's anti-European stance unacceptable and it was really on that issue that I resigned the Labour whip and went back on to the cross benches.

Have you changed your views about Europe since?

No, but I do think that Europe is going too far at the moment towards federalism, towards political union. I never believed strongly in political union; I believed rather in an economic community, the building up of an economic block of 300 million people who would have the same influence in the world as the United States. But I was never in favour of some kind of supranational European government with its own foreign policy, its own bank, its own monetary system. That I think is going too far.

Looking back on your time with Harold Wilson, how would you assess the man?

I have a very considerable affection and admiration for Harold Wilson. I think he was a very clever politician. To say he was knowledgeable sounds rather patronizing, but what I mean is that he did know what was going on all the time, both in foreign and domestic policy. He was not, as some of our political leaders tend to be, orientated towards one at the expense of the other; he saw the task of a government in the broadest terms. He had a number of intellectual characteristics which were fairly unique, an incredible photographic memory, for example, which enabled him to quote speeches which he and other people had made years before almost verbatim. Leaving aside his political abilities which were very considerable, he had an immense quality of loyalty. Once he had given you his trust, put you in a position of responsibility, he would leave you to get on with it, and if something went wrong that was not your fault, you could be sure that Harold Wilson would not let you down. The obverse of that coin is that he was not a good butcher, something which is generally thought to be a desirable characteristic of a prime minister. He hated getting rid of people, and in the hard brutal world of party politics, that was, I suppose, a bad thing. But I didn't hold it against him; I thought his sense of loyalty outweighed that.

People talk a lot about Marcia Falkender and her influence over Harold Wilson. Was she very influential or is this exaggerated?

I think her influence has been greatly exaggerated. She had scarcely any influence in the truly political sense. Harold's political views were far too well honed and thought out to be affected by kitchen cabinets. Where she did have influence was in the sense of controlling his diary, and that meant that the people who got to see Harold were the people that Marcia wanted Harold to see. That was what gave her most of her power.

When you lost faith and resigned your Labour Whip, didn't you urge the then Home Secretary, Roy Jenkins, to break away and lead a new party? This was before the Gang of Four . . .

How do you know that? I didn't think anybody knew that . . .

Would you have been tempted to join them?

Oh yes. It was in 1973. I made a special appointment with Roy and told him that the party was going in the wrong direction, it was becoming anti-European, it was becoming collectivist and moving to the left, to use that rather crude expression. I told him that he was the clear standard bearer of what you might call a social democratic government – I think that was the phrase we were using then. And had he broken away at that time I would have been one of the first people at his side.

Do you think Roy Jenkins would have made a good prime minister?

He would have made an excellent prime minister. He is a man of considerable intellectual distinction. He was a very good speaker, and an intelligent and sophisticated politician. I know that this is the 'What if?' school of history, but if Roy Jenkins had taken his lead earlier he would have been successful. As it happened, it was too late. He didn't seize the historical moment, and by the time the Gang of Four made their démarche, history had moved on.

By 1979 you were supporting Mrs Thatcher. What had prompted such a fundamental change – or were you really returning to your basic political instincts?

I wouldn't say I was returning to my instincts; my instincts are much more centrist. If we approach things in the classic – and sometimes misleading – context of right and left, I could be described as very right-wing on a number of things but quite left-wing on others. The reason why I became a strong supporter of Mrs Thatcher, and remain so to this day, is that she did something which Roy Jenkins failed to do: Margaret Thatcher grabbed the historical moment. Here we were, a nation that was getting very cynical about itself, we had lost our self-respect, our pride in our country, our influence in the world, and morale was very low. Along came Mrs Thatcher, who appealed immediately to my military instincts as a leader. She knew where she was going and she could explain to other people where she wanted them to go. In almost everything she did, certainly in the early days of her prime ministership, she gave this country back its self-respect, its image in the world. I wasn't so much concerned with her political philosophy – I'm not an unreconstructed free marketeer, so in that sense I'm not a Thatcherite – but I reacted very strongly to her leadership qualities, particularly during the Falklands campaign, which sent the message far beyond the Falkland Islands and Argentina that as far as this country was concerned aggression would not be allowed to go unpunished. It was a lesson that needed to be learned by our European allies, as well as the Soviet Union; indeed I've always regarded the Falklands as being a far bigger symbolic incident than just simply the recovery of those islands. I had my own views about the Falklands ever since I went there in the 1960s when Harold Wilson was in power, and I wasn't mad about recovering them for their own sake; but what she did in authorizing the military to put together that task force and recover those islands was a message of extraordinary importance to the rest of the world.

I can understand your backing Mrs Thatcher in the first place, but don't you think that in the last few years of her premiership, she went a bit too far and stopped listening to people?

It's true to say that towards the end there was a sense almost of infallibility, but a great deal of blame for that should be attached to the people around her. There were not many people who were prepared to say to her, 'Margaret, you've got this wrong and I will tell you you've got it wrong'. She was not receptive to polemic, but she was receptive to ideas, and had there been stronger people around her she would not have been allowed to become so arrogant as she appeared to become. The second thing I would say is that these were only the weaknesses that were the obverse of some immense strengths, and I always believe, whether you're dealing with prime ministers or with people in your own business organization, that you must recognize that people are going to have both; you simply have to play to their strengths and try to reconcile yourself to their weaknesses. What happened with Mrs Thatcher was that people started to concentrate on her weaknesses and to ignore the fact that the strengths were still there. Perhaps the sense of infallibility had been allowed to grow too much, but I would never regard that as a reason for performing upon her the kind of political assassination executed by her rivals.

But isn't the Tory Party notorious for that kind of behaviour?

Any political party is prone to this kind of palace revolution style of politics. I just happen to think that on this occasion it was an especially unpleasant political act, the most unpleasant in my time in politics. Mrs Thatcher had great leadership qualities and clarity of vision, something we lack at the top at the moment.

Would you say that in general politicians today lack the intellectual ability of their predecessors?

Yes, but there is perhaps a basic reason for it. The extraordinarily intrusive nature of the media has meant that a lot of people simply will not go into politics because they can't stand the sense of nakedness and vulnerability involved. People of integrity and distinction are finding it much more difficult now to subject themselves to this kind of treatment.

When you became deputy chairman of the IBA in 1989, Lord Bonham-

Carter, a former BBC vice chairman, said it was 'the most flagrant example yet of politicization of government appointments'. Presumably you saw things rather differently?

Not entirely. Let me explain. Mark Bonham-Carter is of course a Liberal, and he has an especially jaundiced view of anything that he regards as a quango, as a politicized public body. The reason why Mrs Thatcher asked me to go to the IBA was indeed political; she believed that the whole world of television was getting out of hand – programmes like *Death on the Rock* and so on – so to that extent it was political, but not party political. I think Mark Bonham-Carter took the view that a Conservative was being appointed to the IBA by a Conservative government – not true, of course, because I was and still am a cross bencher. The idea behind my appointment was to ensure that the regulatory body was tough enough to stand up to the television companies.

Bonham-Carter also said: 'He is an openly right-wing ideologist. His views on broadcasting are unacceptable.' This was a view quite widely shared at the time. Did you at least understand the basis of their concern?

Yes, because I'm ideologically opposed to people like Bonham-Carter on the subject of broadcasting. I'm not being rude about him, because I like him, and I hope I'm not being rude about Liberals, but I don't believe in the kind of liberal attitude to broadcasting which is part of contemporary culture. I think there is far too much freedom in broadcasting, far too much violence in television; I don't think that the sensitivities of older people and much younger people are given enough consideration by broadcasters. Television producers and reporters have begun to believe that they control the political agenda, and I believe this to be dangerous. So I fully understand why people like Mark Bonham-Carter and Paddy Ashdown were horrified when I was appointed to this post. Not only did I understand it; I was extremely pleased by it.

You had of course written the foreword for the Media Monitoring Report *in 1987 which attacked programmes like* Panorama *and* World in Action *for so called left-wing bias . . .*

I think if you look at my actual words, my criticism of the media then, and it remains so now, was that it is not a bias of the left or right, it is a bias against the established order, against the police, against the army, against the church, indeed against everything that's established. It's iconoclastic, it's nihilist and anarchist – that's my objection to it.

But isn't it good to keep the establishment on its toes?

To keep it on its toes, yes, but not try to take its place. There are far too many people in television now who regard themselves as alternative ministers. I've criticized one of them recently for thinking he's the Foreign Minister, because in Bosnia, for example, I think that television is setting the political agenda. They've only got to show some heartrending pictures of a child with its leg blown off with the comment 'Something must be done about this', and the Foreign Office immediately starts to talk about sending in bombers and troops. This is a dangerous phenomenon in our public life. Journalists have become incapable of distinguishing fact from opinion; they have begun to usurp the functions of the elected government in a democratic country. I am a great believer in a degree of regulation of the media, if only to ensure that the aim of journalists should be to pursue the truth and not their own political agenda.

You said at the time that TV was essentially an entertainment medium that should not cover serious issues. Was that designed to be a deliberately controversial remark or was it a belief sincerely held?

Both. It was said on a programme with a man called Michael Ignatieff who is a somewhat opinionated young man. I wanted to provoke him, but it had more than a grain of truth in it. I really do think that a medium which deals in images is much more suited to entertainment than to information. I've always been a believer in the written and spoken word as methods of communicating ideas to people. If you want to communicate images or impressions, then use pictures.

You have been very critical of Radio 4, particularly the Today *programme where you thought there was 'too much editorialization by the presenters'. Why do you regard this as such a bad thing?*

To use those now rather jaded words of C P Scott: 'Opinion is free but facts are sacred'. The most important thing about journalism is to separate presentation of facts from opinion, and my reason for criticizing Radio 4 and the *Today* programme especially was that they confuse fact and opinion. There are people who, by the very tone of their voice or by a comment at the end of an item, will slant the whole news story in a way obviously designed to condition people's perception of the news; and I think that's dangerous.

You singled out Brian Redhead as being one of the worst offenders for letting his opinions intrude in what was essentially a news programme. But as the obituaries showed, this was precisely what he was admired and respected for . . .

Well, he was admired and respected by people who are of the same view. It's rather embarrassing that Brian has recently died – *de mortuis nil nisi bonum* – but I still believe that he was guilty of peddling his own political ideology in his programme. When people are writing obituaries they go over the top in terms of eulogy and don't always present their real views, so I don't take too much notice, but those who believe in the liberal culture in broadcasting would certainly say that Brian Redhead failed to uphold it. His own political ideology shone out of everything he said and did, even in the news programmes.

If I can press you a bit on this business of distinguishing between fact and opinion, which you regard as one of the principles of journalism . . . if you are able to tell the difference without difficulty, is it not reasonable to assume that other listeners can do the same?

I'm going to say something now that is disastrously unwise, but you see, everybody is not as sophisticated as I am. The vast majority of listeners to radio and watchers of television are not sophisticated; they are not political animals, and they do not necessarily recognize nuances and opinion, or distortion of facts. I know as I say this that it will sound very patronizing if it ever appears in print, and I shall be accused of insulting the intelligence of the public. But I'm not talking about intelligence; I'm talking about political sophistication, and it is possible for a large number of people to be fooled and deceived by clever purveyors, by clever communicators. All I am concerned to do is to alert people to the fact that everything they read in the newspapers or hear on the radio is not necessarily true, and what I want from the professional journalist is the presentation of two sides of a question, equally balanced, so that people may make up their own minds.

I know you don't favour censorship but doesn't any interference in the editorial independence of programmes inevitably introduce a degree of paternalism which is inappropriate in the late 20th century?

I don't want any kind of interference with editorial freedom or with editorial discretion; I would be the very last person to suggest that, provided the normal conventions are observed. But if editorial freedom means blasphemy, obscenity, explicit sex, then I think somebody has to – if not interfere – at least try to educate.

But do you think it will ever be possible to have a truly independent broadcasting authority?

I don't see any reason why the present regulatory authorities in this country should not be independent, provided they are properly appointed so that they cover a broad range of political opinion, a broad age spectrum, and a broad culture and ethnic spectrum. It is then perfectly possible through a process of discussion to arrive at decisions which are objective and balanced.

Would it be a cynical view to say that independence will exist only to the extent that the government of the day wishes it to be preserved?

That's absolutely true. If the government of the day wants to control the media, it will control them, and can control them, if only by patronage, or by ensuring that the right people are in the right places. I can only say, however, that I have now been chairman of the Radio Authority for four years and there's never been one single occasion when anybody from the government has tried to press any idea upon me. I have carried out the affairs of the Radio Authority totally independently, and there's never been a hint of any government interference.

Lord Chalfont

Would you say that there is still a left-wing bias in the media today?

I must insist that I've never said there is left-wing bias. Let's deal with newspapers first. It doesn't really matter if a newspaper is biased one way or another, because there is a broad range of newspapers and you know what you're getting when you make a purchase. In local radio, there's no place for bias, but in national radio – I've already cited the *Today* programme – there is sometimes a bias against the established order, a kind of radicalism, an iconoclasm, a wish to knock down everything that smacks of the establishment. The worst danger, however, is in television where there is a great deal of extreme radicalism, the desire to attack everything that is regarded as being traditional and established.

Does it make any sense to talk about establishment and anti-establishment nowadays, when what was regarded as the establishment does seem to be crumbling, or at least in disarray . . . the royal family, standards of behaviour in government, and so on?

The term 'establishment' is a piece of journalistic shorthand which has passed into the language and is of no importance. The establishment in that sense is undergoing a considerable battering at the moment, but I don't care about that. I am interested in the established order rather than the establishment; that is to say, a society in which there are certain values like honesty, civility and courtesy, the rule of law and all the things that traditionally go to make up a compassionate and civilized society. When I say people are anti-establishment I don't mean that they are against judges or the Garrick Club – because that doesn't interest me; what worries me is when they start to question traditional and established values. We're moving now into a terribly debilitated society, in which an unarmed policeman is stabbed when investigating a perfectly commonplace crime; in which private lives are spread across newspapers – whether they belong to the royal family or not is beside the point. I'm not necessarily concerned to keep the judiciary in its present form, or democracy in its present form; there are many ways in which democracy can be preserved without necessarily following the Westminster pattern, but I think we have all been extraordinarily fortunate to have been brought up in a society in which the feelings of other people are a matter of great importance, in which the freedom of the individual is paramount, unless he begins to impinge upon the freedom of others. It's the whole Juadeo-Christian civilization which has come down to us over the centuries; and I don't think that the next generation is going to live in a world nearly as civilized and as courteous and as at ease with itself as the one in which I have been able to live.

In 1991 there were calls for your resignation as chairman of the Radio Authority because you were also a director of a PR firm which was appointed to handle a commercial radio station. Before that you had to leave the Independent Television Commission because the same PR firm was advising two TV companies. You also had to resign from Hamilton Ingram, a private security firm, when you were chairman of the IBA. It does seem as if your career has been dogged by a number of conflicts of interest . . .

Conflicts of interest arise for anybody who is active across a broad spectrum of life as I am; the main thing is to resolve them at once, and in each of those cases I took immediate steps to deal with the situation. In the case of the Radio Authority I ensured that the company with which I was involved resigned from its contract. I chose to resign from the IBA, because the company with which I was concerned had important contracts, which I didn't want them to lose. I also immediately resigned from Hamilton Security, where there was a similar conflict. I'm involved in industry, in business, in quasi-government affairs, I'm also involved in the House of Lords – surely anybody who lives a full life of the kind I live must expect conflicts of interest. What is important is your own personal integrity which will ensure that if a conflict arises you will resolve it in an honest and straightforward way; I have always moved very quickly, within hours, to take appropriate steps, and I think that's all that anybody can do.

Were you upset when Paddy Ashdown tabled a Commons motion saying that your business interests were incompatible with the independence required of your appointment? Did you understand the basis of his disquiet?

No, I didn't. What he seemed to be assuming was that if a conflict of interest were to arise I would in some way attempt to conceal it or to benefit by it; and I find that very offensive, not to say simple-minded.

Lord Chalfont

You were very critical of Thames TV's Death on the Rock. *Was this chiefly because of what you saw as a lack of balance in the programme, or did your criticisms go deeper than that?*

I thought it was a totally irresponsible and seriously damaging programme, because it gave only one view of the SAS operation on Gibraltar. It might have been excusable if they had made another programme concentrating on the violence of the IRA and the fact that if they had been allowed to complete their operation hundreds of innocent people might have been killed. None of that came out in *Death on the Rock*, and that's why I crossed swords with them.

But wasn't what took place on Gibraltar murder, and as such morally repellent?

Well, here I think you have to make some allowances for my military background. If I explain to you that I regard the situation with the IRA as a war, perhaps you will understand my point of view. We should not speak in terms of murder – I think 'shoot to kill' is a totally irrelevant concept. If you have an armed enemy, and that armed enemy is determined to kill you or the citizens of your country, you are totally entitled to use the same measure against him or her. It's a war, and people get killed in wars, and unless terrorists are made to understand that they risk being killed in pursuit of their terrorism, we're going to lose the war.

But aren't you afraid that an innocent man might be murdered?

There is a danger that innocent people will get killed. But I take the view, which perhaps you would regard as too simplistic, that the terrorists are killing innocent people all the time. I am perhaps less worried than you about the possibility of one innocent person being killed in a counter-terrorist operation than the certainty of a hundred innocent people being killed if that operation doesn't take place.

You are regarded as the most controversial of peers. Do you rather relish this public image?

I used to. I used to love controversy, public debate and argument, and I would often make provocative remarks simply for the fun of it. The joy of that has gone to some extent, and I would prefer now to be regarded as a wise father figure in politics. I feel less agitated now, less excited when someone disagrees, more serene. As you get older you come closer to one of the great mysteries, which seems altogether more interesting and important than some of the sideshows here.

How important has your private family life been in supporting you through public life?

Enormously. My wife is a paediatrician by profession, highly intelligent, and she has been extremely supportive throughout the whole of my life. We had a tragedy early on in our marriage when we lost a child, and for various reasons we didn't have more children. So my family really consists of my wife, who has been totally and utterly dependable all the way and especially strong when there have been difficulties.

You must have developed a thick skin over the years in politics . . . have you ever longed for a quieter life, out of the public eye?

I'm beginning to feel that way now. I'm not going to go on forever running large industrial companies, the Radio Authority and the various other interests. As that happens I hope that there won't be so much of the public eye, but I can't pretend that I haven't enjoyed it.

QUENTIN CRISP

QUENTIN CRISP

Quentin Crisp was born in Surrey in 1908. He worked as an artist's model until the 1970s when his book *The Naked Civil Servant* was dramatized for television to great acclaim. Since then he has written several books including a second volume of autobiography, *How to Become a Virgin*, and a book of film criticism, *How to Go to the Movies*. In 1993 he played the role of Elizabeth I in the film version of *Orlando*. In 1981 he left England for New York where he lives in a single room on the Lower East Side.

From an early age you were aware of what you call your predicament. Do you think your predicament was largely genetic or do you think there were other factors involved?

There must have been something genetic because so many people have such absolutely conventional upbringings and they still are peculiar in some way or another, including sexually peculiar. But there may have been other factors involved. For example, you could say that I lacked anyone to tell me how to be a grown person. My mother alternately protected me from the world and threatened me with it; my father took absolutely no notice of any of us, he hardly ever spoke to us.

You obviously had a very difficult relationship with your father. How much do you think this was a symptom, how much a cause of your own problems?

I never tried to talk to my father about anything, certainly never about anything serious, so I think that was a cause. The more appalling I was, the less he talked to me.

You said that in later years you found ways to fuel the furnaces of his hatred. That sounds like a deliberate attempt to do battle.

In some ways, yes. I became more frivolous and more deliberately helpless. I knew I was a hopeless case, and I paraded my hopelessness before my father.

Money always seems to have been a bit of a problem. Yet the impression is of a middle-class upbringing with domestic servants and so on . . . would you say that was the case?

We did have a middle-class suburban upbringing, and there were servants with black dresses and starched aprons, but I now know we had no money. My father was permanently in debt, and there were bailiffs in the house regularly.

Quentin Crisp

In your autobiography, your three siblings are given hardly a mention. Did you always feel apart from them, and they from you?

Yes, I think I was apart from them, and they felt glad that I was apart from them. My sister, who died only about ten years ago, once said long after all the trouble was over, that I had been a terrible child. My brother next to me in age was horrified by having to be associated with me. The brother after that was so much older that he didn't really bother.

As a child, your unhappiness, or sense of being different, manifested itself in all kinds of attention seeking behaviour. Were you aware of what you were doing at the time, was it a means to an end, or did you become aware of what it was only retrospectively?

I certainly did draw attention to myself, and I think I knew that I did, but I would have denied it, I imagine.

Do you look back on that period when you were wetting your trousers and soiling yourself with a kind of revulsion?

Well, I suppose I should. I really don't look back on it at all, but certainly I was a disgusting child, there is no doubt about it. But I don't remember being ashamed.

Boarding school seems to have been a terrible time. You were half-starved, half-frozen and humiliated in a number of ways. Did you never appeal to your parents to take you away?

I didn't. I never tried to get them to take me away. It never occurred to me to challenge my destiny.

You hated boarding school, but you describe it as a dress rehearsal for the treatment you were soon to receive in the streets of London. Would you say in that sense it was a good preparation?

Yes. I think if I had left straight from home and gone out into the world, it would have been like falling over a cliff. I had a doll's house view of the world when I was at public school. I had to learn that everybody was my enemy, and that I would have to find ways of dealing with this if I was going to go on living.

You were so unpopular at boarding school that you say that you came to regard your unpopularity as a gift, and what was originally something you tried to avoid, you later came to cultivate. Deep down didn't you still crave friendship and approval?

I think I must have wanted friendship – it seems so unlikely that I wanted none. I didn't want approval enough to alter myself in order to get any. On some days I would think, I can't bear this any more, I will try and behave like a normal schoolboy, and then I would think, I'm doing this so badly, it's too humiliating, and I would go back to being my horrible self.

Although there was a great deal of homosexual coupling at your school, you said in your autobiography that effeminate homosexuals did not indulge very much in sex with other boys. Why was that exactly?

Effeminate homosexuals tend to want love at the beginning, but they will not find it. It wouldn't have meant anything to me just to go behind a hedge with a boy and do it, and come away again. I wanted the world to care about me, and that included anybody that I met.

So you weren't driven at that time by a sexual urge?

I've never really been driven by a sexual urge, certainly not deeply. Of course I very quickly realized that love was out of the question, that any contact I made with people would have to be sexual, and I tried to give myself up to this, not at school, but later on. I thought at one time that sex would take me away from all this, without knowing where it would take me. I thought that if I could find someone who would cherish me, everything would be all right, but this never happened.

You also wrote of that period: 'What I wanted most of all was to use sex as a weapon to allure, subjugate, and if possible to destroy the personality of others.' That seems a remarkably well formulated analysis for a boy of 14 or 15. Did you actually think of it in that way at the time?

I think I did. I thought I could meet someone who would be sufficiently interested in me to do as I told him, but of course no such person existed. At the age of about 18, that would have been in 1927, I was much influenced by what I saw in the movies. Gloria Swanson, Greta Garbo and Marlene Dietrich were all icons of power, and the great German films were all about vamps – the word has all but disappeared from the language. The women were vamps, and they destroyed men. In one film Miss Helm, the most beautiful woman who ever lived, sits in a tent while the men struggle across the desert, their lips blistered with thirst. She orders some champagne, drinks it, then breaks the glass on the edge of her throne and cuts the throat of one of the men for no reason whatsoever.

When your father died, you say you felt only irritation at having to return for his funeral. Did you ever come to revise those feelings?

No, I didn't really. I had no feelings about his death. I ought to have been pleased he was dead, but actually I had already left home, so I felt nothing. It was just an event. Even now that I can, if I wish, think of my father as a character in fiction, it's still impossible to like him. Why did he saddle my mother with four children when he had no money? When he died, she had to go and live with my sister, there was nothing else she could do.

What was it like when your mother died? Were you more attached to her?

We were all relieved, because she had had such a terrible life. She didn't die until she was 86 and by that time she had to be lifted out of the bed into a wheelchair and at night had to be lifted back into bed. I don't seem to be able to be deeply attached to anybody. It's hard to tell how much people mean when they talk about such things. I don't know how different I am from other people, but I certainly do feel I have fewer of what would be called proper sentiments in regard to other people.

At some point in your youth, you managed to shift homosexuality from being a burden to being a cause. Presumably in some ways, far from making your life easier, it must have been made more difficult . . .?

Of course I know now that it was nonsense to think of it as a cause, but at the time I spent my life in cafés where I sat with other gay boys, most of whom were on the game, and we pulled our tears. They were miserable and for no justifiable reason, and I therefore decided that somebody had to live the homosexual life – it was no good writing books about it, because they would be read only by homosexuals. The important thing was to live it so that people would get used to the idea. The great weapon in the hands of integration is boredom. When you say to somebody, I'm gay, and they say, and then? – you're in the clear. It's while you have to explain yourself and justify yourself, and they try to be tolerant of you, that the problem still exists.

Did you ever dabble in prostitution?

Yes, but I was so bad at it. The reason why men go with boys is usually in the spirit of hilarious research. They want someone who's no bother, someone who doesn't try to weave an emotion into it. I didn't so much want to have sex as to be admired, and of course that was no good. So I gave it up the moment I got any real work to do.

Was the wearing of make-up a kind of acceptance of your own sexuality, a statement to society that this was you, and they had better get used to the idea?

Yes. First of all, I wore very little make-up, but exhibitionism is like a drug – after a while you can take a dose of it that would kill anyone who is just starting out. When you don't get noticed, you think, I must do more. You start to expect to cause a stare, and you're frightened when you can't do without it.

You describe the homosexuals you befriended in those days as 'pseudo-women in search of pseudo-men'. Did that mean it was a disappointment when they had encounters with similarly effeminate men?

83

Yes, that's right, it worried them. They would express to me their disappointment, their indignation at finding out that someone who they thought was going to turn out to be a man was just as effeminate secretly as they were. Nowadays the homosexual world is a world apart, and they don't really want to bother with real people, but in those days we all thought we would reinforce our idea of ourselves by gaining the attention of real men. Of course it led to disaster over and over again.

At what point did you realize that it was pointless to expect people to be tolerant or understanding towards you?

Very early on. By the time I was 30 I didn't really expect anything.

Your early working life was precarious to say the least, spells of unsuitable jobs interspersed with dole money. You must have lived in a state of permanent anxiety . . .

Yes, and I was always hungry. The dole was 14 shillings a week. I had one meal a day and lived in a room which cost 6 shillings a week. The room was long enough to lie down in one way, not quite long enough to lie down the other way, and not quite high enough to stand up in. It was a very difficult period.

You turned your hand to writing – poems, libretti, stories – but you describe the problem as being one of having a genius but no talent. What did you mean by that exactly?

My genius is for the smiling and nodding racket which I can now practically live on. If you can get by on peanuts and champagne in America you need never buy food again, but in England you can't do that; you need to be able to do something and do it well, and possibly even study it. I've never studied anything in my life.

At one point, in The Naked Civil Servant, *you liken homosexuality to an illness. That implies that it cannot be helped but in some cases it might be cured. Was that your view?*

I suppose it still is my view. I don't remember what I thought at the time, but I have known homosexuals who have got married because they thought it might help. I didn't ever say, 'help whom?', and indeed since they remain married and they have children, it obviously did help. The idea that people are either heterosexual or homosexual is nonsense; they will sometimes drift backwards and forwards for an hour or a week or for years, it depends. The more the gay people now insist on their rights, the greater the distance becomes between the gay world and the straight world, and this is such a pity. I suppose I have to be careful about calling it an illness, but homosexuals seem to me to be people standing on the bank watching other people swim. In some way it takes you away from real life, away from the main stream, so if it isn't an illness, it's certainly like having an illness.

Did you ever sleep with a woman?

Never. I don't think it could have worked. Sexually I have no interest in women at all. I don't shun them, I simply have no interest in them.

You say at one point in the book that you regarded all heterosexuals, however low, as superior to all homosexuals, however noble. What did you mean by that?

The world belongs to straight people, and they must be regarded as superior. The superiority of numbers, of power, of know-how, of worldliness is all with straight people – that's the sense in which they are superior.

Do you have a secret admiration for heterosexuals?

I suppose I do, yes. Especially the ones who seem so totally at ease with themselves.

During the 30s you began to meet a greater number and variety of homosexuals, but because you did not conform to their rules you were ostracized by them too. It must surely have been much harder to bear the hostility of homosexuals.

Yes, I was very disappointed when I first found that the homosexual community distrusted, disliked, even despised me. I got used to it and I suppose in England most of my friends were straight women, because they expected nothing of me, and in any case these were women in happier times, before they decided they had to be people. When women were women, one of the things they liked to do was chatter, and I'm a born chatterer, so I could sit with them, and entertain them and they could be nice to me. I didn't really ever get on with men because they only ever speak about money and politics and sport, about which I know nothing.

It seems that because you publicized homosexuality and flaunted your own, you angered a great many homosexuals who preferred to remain incognito. Did you not sympathize with their position?

I understood their position but I don't really believe that my being obvious made any difference to them. Everything is so changed now. Nowadays if two men take an apartment in any big city in the western world, it is assumed they are gay. In a time gone by, people would have assumed they were sharing a place and halving the rent. Friendship is disappearing altogether and sex has taken its place.

From where did you derive the courage to display all the trappings of homosexuality at a time when it was firmly in the closet?

I couldn't do otherwise. I was hopeless at being a real person, and even when on occasions I was not wearing make-up, it made no difference. People still stared at me.

When the war broke out you were turned down by the medical board on grounds of sexual perversion. Did you receive that as an accolade or were you humiliated by it?

I wasn't humiliated. People had told me I would never get into the forces, but I hadn't believed them. I had no money, I couldn't get a job, and I imagined it would solve all my problems.

What were your feelings about the war?

It was very nice when it came. First of all, there was a whole year in which you never saw any war whatsoever, and you could only read about it in the papers. But then the war came to London and the sky was pink with doom, the ground shook with the anti-aircraft fire, and you could hear the shrapnel falling. And that was very exciting. I decided I wouldn't accommodate the war at all, so if I was invited out I went out, whether there had been the air raid warning or not – it was all a lottery in any case.

The war seems scarcely to have impinged on you – at least it hardly figures in your account of those years. How did you manage to avoid thinking about it, worrying about it?

I just didn't alter my life, I went on exactly as though there were no war. The only wonderful aspect of the war was the American soldiers. Americans listen to what you say; Englishmen never do. It felt you were being courted to some extent.

When you found unfurnished accommodation you discovered that squalor was your 'natural setting', as you called it. Was this primarily a reaction against your mother's domestic orderliness?

I don't think so. It was just natural laziness. I didn't want to clean everything, and so I thought, I won't, and we'll see what happens. Then I formulated the idea that after the first four years the dirt doesn't get any worse.

Is that what you truly believe, or was it something you said primarily to shock people or to amuse them?

I never say what I don't mean. And I'm not the only person to think that way. There was once a woman called Nancy Spain who went on to

Woman's Hour, and said that only a fool would make the bed every day. It shook England, but in fact it was a message of hope. I once watched a woman dust the rails under the chairs, and I told her there was no need to do that. She said, 'I know there isn't, but if I don't do it they haunt me.' And that is the way women feel. Women in England are all in a blind rage by half past ten in the morning, because they've had to skirmish round the house, and dust everything, and put everything right, wash everything. But there's no need.

You criticize the advertising industry for spreading the idea, against all evidence to the contrary, that sex leads to happiness. Would you at least concede that it leads to pleasure, perhaps the greatest pleasure of all?

It leads to pleasure, but with penalties. Homosexual intercourse is often actually painful, sometimes uncomfortable, sometimes nasty, so you have to think, do I really want this? There was once a programme about hepatitis, and a woman interviewed a young man and asked how many times on average he had sexual relations. He replied 'six', and she said, 'six times a week'? He replied, 'No, six times a night.' Now at that rate, it can't go on being a pleasure – it must simply be a score. I think it's a form of pleasure which some people cannot do without, but I don't believe it is a form of happiness.

Could you yourself do without it?

I can do without it now, and I have done for the last twenty years or so. In the past if I felt sexual urges I usually masturbated, which is less trouble. And so much cheaper.

Why is the homosexual generally more promiscuous than the hetero-sexual?

I secretly think – though I have been shouted down on this – that it is because it is not very satisfactory. Just as if you eat food that doesn't nourish you, you eat more food, so people who indulge in unsatisfactory sex are often extraordinarily promiscuous.

You seem very cynical about sex, calling it 'the last refuge of the miserable'. Was this some sort of defence mechanism operating?

I don't think so. It's just that I don't set much store by sex, and I have had less sexual experience than most people. But certainly it is a refuge of the miserable insofar as people who are not content with their lives have to go out to look for sex. And that applies to the heterosexual man as well.

Have you ever had a happy sexual relationship?

I've had pleasant sexual relationships. I couldn't say I ever met anyone who fulfilled my dream which was to be admired for sexual and other reasons. I suppose the truth is, I do not deserve it, but you don't realize that in the beginning.

Your relationship with the American GI seemed to be one of the most satisfactory but even then there was no love. Was there affection?

There was affection, and he was friendly, which is rare in homosexual relationships.

But you never really fell in love . . .

I don't think I quite know what the phrase means. I understand that you can fancy somebody, or wish them well, or you can enjoy their company, but I don't know anything beyond that.

Towards the end of the war you became a model and posed for art students. I imagine that had greater appeal than your other jobs . . .

It did. In the beginning I really liked it in spite of the terrible suffering involved in sitting. There was hardly any limit to the discomfort I could endure, but you can only get better at it for the first two or three years. When you begin, you think, I wonder if I'm going to faint, but after a bit there's nothing you can't do. I did it on and off for 35 years

---

Quentin Crisp

and in the end I was half asleep half the time. But yes, I liked it in the beginning.

One imagines that you might have lived a rather promiscuous life, but this seems not to have been the case in the early days. For many years you were able to live without sexual encounters at all. Was this primarily lack of opportunity or lack of desire?

I never really desired much sex. I don't ever remember thinking, 'I've got to get a man from somewhere'. If it presented itself to me, fine, if it didn't, I went without it. Now I haven't had any sex for at least 20 years and this doesn't worry me in the least. My appetites are in general much weaker than other people's – I've never been drunk, I never overeat, I have never done anything to excess. Even at my worst I was never as promiscuous as most homosexual men are.

After the war you took to the movies and watched anything as long as it wasn't English. Was this a kind of escapism or was it a genuine passion?

It is a genuine passion. Nothing ever happens in English movies, which is why I dislike them, and in any case I've always been American in my heart. When I was a child my mother took me to the movies in the spirit of ostentatious condescension; the cinema was for servant girls, and people with taste went to the theatre. She told me America was nothing like how it looked in the movies, but she was wrong. Everybody who comes from England to America agrees it's more like the movies than you'd ever dream.

Are you lonely ever?

I like solitude, but of course I've never been put to the test because I've always lived in big cities. If I spent a whole week in my room doing nothing, I would reconstruct myself, go out, walk from where I live up to 14th Street and back again and I would be really surprised not to meet somebody with whom I could have a cup of coffee and discuss the secret of the universe. I've never lived in a village and I hope I never shall.

Your first major writing success was The Naked Civil Servant *which was soon made into a TV movie. Was that the first real flush of success for you?*

Yes, but it was only a mini-success. It did not lead to any work, I wasn't invited to review other people's books and say they were worse than mine, and no one asked me to write anything else. It wasn't until it was made into a television play that my whole life changed. That was in 1975, and the book came out in 1968, so there were seven long dark years in between.

John Hurt's portrayal of you was widely acclaimed. Were you yourself happy with it?

I was indeed. It was a marvellous reproduction of my voice for one thing. He was slightly more defiant than I ever was, but only minimally. He's born to play victims. After he played me he went on to play Claudius, which is really only me in a sheet, and then he was the Elephant Man. People sometimes ask me if I feel like an elephant man, and I do, I do.

One success led to another, and you soon had your own one man show at the Duke of York's. Did your life change as a result?

I felt my way of speaking, my way of expressing myself, had started to pay off, yes, but my life didn't change much. I didn't branch out, I didn't spend a lot of money. I went on living in one room, and I still live in one room.

Your success in England was readily exported to America. You say you have always felt your natural milieu to be American. It must have seemed like a dream come true . . .

To come here was quite quite wonderful. Happiness rains down from the sky in America. I agree with Millicent Martin who is now an American by marriage. She said the difference between America and England is that in America everyone is always in favour of whatever you propose to do, and this is absolutely true. If you stand up in a bar and announce that you're getting up a cabaret act, everybody will ask, where are you gonna appear? what are you gonna wear? In England if you told your friends you were getting up a cabaret act, they would say, for God's sake, don't make a fool of yourself. Everything is a warning in England. I didn't know there was any happiness in the world, till I got here.

You say, the English have etiquette, and the Americans have manners. How would you explain the difference?

Etiquette is a process of exclusion. The English have rules, and if you don't know how to eat an artichoke then you're not one of us; if you call a table napkin a serviette, you will not be invited again. In America you have manners, which are a process of inclusion. When you're with Americans they want you to feel you can do no wrong; that's the difference.

Your performance in Orlando, *as Elizabeth the First, has been widely praised. Was that something you enjoyed?*

It was absolute hell, but being in a movie is always absolute hell. I wore two rolls of fabric round my middle tied with tapes, and then a hooped skirt tied with tape, and then a quilted petticoat and then an ordinary petticoat and then a dress, and I had a bodice so tight that it blistered my stomach. No wonder Queen Elizabeth was always chopping off people's heads – she must have been in a permanent rage from having to wear those clothes.

Presumably now, with your writing and lecturing and TV and film appearances, you are better off in your 80s than you have ever been. Do you feel there is an irony there?

I suppose there is. I am better off, but not very much better off. People assume that if you're famous you're rich, which of course is not necessarily so, but provided I die in the next two or three years, I'm in the clear. In America everybody is your friend, but the system is ruthless. Once you're unproductive you will end up living in a cardboard box on the street corner. So you have to get into your grave fairly quickly.

In your autobiographical writing you seem much concerned with the notion of happiness and what it consists in . . . for example, you think money is a prerequisite, or to look forward to the future spells the death of happiness. How would you describe the state of happiness, and have you achieved it in your life?

I've achieved a little of it. Happiness, I would say, is to live in the present, not to think about the past, not to think about the future, but to be here and to be now, to be aware, to live inside your body. I think happiness is a physical thing.

Most people would define happiness in terms of loving and being loved. Does that strike you as being completely alien?

It's alien to me. My happiness is a relationship between me and myself, not between me and someone else, which is always full of uncertainty.

You have described yourself as doing deliberately what you used to do by mistake, a way of getting the joke on your own terms. Have you arrived at a kind of contentment now, would you say?

Yes. Now I can behave in a way that is perfectly natural for me, and other people accept it, or appear to accept it. Perhaps it's all an illusion, because in America if they don't like you, they don't say so, whereas if they do like you, they tell you. It's completely the other way round in England – there you feel terribly disliked, but here in America it's easy to get the impression that everybody adores you. But I would say that I'm happier than I ever expected to be.

You were a martyr, weren't you, but your martyrdom was partly self-inflicted. You got used to living in a world which scorned and hated you. Did you become a willing martyr in the end?

I suppose I expected the world in general not to accept me, not to like me, and to throw things at me and shout at me, so yes, I suppose I was the willing kind.

Would you have had the sex-change operation if it had been available at the time?

Quentin Crisp

If it had been available when I was in my late teens, and I had had the money, I would certainly have had the operation. Then I could have gone away to a provincial town and run a knitting wool shop, and nobody would ever have known my terrible secret. I would have been free.

You have been much preoccupied with the business of death, and have been predicting your own for some time now. Do you look forward to it?

Yes, it's the next big event in my life. Like most people, I imagine, what one is concerned with is behaving nicely when you're dying. A lot of people think it terrible to die alone, but if you die in the presence of other people you have to be polite while you die, which must be very difficult. So that is one of my chief preoccupations: how to behave nicely while dying.

What is your attitude to religion . . . has it changed at all over the years?

No, I think it's always been the same. I don't want to say anything that might give offence, but I can't believe in a God susceptible to prayer. If God is the universe that encloses the universe, or if God is the cell inside the cell, or if God is the cause behind the cause, this I can accept. But I think it is actually wrong to teach children to bargain with whatever they think is God – for example, if you don't eat sweets in Lent He will give you a bicycle with ten speeds. This is undignified. If there is a force that keeps the spheres moving in the heavens, why would it be preoccupied with us, and why would it be endowed with such wretched human characteristics? Why is it angry, why is it jealous, why is it forgiving? No, I don't believe in that sort of God.

But do you expect any life after death?

I can't afford to. What little I can, do, say and be is complete, so it would be very dreary to have to come back. I can't really imagine what life after death would entail; I can only imagine more of the life that I've already led, and that has been long enough.

Your life has been extraordinary by any standards, but it strikes the outside

94

observer as having been a tragic one in some measure. Would you agree?

Yes. I don't know how it could have been changed to make it less tragic. Other people grow up with their brothers and sisters, and they get on fine for the most part with them, and then they go to school and make friends, and then they go out into the world and acquire workmates. None of that happened to me. I was alone, and I had to invent happiness.

Your autobiography ends with the words: 'I stumble towards my grave confused and hurt and hungry . . .' Would you use the same words today?

No. Today I am less confused, my hurts have been mostly healed, and I am well fed.

RUMER GODDEN

RUMER GODDEN

Rumer Godden is author of more than sixty books, mostly novels for adults and children, but also biographies, plays and poetry. She was born in 1907 and spent most of her childhood in a remote village in East Bengal where her father worked for a steamship company. She first went to school at the age of twelve in Eastbourne but soon returned to India. She married in 1934 and had two children but later divorced and returned to England after the war where she devoted her time to writing. Her novels *Black Narcissus* and *The Greenage Summer* were made into films, as was her Indian epic *The River*, directed by Jean Renoir. She has written two volumes of autobiography *A Time to Dance, No Time to Weep* (1987) and *A House With Four Rooms* (1989). She now lives in Scotland with her daughter.

From India to Dumfriesshire is a long journey in any life. Have you been able to regard Scotland as home, or is India still where you belong in spirit?

I'm always divided. I've never regarded Scotland as home, but I'm deeply attached to England. I'm like the character in the Gilbert and Sullivan play who was a fairy up to his waist and a human above. I have India in my bones and when I'm in England I'm homesick for India and when I'm in India I'm homesick for England. It's very difficult.

When you were 19 you read Forster's A Passage to India *which changed your life. It made you ashamed of what you call your 'blindness and ignorance' – how little you understood of the India you inhabited. Can you recall those feelings?*

When I was a child in India the old shibboleth still prevailed, that the men had contact with all the Indians, but the women and children were not supposed to mix. My father spoke Bengali and Hindi, but we were not allowed to in case we caught the accent and became 'chichi', as they called it. We were not allowed to play with Indian children, nor they with us, and as for the Anglo-Indians, those of mixed marriages, they were absolutely outré. We sometimes used to escape and get over our garden wall into the bazaar without anyone knowing. And so even as a child I saw perhaps more of India than my mother, but if I asked questions they were never answered. It was *A Passage to India* that suddenly made me see that we were like the Turtons. After that I astonished my father and mother by insisting that I was given lessons in Hinduism and allowed to visit Indians and speak to them.

Later on you wrote: 'In India, for many people, especially women, the pastiche was their life, and nearly was mine.' Was this pastiche a reference to the hierarchy of colonization?

Probably, but it was unconscious. For instance, I never heard the word British Raj; that was an invention that came after independence. And my father had deep compassion and fellowship with his employees. What enabled me to avoid the pastiche was that I was a born writer and writers are very curious; they like to understand where they live and not feel shut off. Later on I broke away from my family and after training as a dancer, I

Rumer Godden

outraged everybody by opening a dancing school in Calcutta, an unheard of thing. My father was shocked and told me that I would be ostracized by my fellow English. These attitudes lasted a long time. Even when I went back to India as a married woman with my children, the Swiss Italian nanny, who was very dark, used to take the children swimming. I was soon rung up by the secretary of the club to say that my nanny had been seen swimming in the pool and since she was half-caste, that was not allowed, not even with the children. The narrowness was incredible.

Much of your writing is related to the extraordinary events of your life, and in a sense writing was not a luxury but a necessity, a means of earning a living. Do you think there was an element of necessity being the mother of invention?

I think it brought it to fulfilment, but I believe writers are born. My sister was far more gifted than I was, but she married an extremely rich man and was very spoiled. I had no option, I had to work, and I had a very stern apprenticeship when I got back to London after the Second World War. I was practically penniless, and I wrote anything I could, articles, essays, anything that came my way, and it was a wonderful training. It was something I had to do because I had two children and no husband.

Certain books you read in your younger days seem to have had a very significant effect . . . Mr Darcy from Pride and Prejudice, *for example, made such an impression that for a long time no man could measure up. Can you recall the intensity of that feeling, or does it now strike you as absurd, looking back?*

No, I have it still today. I've read *Pride and Prejudice* 13 times and every time I fall in love with Mr Darcy. Nothing has changed. There is still a lot of the child in me, and though I've been through a lot of adversity, I have retained that feeling of wonder which enables me to fall in love with Mr Darcy again.

Your own romantic path did not run smooth. How much do you think this was to do with colonial life and the restrictions and expectations placed upon it?

Not much. I don't think I was in love with my first husband but I was in love with the idea of being married and he was a very charming person, though he was not all he should have been. But my second husband was wonderful to me, absolutely wonderful, the most understanding man I ever met, and totally unselfish.

You broke off your first engagement, and wrote of your fiancé: 'I hurt him abominably, but not as much as I would have done had I married him.' It must have taken tremendous courage to do what you did, especially in the face of family opposition . . .

Yes, my parents were furious with me. In fact I left home for a while. They so wanted me to marry him. He was a very desirable match, and it seemed to be so perfect, because he fell in love with me when I was only 8, and he waited all the time that I was at school until I came back to India with the unwavering conviction that he was going to marry me. I was barely 18, and I just knew I couldn't.

In 1934 you married Lawrence Foster, whom you described as 'unfailingly kind'. That description seemed to condemn rather than to praise . . .

Well, it wasn't meant to. I just didn't know what else to say about him. When I first wrote my autobiography I left him out, but my dear publisher said I had to include him. He was absolutely charming and like very many charming people, not to be trusted. I have a deep distrust of charm. I was never really in love with him, but I tried again and again to save the marriage, because I had the children and he was their father. He had perpetual money trouble, but by then I was earning quite well from writing. *Black Narcissus* was a real bestseller and brought in a tremendous amount of money which is why I thought I could afford a nanny and a nice house. This was before I realized that my husband had gambled on the stock exchange and was deeply, deeply in debt. I used up all my money in paying off his debts, which was perhaps the most foolish thing I ever did because it didn't save the situation. But I was very pleased by my father's reaction when I told him what I'd done. He said, 'He's your children's father. It was the only thing you could have done.'

Rumer Godden

*You were pregnant when you married . . . was that a rather shocking thing
in the 30s?*

Oh frightful . . . dreadful. And had I not been pregnant the marriage would
not have taken place.

*Sadly that baby lived for only four days, 'a piercing grief' as you describe
it . . .*

Yes, it was a sadness I have carried around for the rest of my life. And he
was the only boy. I went on to have two daughters, but he was my son. I
was so alone because nobody would have anything to do with me. My
mother rallied to me, but my father was very shocked. What I should have
done was to go back to England and have the baby and not get married; but
I hadn't the courage.

Do you believe that suffering helps the creative process?

Yes, I believe in the garret. This is what makes me so sad about young
writers nowadays who won't do anything till they've got a commission.
Money and safety are more important to them than creativity, and of
course they put themselves into a straitjacket. I try never to take a penny
until I've got the book approved and finished, and I can say to myself, now
there is a book.

*In your autobiography you write: 'It's frightening what intensity of feeling
is aroused when anyone derides or desecrates something holy or simply
beautiful – I cannot stop myself burning with anger.' These words were
written with reference to your first husband, but is it something which
extended beyond the marriage, something you have felt all your life
perhaps?*

Oh yes. People spoil and desecrate things, they take away a child's
innocence. When I see mothers shaking their children and telling them not
to daydream, I really feel like shaking them. It outrages me, I cannot bear
it. It especially grieves me with religion. In Scotland where I live there is a
lot of intolerance. I am a Catholic convert, and the feeling against Popery,

as they call it, is very bitter. I once had to meet a nun, a very fine woman, travelling back from London to the convent near us. When she got off the train she was very pale. I asked her if she was all right and she told me she'd been standing by the carriage door waiting to get out – because I had warned her that the train only stopped at this little station for two minutes – and two women came by, and when they saw her in her habit they called out 'Satan!', and spat all over her. Now that is a terrible thing.

Why did you convert to Roman Catholicism?

I searched for a religion for a very long time. I nearly became a Hindu. Then I tried the Anglican church which my grandmother was a great supporter of, but it seemed to me full of hypocrisy. When I went up to the altar rail to take communion I saw that people were looking at me. I went to the vicar and asked him why, and he told me it was because I had been divorced. He then said that he would prefer me not to come to communion on any of the big feast days at Christmas or Easter when people would see me. It was then I realized that the Anglican church was not for me. With the Catholic church, you know where you are. It was about 16 years before I could become a Catholic, because of my divorce, and I believe that a church which lays down such rules is not a hypocritical church. It is also the only Christian church that was founded by Christ; all the others were founded by men for expediency.

You have always been captivated by beautiful places and have written very movingly of the beauty of India. That country also contains a lot of ugliness, squalor, deprivation, hunger. How did you reconcile the two aspects?

By living with both. When I had my little house in Kashmir, I became the village wise woman in the sense that they all came to me if anything went wrong. The suffering in winter was simply terrible there. Women wore just a quilted cotton garment, nothing underneath, bare legs and bare feet and straw sandals. I tried to alleviate the suffering, though I couldn't do much. And when I was running my dancing school I took the Anglo-Indian children, which shocked people of course, but I wasn't going to have that kind of discrimination. I trained a troupe of very poor Anglo-Indian girls so that they could do cabaret and earn money. So one knew all about the squalor and the filth. Quite a lot of us women who had a conscience did.

Apropos the number of broken marriages in India during the 30s, you say: 'I cannot understand now why we could have broken those vows we made, though then there seemed nothing else we could do.' There seems to be an enormous amount of pain behind those words . . .

Yes, that's true. A broken marriage is a very dreadful thing but I didn't know what else to do. My father said to me, 'You will never bring up your children properly while you're married to that man.' Of course if I had had the belief then that I have now, I would never have divorced; but then I would never have met James, and I had such wonderful years with him.

Both you and your sister Jon divorced. Was there a degree of stigma attached to divorce in those days?

Not in India. It became extremely common. Calcutta is a terribly corrupt city, you know. They say if you put a bag of Calcutta dust under the bed of a virtuous woman she becomes corrupt overnight. There are a tremendous lot of broken marriages and unfaithfulness and affairs going on . . . it's a rotten society.

After the separation there followed some difficult years in India on your own with the children. Since it was wartime and the men were in any case away, did that make your own circumstances appear more normal?

My circumstances then were absolutely abnormal. We were what they call an abandoned family, though we were much more abandoned than most, because the custom was that if the husband was taken away or volunteered to go to war, his firm paid the wife half his salary and kept his position open for him. My husband had been sacked, and I had no money, absolutely none, which is why I went and lived literally like a peasant.

Looking back on that time when there was illness and shortage of money and uncertainty about the future, do you wonder how you had the strength to come through it all?

I cannot imagine where I got it from. Everybody said to me that I must get a job, but I knew I had to get my writing established. My dear father and mother who were then living in Cornwall offered me their home, but after thinking very deeply about things, I decided to live in London and write.

The 'Four Rooms' of your second volume of autobiography divide into the physical, mental, emotional and the spiritual. Have these rooms all enjoyed equal importance?

No, the physical room is very barely inhabited, because I injured my back when I was very young and I've never played a game in my life. The mental room of course is the one I'm tempted to spend a lot of time in, but that is now balanced by the spiritual. The emotional has always been there.

Your future looked bleak when you stood on the Liverpool docks with two small children after losing nearly all your possessions . . . were you despairing or did you manage to remain hopeful?

I think it was determination more than anything else. I knew I had to do it for the sake of the children, quite apart from anything else.

You wrote then: 'To despair is traitorous to your gift.' Do you think that creativity requires hope?

I suppose it does. You see, I am a strange person – I don't believe in self-expression. All these young people, and particularly women say, oh we want to express ourselves, but writing is not self-expression. The writer is simply an instrument through which the wind blows and I believe it is the third part of the trinity, the spirit, the holy spirit, that makes the artist creative. My writing is something outside me that I've been chosen to do, and I think that is what has enabled me to go on.

It seems you had a very practical unsentimental approach towards life.

Rumer Godden

Most mothers would have clung to their children in your circumstances, but you sent your daughters off to school, knowing that it would be best in the long run for both of you. Did you ever regret that?

I regret that I couldn't find a way to keep them at home. If I had been able to find a good governess or nurse, I would have sent them to day school, but just after the war domestic help was terribly difficult to sustain, and I couldn't expose them to the kind of life I led when they were at school. It would have meant hours and hours shut away from them.

Black Narcissus was made into a film and has become a classic, but you thought it was a travesty of the book. Did there come a time when you stopped minding about that?

No, I've minded about it always. I won't see it. I saw it only once, but never again. It is an absolute travesty of the book, I cannot bear it. Micky Powell, the director, said he saw it as a fairy tale, whereas to me it was true. I stipulated that they should send a unit to India, which they did, but they never used a foot of what they shot there. They might just as well never have been near India, and my young Rajput prince was played by some coolie boy with a snub nose and lots of charm, but no more Rajput than I'm Rajput. The whole thing was an abomination.

You vowed you would never allow another book to be made into a film, but relented in the case of Jean Renoir and The River. *Did you ever regret that decision?*

No, it was the greatest two years of my life. What I learned from Jean was absolutely extraordinary, and I could feel myself growing as I worked with him. He was a wonderful man, a real genius. In Paris the film broke all records, and now it goes on and on and has become a classic. It's also beginning to go in India now.

Before long James Haynes-Dixon came into your life, but you held out for a long time against marrying again . . . why was that exactly?

Because of the experience I'd had before. I wasn't going to tie myself down.

It seems that marriage came about more through perseverance and persistent kindness on his part, rather than a passionate romance. There was certainly no coup de foudre. *Do you think perhaps that made for a stronger basis in the end?*

I think it did. After being very patient he laid down an ultimatum when I went to Beverly Hills to do the script for *The River*, and he said that if I would not agree to marriage he would not be there when I got back. The idea of life without James was more than I could bear, so I married. I needed him. I'd been fighting so long on my own, and he was like a wall behind me, always supportive and entirely unselfish.

Do you still miss him?

Oh terribly . . . and I never want to be consoled. It's not given to many women to be loved like that . . . absolutely selflessly.

Marriage then seemed to weigh rather heavily for a time and you missed your freedom, but as you put it, 'we grew content'. Did this take a long time?

About three or four years, I think. I hadn't been prepared for James to take complete authority over me and the children; we weren't used to it, and the children didn't like it, so life was very difficult. They were very fond of James before I married him, but then he started feeling responsible for us and asserting his authority. My mother helped a lot and used to talk to him about this. The children eventually had to come round to him because he was so extraordinarily good to them, though I think they always had reservations, even to the very end. But they were terribly affected by his death.

Pekinese dogs have always been important to you. I was struck by the story of the two sad dogs you inherited and how you did not try to cajole them out of their sadness, but instead respected their grief. Have you applied the same philosophy to people?

Yes, when I'm with people who have had a tremendous grief I always say to them not to try and be too brave. Grief is good, but not self-pity. I can't stand people saying 'why should this happen to me?' when it's the law of life.

Twice in your life you lost all your possessions – once in India, and once when your house in Sussex burned to the ground. Do you think people who have experienced loss on this scale have a different attitude to life?

Oh yes, it changes you completely. I don't want things now . . . I know they're going to be taken away. As you get older, you've got to shed your possessions as fast as you can, and I have arrived at that critical time of not wanting things. I want books of course, but those are part of living. I like my house uncluttered. I like space, I like emptiness, and I like silence.

You set great store by the power of prayer. Have you ever been troubled by wondering what kind of God it might be who is persuaded to change His mind on certain matters, as a result of people praying to Him?

I've seen wonderful things done by prayer. I think that He can be swayed. And I also think you're meant to pray, to put yourself in touch with God. Everything may be preordained, but I have actually seen the most wonderful things happen after prayer.

What is your attitude towards death?

I'm not afraid of death. My mother put it to me wonderfully when I was a little girl. I was a very sensitive child and although I wasn't afraid of dying myself, I was terribly afraid of my mother or my sister dying. One night when I was crying in bed my mother came, and said to me, 'We can't understand what is going to happen to us after death, in much the same way that if we told a little two months old baby that we were going to take it to America, the baby wouldn't have the faintest idea of what we were talking about.' And that's how I think of death – we have no idea what's going to happen to us.

Do you think that without pain and suffering it's not possible fully to appreciate the great joy in life?

Some people seem to be born with the spirit of joy, and they don't seem to have much trouble in their lives, and people always wonder why. It may be that they are what I would call very old souls, they've been here before, quite often, and they're very happy and joyous. For most people, however, the pain and suffering make them prize the joy.

SIR ERNST GOMBRICH

SIR ERNST GOMBRICH

E H Gombrich was born in Austria in 1909. He studied at the University of Vienna, taking his PhD in 1933. In 1936 he emigrated to Britain where he joined the staff of the Warburg Institute in London, becoming its director and professor of the history of the classical tradition from 1959 until he retired in 1976. During the war he monitored German broadcasts for the BBC. His books, for which he has received many awards, include *The Story of Art*, (1950), the world's best-selling art history book, *Art and Illusion* (1960), a study of the psychology of pictorial representation, and *The Image and the Eye* (1982).

You were born in Vienna in 1909. How important were the place of your birth and the culture of your upbringing in determining the pattern of your life?

Immensely important. I'm still an Austrian, of course, I am a product of the Viennese middle class and culture, and I have never tried to conceal this.

Vienna has entered the public perception as the cultural and intellectual centre at the turn of the century, but you have always rather rejected this view . . . why is that exactly?

Because I think it is an exaggeration. Vienna was an important centre, but so was Paris, so was Berlin, and other places too. Intellectual fashions play a certain part in putting some things into the limelight and neglecting other very important influences, and I think this happened with Vienna. One cannot say that Europe owed everything to Vienna at that time.

Although you are of Jewish extraction you were not educated in the Jewish tradition. Have you ever had reason to regret this?

No, which doesn't mean that I have no appreciation or esteem for certain aspects of Jewish education. But I have been quite happy with my own formation, which after all was the choice of my parents – and why should I criticize my parents?

You say it can only be of interest to racists that the Viennese contribution to the modern world was in large measure Jewish. Why do you think this is a racist issue and not just a matter of fact?

There is an element of fact of course, but always to ask whether an artist or a writer was Jewish or not Jewish seems to me very much beside the point. In my youth, nobody asked whether they were Jewish or not; it was only after Hitler invented the term Aryan that one began to wonder where they came from.

You belonged to the middle classes, but you knew hardship and poverty from time to time. Do you think this is the kind of experience which remains with one always, no matter how one's fortunes change?

I'm sure it does remain up to a point. For example, I was surprised that I managed to live quite comfortably on a job in which I never expected to be able to make any money at all. I'm grateful, but I never expected it . . .

At one stage you were evacuated to Sweden, suffering from malnutrition. How much do you remember of that time . . . do you remember feeling hungry?

No, not actually hungry, but the fare was very drab – lots of turnips and potatoes – and certainly not what one would expect a middle class child to have. I still remember my Swedish years with very much pleasure. I learned the language, I read children's books and certain things – the full text of the national anthem of Sweden, for example – remain with me.

Your childhood was steeped in music in the classical tradition. Was this the first sort of aesthetic response you were aware of making?

Probably, though my father also took us to the great museums of Vienna, in particular to the Art Historical Museum which was only ten minutes' walk from our house, and we also had a great many books on painting. My older sister began to look at these books and then to draw, and that also played a part in my response. But certainly classical music was and remains my central aesthetic experience, even now.

You have sometimes said that the time you spent in Austria was not a happy time, and yet your childhood and adolescence seem to have been secure and enriched by caring and intelligent and cultured parents. What was it that made you unhappy?

The general atmosphere was one of depression, the political tension was enormous, there was a lot of unemployment and terrible inflation. Vienna was largely socialist – its working population came from Bohemia and Hungary, and elsewhere – while the countryside was still very much dominated by the Catholic Church. Therefore the tension between the partly atheist Marxist Vienna and the peasant farming communities became very acute, so that one could say there was a latent civil war even before real civil war broke out. There was certainly mutual contempt and hatred. The conservative farmers and their representatives accused the socialists of being entirely Jewish led, which was not completely true, though there was an element of truth. So the general atmosphere and the expectations were far from happy, and one was also very much aware of the impossibility of ever leading a normal life in the future.

When did you first become aware of anti-semitism?

When I first read anti-semitic posters on the hoardings. They were probably put there not by the Nazi party, which did not yet exist in that form, but by radical nationalist groups who agitated against the Polish Jewish immigrants. I remember the headlines referring to the Jews with their sidelocks and their kaftans, and the question: where are they now? The answer was given below: they are now the bankers and the rulers of finance and they swindle us.

Was the university in those days open to everyone who qualified, or was it a question of fees and who could afford to go?

They were open to everyone who did the *matura*, which was the final exam at school. There were fees but they were minimal. The number of students was therefore very large, too large, but they crowded into fields where they hoped that they would at least find teaching jobs. By the time I went to university, which was in 1928, anti-semitism was highly organized – this of course was long before the *Anschluss*. There was a Roman Catholic league and there was a nationalist league and gradually they saw their main job, particularly the nationalists, as hunting Jews and beating them up. Because of an old medieval privilege, universities were extra-territorial, which meant that the police were not allowed to enter, and these thugs abused this privilege by gradually introducing a reign of terror against Jews within the university. The atmosphere was very tense, and as we all know, the professors, while not exactly approving, closed more than one eye; they were cowards and they themselves had certain nationalist leanings, so they minimized the criminality of these groups.

115

Sir Ernst Gombrich

Were you ever assaulted?

I looked sufficiently Jewish to have been in some danger, and yes, I was assaulted, but I was not beaten up. However, one of my best friends was badly wounded in an attack with a steel rod while he was working in the university library.

To embark on a career in art history strikes me as a brave thing to have done at that time . . . was there no parental opposition?

My father was very dubious. He would very much have liked me to follow him and become a solicitor, and he was certainly not happy when I told him I was very interested in the history of art, but he was much too humane and kind to oppose it. He only wondered whether I would ever be able to make a living that way, and he was quite right to wonder. No, there was no opposition, and in fact my sister studied law and she eventually took over the office.

You said that you were never very interested in mainstream art history – connoisseurship and attribution – you preferred explanation. What sort of explanation is relevant to a work of art? Is it possible or desirable to reach towards the artist's psychological state?

There is no bar on hypothesis, on anything one might try to find to explain a work of art. I don't think that we know enough about the artists of the past to make an elaborate psychological hypothesis about them. What we do know is what one might call the social context of the work of art, who commissioned it, who bought it, who the artist's teachers were and what he was trying to do.

You said once that you were dissatisfied with traditional explanations of style, those which emphasized 'the spirit of the age', and you mentioned in opposition to that the importance of 'formulae' . . . could you tell me something of that?

At the time when I studied there were some very eminent art historians who treated art as an expression of the spirit of the age. So you heard about the 'spirituality' of the middle ages, and the 'sensuality' of the rococo. Now I don't want to say that all this is wrong, I only say that on the whole it is pretty vacuous and empty. It has always been true that people were occasionally sensual and occasionally spiritual – even at the time of the rococo – and the idea that medieval man as he is sometimes called was a kind of different species from us seems to me slightly ridiculous. People were always people, they had their own impulses and their own ideas. Naturally there are intellectual and religious movements which one must take into account, but one shouldn't exaggerate the differences between ages and periods. The main reason why I have opposed these stereotypes and clichés is that they are insufficient – they really tell us very little.

You have always had an urge towards the scientific, but how does that mesh with an aesthetic response to art? What part can science play in judgements of this type?

Science cannot explain, and I don't think science will ever be able to tell us why a work of art or a piece of music is so great, but science may be able to explain why a tradition is necessary in art. Every artist has to start from something, the formula you mentioned before, and this science can explain. But the aesthetic experience remains outside the region of science; in other words, if somebody hears a beautiful tune by Mozart and asks me why this is so beautiful, I can have no scientific answer.

You arrived in London in January 1936. Did you think you were leaving your country for good then?

No, but I was aware of the possibility. One never thinks of the worst and the worst would have been, as indeed happened, that Hitler would invade Austria. At that time it did not seem so likely because Austria, that little state with very bad diplomacy, was vaguely protected by Mussolini who didn't want the Germans at his frontiers. There was a very precarious balance of power, and one just hoped against hope that this might hold.

You must have felt very isolated when you first came to England, and quite soon England was at war with your native country. What did you feel in those early years?

117

Sir Ernst Gombrich

I wasn't as isolated as perhaps others may have been because my mother, who was a piano teacher, had a number of English students, and when I went to England some of them became family friends. But it is true that the lack of knowledge of the language, and of ordinary habits and customs, isolated the little enclave of scholars who had arrived at the Warburg Institute. These were very tense years because of the constant awareness that war might break out. Hitler was making one demand after another, and one was very conscious of the possibility either of appeasement or of war, and neither was a pleasant alternative.

Did you think you had come to a safer place when you came to England?

Yes, originally when I arrived, but very soon people started talking about what would happen if London was bombed and so on. People exaggerated the power of incendiary bombs, some of which could be stamped out with the foot; they talked about them almost as they now talk about nuclear bombs.

Were you conscious of any psychological change in yourself because of the war?

Yes. During that time I was really interested in the war and had very little time or inclination to think about the history of art. I was working at the BBC, very hard, long hours, terribly intense. We probably overrated the importance of our work which was to listen to foreign broadcasts, particularly German Nazi broadcasts, and the tricks of propaganda they used. Of course one listened with a certain detachment, one didn't believe a word of what they said, though sometimes, if one didn't believe it, it happened unfortunately to be true, as in the case of Khatyn, for instance, though even then I had my doubts. On the whole one was completely absorbed in this work and in the problems of translation. It was almost like being on a ship – there were people from all parts of the world who were members of the team because they knew Greek, or Turkish, or Albanian, or Estonian and we all just sat there listening to the wireless. After a time I became a supervisor and my job was to check the translations before they were passed on to a unit for publication. So my interests in that time certainly changed. The psychology of propaganda fascinated me. For instance, I listened very often to Goebbels' speeches. There was something

Sir Ernst Gombrich

definitely diabolic in him, in the way he talked, in the way he insinuated himself, in the way he could apparently control his emotions. He was able to manipulate argument, and he was certainly an educated man. In that respect he was very different from Hitler who was much more vulgar and exploited his vulgarity as a demagogue.

Your parents decided to join you in London in 1938 . . . was that an agonizing decision for them?

Absolutely. It would not have happened if my father hadn't come to believe that he was in personal danger. They had both believed they were safe, but one day my mother was summoned to the Gestapo in connection with a letter she had given to a student of hers. The letter had been intercepted at the frontier so she was called upon to explain what she had written. Nothing happened to her, but it was a real warning signal. Also my father's passport was taken away for a time because he had been a freemason, so gradually they saw that really it was necessary to leave.

It must have been very depressing to be classified as enemy aliens. How did you cope with that?

Well, one had a certain detachment, and it was after all true up to a point. I don't think it was particularly depressing. It even had its funny side. As an enemy alien a curfew was imposed and I wasn't allowed to go out after sunset. On every normal day of the week, however, I went on my bike to engage in secret work at my listening post, but on my days off I wasn't allowed to go out. Obviously ridiculous.

Did you have ambivalent feelings towards Austria at that time?

I still have. Of course I was perfectly aware of the situation, not that I knew all the horrors, but sufficiently aware to know something of what was happening. My feelings were torn, and still are, just as when it came to the destruction of beautiful cities by British bombers. For all of us who valued the European heritage, the destruction of Dresden or the blowing up of the bridges of the Arno in Florence were very painful events.

119

Sir Ernst Gombrich

It must have been a strange experience to find yourself monitoring broadcasts and contributing to an effort to overcome the people you had just left. Did you find it disturbing?

Not at all, but then – though there is an element of fiction in this – Austria regarded itself as an occupied country, occupied by Hitler and the forces of expansionist Germany. Traditionally Austrians never liked the Germans very much – this was based on a slightly silly jealousy – but the Austrians like all nations considered themselves superior. For example, a German tourist was always slightly looked down upon in Austria.

Have you ever had strong political leanings?

No, never. I have a horror of mass demonstrations, and whenever I see people marching through the streets and shouting I see them as parrots who cannot think for themselves. I find all that very depressing, and therefore I've never been at all inclined to join a party. Many of my friends in Vienna leaned strongly towards the socialists, but I always stayed aloof.

After the war you returned to the Warburg Institute and wrote The Story of Art, *which was to change your life, and yet you had mixed feelings about writing it, and despaired of completing it. Had you any idea of how successful it would be?*

Not the slightest idea, no. I had written a world history in German before the war, also a surprising success, and then the publisher wanted me to do a history of art. I started tentatively, and then the war came, and I didn't do anything for a while. Then I accepted a contract, and so I wrote it, but a little *contre coeur*.

Now, some 40 years later, you seem to have mixed feelings about the success because you are always, perhaps too narrowly, associated with it. Is that a sore point with you?

It's not a sore point at all. I mean, I'm quite happy if people tell me that they've read it at school, or at polytechnic or whatever, and sometimes I get very nice fan letters. I think my mixed feelings may have been exaggerated. After all a good many people do know that I am also a historian who has done genuine research.

But you became Slade Professor of Fine Art at Oxford, you were invited to America and became extremely famous, all because of that book. Is it that you feel in a sense it sold too many copies, it appealed too much to the masses?

No, I don't think that at all. I am very happy about that – after all I wrote it for that purpose. What I feel sometimes a little dubious about is when it is used as a textbook. I prefer it to be read at leisure as a book to be enjoyed, rather than as a book to be swotted up and learned for facts.

At one point in the preface to The Story of Art *you distinguished between what you call real works of art and examples of fashionable pieces. How is that distinction made?*

That is a subjective distinction, I entirely agree, though most of us would know examples of works which are sort of nine day wonders and suddenly disappear again as fast as they appeared. They are examples of fashion rather than any real intellectual or emotional effort. But I don't think anybody can absolutely draw the line . . . I mean, Picasso became very fashionable, but he was also a real artist, and the same is true of many others. In the case of Dali, I feel that he is more a case of fashion, although he was very skilful; certainly he was not contemptible, he could really paint.

I should like to touch on what I suppose is a central difficulty for art historians, and indeed anyone interested in art: the matter of taste. Unless you allow that all artifice is art and do not distinguish the good from the not so good, are you not obliged to offer your own taste as a reliable yardstick, and to explain that what you like, everyone ought to?

No, I don't think that is true, though I think it is a very understandable attitude. Most of us who are interested in art can say this work is not to my taste but I recognize it is a very respectable work of art. Taste is something which fluctuates enormously . . . even in my time taste has changed radically; for instance certain artists like the Bolognese of the 17th century were considered much too theatrical, much too cheap in a way, and I had friends who helped in rehabilitating these painters and now we all see that they are really masters in their own right, even if they don't appeal to our present day taste. But one has to have a basic interest in the art for taste to be able to develop. For instance, I have no taste for ballet, so I wouldn't set myself up as a judge of ballet or be able to distinguish between various ballets. When your taste is not involved you have no discrimination, no involvement in any way. Music is another good case in point: for various reasons I have no taste for Richard Wagner, but one would be a fool not to acknowledge him as a master in his own right.

You often speak of 'great' works of art, but can that mean anything other than that they have become canonical – admired in the end just because they have been admired before?

That is certainly an important element, that we learn to admire them because we learn from our parents, and from tradition, and from books. That Michelangelo is a great master I have not the slightest doubt, but it's true that we do not always sufficiently test a reputation, simply because we are conditioned to admire, and therefore we may not be sufficiently critical. In fact I recently attended a lecture on the new restoration of *The Last Judgement*, where we saw many details which they have now cleaned, and I actually think that some of it is pretty repulsive. But of course Michelangelo was a towering master and nobody can deny this.

I have heard it said that the Chinese apparently do not distinguish between an original art work and a copy which cannot be distinguished from it . . . is there any virtue in an original if the only way you can tell it is original is by testing the chemical composition of the paint?

You are right . . . it is a genuine problem. I don't think that what you say about the Chinese is completely true, but certainly they have much more respect for a masterly copy than people have here. Equally if it bears the signature of a famous artist of the past and it is really authentic, they would have a great respect for it. There is, however, an element of the attitude one has towards a sacred relic, the idea that Rembrandt's hand really rested on this paper and he drew it. But even though a totally faithful copy of a large painting is very hard to get, I agree with you that a perfect reproduction on the same scale can give the same effect. A Rembrandt etching is a Rembrandt etching, and whether it turns out that it is actually a photo-electric repeat of the copperplate and it is reprinted from another edition, it hardly matters.

You have spoken of connoisseurship and attribution as the mainstream of art history, but is it not precisely that professionalism which feeds the art market and distorts value as it enhances prices?

We couldn't have a history of art if we didn't know the dates of the masters. If you go to a museum you don't want to read on every frame: 'might come from any period'. In other words, when we go to a museum we get a kind of prospectus of the history of art, we want to know who painted the works exhibited there, and any collector has the right to information about a painting. I think the connoisseur has a very real function – he is really at the foundation of what one calls the history of art. We must first have the knowledge of what actually happened, and the hypothesis of who painted what is extremely valuable – except when it becomes authoritarian.

You speak at one point of 'the artist's probable intention' as a starting point, but what would or indeed could count as evidence for that?

Only the context and what one knows about the time and judgement. We would know for instance that in a religious painting the artist's intention would have been to evoke a feeling of devotion, and that he would have wanted his Holy Virgin and Child to be a moving experience. We would know that because that was part of the period in which he lived, and the same is true of many other decorations . . . the wish perhaps to shock, or to entertain, or to paint an erotic picture are all pretty clear in the context of their time.

Something that interests me particularly, because I suppose I have never understood it, is the idea of 'artistic aim'. You used a phrase once, 'a master's artistic aim' . . . is that a definite thing? It suggests a target, some definite end-point, but I would not have supposed an

123

artist works like that. Can he really know beforehand what he will produce?

Not always. Certainly there is an element of what in engineering is called feedback, what he produces suggests to him other possibilities of which he may not have thought before. There are enormous differences in the various media. If you carve, for example, you have to have a good idea of what you want to get out of a block, while if you model you can at any moment respond to the clay and change it. In watercolour, accidents can very easily happen if the paint runs, though Turner told his students never to use an accident. The medieval master who built up his paintings very carefully to the last moment of varnishing certainly had a much stricter idea of what he was doing than the impressionists had. Similarly, in ancient Egypt an artist probably intended his statue or relief to be very much like that of his predecessor, and the icon painter in the East also had a very clear aim of what he was doing; the 20th century artist often much less, if at all, so there is an interesting spectrum between these various media. But I think one can still speak of an artistic aim because every artist is also free to say, 'No, this isn't what I wanted', and to throw his work into the wastepaper basket.

You emphasize two possibilities for the individual artist, to continue a tradition or to oppose it, and you say that we must understand something of his sense of newness. But how can we do such a thing except in our own time? We can't feel as someone felt in 1550 or 1720, can we?

Up to a point I hope we can. That is to say, if you are reasonably well versed in the history of painting and Quattrocento in Florence, for example, you can understand that when people saw the paintings of Perugino, they thought nothing better could ever be done. Of course they were proved wrong when they saw the paintings of Leonardo da Vinci, but I think one can appreciate that there are quite a number of such utterances in the past which show how the novelty struck. There is a very nice remark by a contemporary of Rembrandt who said that when *The Night Watch* was hung alongside other portraits, the others began to look like flat playing cards compared to the vividness and depth of *The Night Watch*. One can up to a point recapture that feeling of novelty, the thrill of innovation, what Giotto must have meant to people who only knew the earlier manner. But I agree with you that this is slightly the preserve of a historian.

It is an old question, but one fashionable at present: why have there been so few women artists? After all, some women became novelists precisely because they had leisure . . .

Yes, but to paint, you needed a workshop, you needed apprentices, and it would not have been very easy for a woman to set up a workshop and to hire apprentices, nor indeed to become a painter of murals – it was hardly within the role expected of women, it was outside the range of possibility. It is therefore all the more impressive that a few managed to overcome this barrier, but on the whole, just as women didn't become soldiers, they didn't become painters, or architects. I don't say that women have less talent for painting; perhaps Michelangelo had a sister who was as gifted as he was, but we shall never know.

Speaking of Dürer's drawing of his mother, you propose sincerity as the mark of a great work of art. But what can sincerity be? After all, any number of artists have been commissioned to paint portraits, some have even worked from photographs. What sort of sincerity can be involved in such cases?

I entirely agree with you that sincerity is a very elusive term because we shall never actually know. There are many things we shall never know, but that doesn't stop us having the feeling that Dürer in this case was sincere. Why otherwise should he have done it? Equally it is possible that a work could impress us very much, and not be sincere. For example, there is a beautiful portrait of an art dealer by Titian, but in a letter Titian makes fun of the man and expresses contempt for him, though that didn't prevent him from painting a very good portrait. So I agree with you that sincerity, though it is often used in criticism and perhaps I shouldn't have used it, is not something we can ever demonstrate.

How does it help to understand a picture like Memling's Angel, *to be told that it is infinitely lovable, and then invited to agree . . .?*

It doesn't. But we are all suggestible and therefore if somebody tells me, 'I am very fond of this picture – isn't it very lovable?', unless I am very distrustful I will make an effort to see it that way.

Sir Ernst Gombrich

You once used an analogy with language when you explained that learning an artist's method of drawing would help us to understand his feelings, but I do not altogether see the analogy. Language depends on system, so the choice a writer makes of vocabulary will suggest his feelings, but in what sense can drawing be thought of as a system with alternatives?

Drawing is actually a system of alternatives, because various artists of the same period use different strokes and different formulae. But I agree with you that language is very special because it has a fixed range of repertoire, while in the language of painting and music – though there certainly are alternatives – they are always metaphors. They may be revealing metaphors, but they are metaphors nevertheless.

In Topics of our Time you publish a fine photograph by Henri Cartier-Bresson, 'Le Palais Royal', but its very quality does seem to suggest that the time may have come for representational art to be handed over to photography. I can see the great practicality of painting before the early 19th century, but must painters now look towards something else?

You are absolutely right. I agree with you totally that the perfection of photography was a trauma for the artist; some would like to minimize it, but I'm not one of them. The trauma was decisive in creating 20th century art, the looking for alternatives and things the photograph could not do. It remains a real challenge.

You have employed an analogy with tea drinkers to suggest something about taste in the arts, but does it follow that our greatest enjoyment derives from the finest blends? Is enjoyment not rather dependent on occasion and context?

It is also dependent on occasion and context, I have not the slightest doubt, in that you may enjoy tea when you are very thirsty, or offered tea by a nice person. But there is still discrimination in tea drinking, and the same is true of works of art.

You have deplored the notion of cultural relativism, but is not that the future, the inevitable outcome of the world as global village? Why do you think it a bad thing?

It all depends what you call cultural relativism. I think it is a very bad thing if it leads to a levelling of human achievement, or the appreciation of human achievement. There is a tendency in teaching, particularly in the United States, to say that Michelangelo is no better than any folk art which you find in the Ukraine or anywhere else. I deplore this kind of cheap relativism. Of course it doesn't mean that we should despise the simple madonna painted by a Ukrainian peasant, but there is still a difference in achievement. It is the same in music. It is an objective fact that Bach could write incredible fugues . . . there is nothing one can relativize in this.

In an essay called 'The Embattled Humanities' you speak of 'the Moloch of society' on whose altar academic research is to be sacrificed. Your plea is eloquent but why should research in the humanities not be subject to the same sort of restrictions as other public spending?

They can restrict it and they do restrict it, but they may regret it very soon, because the quality and the stature of British universities will suddenly suffer and gradually they will become just glorified schools instead of having there people who through their research and discoveries show the young how to advance. Research like everything else is also partly a question of attitude and tradition. A young man who enters, let us say, the Warburg Institute, or any other research institution, does not know how to proceed; his future will depend very much on the example of his elders. It is vitally important that research is supported, and if it is not inertia will set in.

You quote one public institution saying that it is not enough that we be a rich society, we must also be a civilized one. Everyone would agree with that, but it is not really self-evident that those who attend art galleries or the opera are more civilized than those who don't. In Yugoslavia poets and artists are waging a brutal civil war. What part do the arts play in civilizing us?

Very little. I entirely agree with you that there might be a person with very fine tastes who is also a brute. Goebbels may have been appreciative of poetry, just as Goering may have been. There is no reason to think that the arts in that sense are good for you, that they civilize you. They may divert certain impulses into better channels, but I'm not sure. Some optimists make too much of the link between art and civilization. The Chinese have a marvellous civilization but they were also terribly cruel.

Don't you think it likely that the scholar will also be confronted with the suspicion that behind the talk of cultural values is the urge to private satisfaction, the wish to be well supported by public money while he does what he likes?

Yes, if people want to suspect that, you cannot prevent them from doing it, but it's very rarely true. The life of the scholar, or the vision of the artist on the whole do not depend on material rewards. They are most interested in what they feel they have to do, the book they have to write, the picture they have to paint. Very few are rewarded in any comparable way to businessmen, although I don't object to that.

This is perhaps a bit provocative . . . but if cultural values are what is at stake, might it not be more sensible to spend public money on artists rather than historians of art?

It is not provocative, you are quite right, but who is to say who the artists are? I am afraid that the record of the last few years – think of the Turner Prize – is not very encouraging. Anybody can say, 'I am an artist', because there are fewer tangible standards, but in contemporary art it is sometimes very hard to tell whether he is actually a poseur or not.

You have a very clear idea of what sort of education a university should provide in the humanities, but it does seem based on your own experience in Vienna before the war – the mastery of foreign languages, the destruction of any barrier between undergraduate and postgraduate, a high failure rate, and a very advantageous staff/student ratio. It seems a very élitist system and would no doubt make for high standards, but is it right to tax people to support a system from which their own children would be

Sir Ernst Gombrich

excluded? The alternative would seem to be private finance and another (and surely worse) sort of élitism.

You are right. I am of course partly influenced by my own experience in Vienna, though I wouldn't say that the universities I attended corresponded exactly to the model I sketched in the particular lecture you refer to. But the question of whether children are excluded is the wrong question, for it depends on the children: if they are gifted they should certainly not be excluded. There was an exchange in parliament not long ago when the question was asked why should a bus driver support anybody who becomes a lawyer? The correct answer is of course because his son might become a lawyer. There are no longer the same barriers. In questions of excellence, there must be élitism in the sense that some are better and some are less so, but not everybody is an Einstein, and that stands to reason.

I understand your distaste for what you call 'cultural relativism', but if the business of the scholar is 'truth', what counts as evidence? Is not every judgement an interpretation, every conclusion one way of seeing?

Absolutely. Every interpretation is a dominant factor in what we call truth, but if somebody finds the terracotta army it is not a question of interpretation. If you find a document which happens to fit a certain picture, there may be a leeway of doubt, but there may not be, and you cannot disregard proper evidence. I'm certainly on the side of Popper who always claims, and rightly so, that our theories are interpretations, but Popper wouldn't have wanted this to count against individual facts.

I remember your saying that it was a commonplace observation that the principal subject of art in the 20th century was art itself. Do you think that sort of introspection is healthy, the endless concern with methodology?

I think your answer implies quite rightly that it may not be healthy, and I agree with you. If you look at the end of my *Story of Art*, or at the last chapter before the postscript, you will find that I have postulated that what would be important for artists is to get commissions so that they really would have to prove their mettle, rather than contemplating their own navels, as it were. And the same is true of methodology. I am not a believer in discussions of method: go out and do it, and then we will see what you can do.

You have had an immensely distinguished and successful career . . . how much has that success owed to the happiness and stability of your private life?

Very little, I think. On the contrary it can sometimes be a nuisance.

You have always rather avoided talking about yourself. Does that come from a basic shyness, or is there some other reason?

The reason why I don't really want to talk about myself is that I don't think I'm very interesting, there's very little to say. What I try to do is in my books, so my private life is not of great interest to others, not even to me.

I read somewhere that you have had a prolonged battle against anxiety for most of your life. Does this have its origin in the political turbulence of your childhood?

I don't think that's quite true. I'm perhaps a slightly anxious person, I'm not a hero, I'm not courageous, but I'm not aware of any battle against anxiety as such.

What part, if any, has religion played in your life?

That's an interesting question, but I cannot answer it simply. I have a certain respect for religion because of the way it inspired great art. The same is true of music – Haydn's Masses, Bach's Passions. If one has absolutely no sense of religious awe, one may find it very hard to enter into the feelings which great music and art inspire. At the same time I must confess that I have very little patience for religion as it is practised today because of the intolerance it preaches; it is a great misfortune that religion so often instils in people the conviction that they are right and that all others must be wrong.

Do you believe in the existence of God?

I don't believe in the existence of God in any traditional sense, and I do not belong to any established religion. I can look at the universe and the workings of nature, and experience a sense of awe and have a feeling for the mystery in everything, but that does not make me believe that there is a man with a white beard who regulates our lives.

Are you afraid of death?

No. If you tell me I will be shot in an hour's time, I should not be very pleased, but I'm not afraid of what will happen to me after I'm dead, because I'm convinced nothing will happen. Death is simply when life is over, and in a way it will be a good thing since there are too many people anyhow and if we all went on living life would be intolerable. It may be a bad thing for one's friends and relations, but it is in itself something to be desired. One doesn't want to live for ever.

LORD HEALEY

LORD HEALEY

Denis Healey was born in Yorkshire in 1917. He was educated at Bradford Grammar School and Balliol College, Oxford where he took a double first class degree. He served with the Royal Engineers in North Africa and Italy (1940–45) attaining the rank of major. After the war he was secretary of the Labour Party's international department for seven years before becoming MP for Leeds in 1952. He was a member of the shadow cabinet for five years after which he became secretary of defence in the Wilson government of 1964, a post he held for six years. From 1974–79 he was chancellor of the exchequer, a period marked by a sterling crisis. In 1980 he was elected deputy leader of the Labour Party. His autobiography *The Time of My Life* was published in 1989. In 1992 he entered the House of Lords as Baron Healey of Riddlesden.

In your autobiography, The Time of My Life, *you are wary of over-romanticizing your childhood or – like Thomas Traherne – casting too rosy a glow over it. But if we accept your own definition of childhood, 'the capacity for wonder and joy', yours seems to have been wondrous and joyful . . .*

Yes, it was a very happy time. There is of course a tendency to look through rose tinted spectacles, and not just at your own childhood: I see the children playing in the gardens outside our flat as moving jewels, but I know they're little bastards as well. But mine really was a very happy time, although I had a black dog at that period in adolescence when I was trying to come to terms with a total change in physical and psychological make-up, but that only lasted about a year.

You were closer to your mother than to your father. Did this largely have to do with the fact that your mother was much more of a physical presence than your father, or did the affinity amount to much more than that?

It was largely determined by the fact that she was always there and he was rarely there. The other thing was that mother had interests in literature and the arts and music which I shared and which she communicated to me. In later life I think I have a great deal in common with my father, particularly a sort of sentimental romanticism which mother didn't have at all. She was extremely pragmatic.

Did your parents get on well?

My father and mother's relationship was not a perfect one, partly because she never responded to his romantic side. She wasn't capable of it. They had a satisfactory sex life but she wasn't an emotional person, and in a way he was too emotional, with the result that he found it very difficult to have a friendly human relationship with his own children, though very easy to have it with his students. The first time he ever talked to me about himself was the day I got married in London, and he told me he had been terrified on his wedding day. He masked this excessive feeling with a sort of rueful facetiousness, which I now have too.

You say that it is impossible for a child to see his parents as they really are, or even as they appear to his contemporaries, but whatever takes the place of 'reality' surely makes an indelible impression on us, perhaps in a way that even 'reality' could not, and this has a lasting effect on us. Would you not agree?

I do agree. The trouble is when you use a word like reality you beg every conceivable question. The American cartoonist Steig has a wonderful cartoon of a child's view of his father, in which there is a naked man with a very large sexual organ and an enormous amount of hair on his face.

As a child you found your father 'curiously sentimental', as you put it – that criticism comes over as a rather adult construction of something which you presumably perceived rather differently at the time. Was it embarrassment you felt, or what?

No, I wasn't embarrassed really, and I did feel it at the time. One of his great ejaculations was, 'Ah, the wistful years . . .', and there was indeed a wistfulness about him which he always put on for a photograph. I have pictures of him when he was a boy, and when he was a young man, and I was very conscious of that, even at the time.

You say that your father's literary romanticism made it difficult for him to communicate directly with you . . .

It was basically that he was frightened of too direct an emotional relationship with his children, so he tended to avoid conversations of that nature, to a degree that mother didn't, but then she didn't risk anything in having these conversations. My father remained difficult in his relationship with my mother right to the very end, and he was appallingly rude to her when he was in hospital, just before he died at the age of 92 . . . and what wholly lay behind that it's very difficult to say. An interesting thing is that when he was cremated, and we had 'Pie Jesu' from Fauré's *Requiem* played, she burst into tears afterwards. It was the first time we'd ever seen her weep.

Your parents in some ways were very much ahead of their time. To have a trial marriage in those days, unless you were part of the Bloomsbury set which flouted convention, must have been very unusual . . . where do you think this independence of mind came from?

It wasn't Bloomsbury – their trials were usually homosexual. Mother always reminded me of one of the heroines of H G Wells, and the idea of a trial marriage was very much in keeping with the feminist movement and suffragette struggle in the early pre-war years.

You say your mother was filled with enthusiasm for the Bloomsbury group. I would have thought that she might have found their élitism rather off-putting . . . was it chiefly their intellectual rigour which appealed?

Oh no, not intellectual rigour; she herself wasn't in that sense intellectually rigorous. She didn't go to university, she went to a teachers' training college, and nobody would have regarded her as a great brain, but she had a very enquiring mind, and she was led to the Bloomsburys by the talks given by Harold Nicolson on the wireless in the early 30s. Nigel Nicolson was my friend at Balliol and he was also with me in the House until he was sacked by the Tory Party for opposing the Suez campaign, and deselected by his constituency. I once took mother to Nigel's house in Sissinghurst, and for her to meet the son of Harold Nicolson was one of the things she most enjoyed in her old age.

It seemed astonishing that what you describe as your first real contact with your father came on the morning of your wedding. Did you regard that as a breakthrough, or were you saddened that it had taken so long?

I was surprised and pleased, not saddened. I did a radio interview with Anthony Clare recently and he kept trying to get me to admit that I was unhappy or sad or something. I never was very much; I tended always to look forward rather than backwards, and of course at that time my interest was in my new life with Edna.

In many ways your childhood seems to have been a perfectly ordinary one, except for the way the arts – music, painting, literature – dominated your early life. That must surely have singled you out as being rather unusual among your peers at Bradford Grammar School?

It was actually a very good school, and Bradford was buzzing with intellectual energy. We had the Hallé orchestra playing every month there, and we got cheap seats as schoolboys. We had a very good civic theatre in which Fyodor Komisarevsky from the Moscow Arts Theatre used to produce Chekhov. And of course boys who were at school with me had the same pleasure as I had. It's true that people didn't go for the visual arts much at Bradford, nor indeed at Oxford when I first went there. Nobody was interested in painting, until with a couple of friends with whom I'd nothing else in common we formed the New Oxford Arts Society. We got some Picasso etchings over and held one of his early Surrealist exhibitions. But Britain is a country even less interested in the visual arts than in music.

Your scholarship to Balliol from Bradford Grammar School was an enormous achievement at that time. How far were you yourself aware of that?

Balliol was regarded as the best Oxford college, as indeed it was, and I don't think we'd had anybody at Balliol in my period. Alan Bullock whom I greatly admired would like to have gone to Balliol but went to Wadham, and so I was conscious of achievement. Mind you, I only got an exhibition; I didn't get a full scholarship.

Your political awareness developed in 1936 during a cycling trip to Germany and Austria . . . were you immediately opposed to Hitler, did you sense the dangers, or did you have some appreciation of his charisma and the spell which he cast?

Both. But I was mainly conscious of the dangers. Germany was a war society when I cycled through, and there were air raid adverts in every village green. *Der Stürmer*, that filthy anti-semitic paper of Streicher's, was posted up on every town hall and of course a lot of the youngsters I met in the youth hostels were Hitler Jugend; so I was conscious both of the danger and of the charismatic appeal Hitler had for Germans. But at the same time quite a lot of the youngsters I met were anti-Hitler, and they told me that most working people in Germany were what they called beefsteaks – outside brown and inside red. So the interesting thing is, I left Germany after this wonderful holiday, deeply conscious of the threat to peace and to our values, but not disliking the Germans. Even those who were Nazi weren't of the aggressively jackboot stamping type, and I've always been able to draw a distinction between the opinions people hold politically and their personality. It was a good background for evaluating some of the things that are happening now. Weimar Germany was an appalling mess, morally as well as economically and politically, and you could see why many Germans saw Hitler as a chap who was taking Germany, if I can use a phrase, 'back to basics', restoring core values – *Kraft durch Freude, Kraft durch Arbeit*, and so on. There's no doubt this gave a lot of Germans renewed confidence in themselves and in their country. I could see that, but I didn't admire it.

With the unification of Germany today, could it ever happen again?

Oh yes, of course it could, but the particular experience of Nazism in Germany in the 30s won't happen in quite the same way. The big characteristic of the post cold war world is the revival of nationalism, and not only in the ex-communist countries. The constant theme in my political activity has been the need to find some way of preventing war and of controlling the enormous unique power of nationalism and directing it into constructive areas. When nationalism is allied with religion, it is an even greater danger, as in Yugoslavia and in India today. Every country is vulnerable to this, and when the political situation is bad, we hear slogans like 'back to basics' and 'core values' and the cry: 'what does a nation really stand for?' Yet the people who destroy all the nation's institutions are the loudest in praising them; like Mr Portillo today, the great Spanish prophet of the British institutions.

It must have been a considerable culture shock for someone from the respectable working class in the North to enter the Oxford cloisters. You say that Balliol was above all a meritocracy – the snobbery was intellectual rather than social – but there must surely have been class snobbery in some measure?

The first term I was there I would cringe internally when I heard the easy conversation of Etonians in the quad below my rooms. Britain in the 30s was very class-conscious, and for that reason a lot of my friends tended to be Americans, Canadians or Indians, but that only lasted a term or two, because after that people judged one another not according to class standards at all. The class thing was strongest among the Etonians, who tended to stick very closely together. Julian Amery, Maurice Macmillan, Harold Macmillan's son, and Stephen Tennant, son of the then Postmaster General, tended to see more of one another than of anybody else. The Wykehamists were very different; they were meritocrats and they mixed very easily into this new society.

You were persuaded to join the communists in 1937 because, as you said, the communists were the only people unambiguously opposed to Hitler. Was there also a degree of idealism involved – the brotherhood of man?

Oh yes, there was a lot of that. Post-war communism, even pre-war communism, shouldn't obscure the genuine idealism which took a lot of people into the communist party, not just to fight Hitler but to fight for a better world. It was anti-Hitler but it was also belief in the brotherhood of man. We totally refused to accept that there were concentration camps in the Soviet Union, or that a lot of these trials which were taking place in the 30s were totally phoney; and the analogy I make with that is the enormous power of Mrs Thatcher in the ex-communist world. Nobody has a good word to say for her in Britain, except in obscure recesses of her old party, but she is still by far the most popular politician in what used to be the Soviet Union, and in Japan, and that's because people tend to react to the other extreme from the thing they see. The young Wordsworth, with whom I find I have more and more in common, was swept away by the French Revolution – 'Bliss was it in that dawn to be alive . . .', and then he had the shock of seeing Napoleon crowned emperor by the Pope, and seeing all the things he most disliked in politics arising out of the French Revolution.

Was your move away from communism painless or was there an element of disillusionment?

I never went for the ideological element in communism, especially the dialectical materialism. It was really the stupidity of the Russians in imagining that they could make a deal with Hitler that would stick, and continuing to do so after the fall of France, which made it very easy for me to leave. But my sympathy for the communists was increased by my experience in Italy where the communist party was the backbone of the resistance movement under fascism especially during the war. However, what killed any lingering sympathy was my experience as international secretary for the Labour Party, trying to keep the socialists in Eastern Europe alive under the communist regimes. I became very anti-communist at that time; indeed I was the chap who persuaded Morgan Phillips to make the affiliation of the communists to the Labour Party un-constitutional. The amazing thing is that right up to 1946 the communists were applying to affiliate to the Labour Party, although they were putting up candidates against Labour all over the country.

You say you are not proud of your political activities at Oxford. How would you rather have conducted yourself?

I was far too uncritical, as most youngsters were. At that time the undergraduate body was only 4500 at Oxford and 1500 were in the Labour Club which was run by communists – over 250 people were communist party members. Almost anybody on the left became communist, including people who later became prominent Tories, like Biggs Davison, and I only mention him because I asked him before he died if he minded being named – whereas the others I don't mention. The only democratic socialists who stood up to the communists were a Catholic called Michael Fogarty, who teaches economics in Glasgow, Chris Mayhew, and people like Roy Jenkins and Tony Crosland. Tony could easily have joined the CP, for his views were very much the CP views, but Roy was never tempted; and of course his father was Attlee's parliamentary private secretary. And there was the same CP domination of the literary world; all the young poets were members of the CP or flirting with it, except Louis MacNeice. Spender and Auden flirted with it, and half of the young painters were communists, both in France and in Britain.

One imagines that despite what was happening in Germany there was still the residual conviction, from less than 20 years before, that the Great War had been the war to end all wars. When did you stop believing that?

Lord Healey

Oh, I never believed that. My generation in England became conscious of these issues in the early 30s when we took the school certificate at 14. We were swept away, my lot, by the poetry and novels against the First World War, which said it was a racket, a view held very strongly by Kipling, who wrote that wonderful couplet: 'If someone asks you why we died/ Tell them because our fathers lied . . .' So we didn't regard the First World War as making the world safe for democracy, and indeed, as we were growing up to political consciousness Mussolini was already in power. Before I went to Oxford we had the invasion of Abyssinia, and then the civil war in Spain during the holiday when I was cycling round Germany. My generation, after we'd fought in the Second World War, were determined not to make the same mess of it as they had after the First, and it was this feeling which was responsible for the tremendous Labour victory in '45. And to be fair, the Labour government of that time did carry out the policies on which it was elected. Trouble is, it's not found very many new policies since . . .

When war was declared you did not hesitate to volunteer. Did you ever consider any alternative to fighting?

Oh no, not at all, although it's true I had been a pacifist and resigned from the OTC at school when I was 16. But at 21, when war was declared, I rang up immediately to ask to volunteer. And so did all my friends, even though we were severely upbraided by our CP mentors and told that it had suddenly turned into an imperialist war instead of an anti-fascist war. We told them to sod off.

Did you consider the case for pacifism to be an honourable one?

Not at that time, no, because it was a question of fighting a patent evil, and those of us who were at Oxford at that time had met refugees from Nazi Germany. My generation knew there was a terrible evil which must be stopped, and we had no doubt about that. Even when the bomb was exploded in Japan – we had no details of course – all I said was, thank God I don't have to go out to Asia now.   DEAD RIGHT

After the war you decided to forgo the academic career you had planned

and you went into politics because, as you say, there seemed no other way of helping directly to prevent a third world war. Was this resolve shaped largely by your experience of war?

The war and the failure to prevent the war with Hitler. My youth was dominated by the inevitability of war with Hitler unless people stood up to him, and then because they didn't, we had the war. We felt it was an unnecessary war, and I still feel that about every war in my lifetime; the Falklands, the Gulf War – none of them would have happened if the people who finally stood up to aggression had made it clear to the aggressor in advance that they'd do so; but they didn't.

Did writing your planned work on aesthetics suddenly seem too trivial an activity to engage in after the war?

I didn't regard it as trivial, nor do I now; in fact I may still write, not a major work, but a trifling essay on the relationship between art and life. There is an argument which is perfectly respectable, that governments make very little difference to what happens socially and economically in a country. All the countries of Western Europe have developed social democracies, using those words in the most general sense, whether they've had right-wing governments or left-wing governments, or no government at all like Italy. But wars are made only by governments, and it's only by engaging in an activity which directly impacts on governments, i.e. politics, that you can hope to prevent them. And I still feel that very strongly.

You met Edna in 1940 . . .

Oh no, I met Edna as soon as I went to Oxford, because she used to go to the Ruskin dances, the only permitted contact between male and female of a social nature. I remember her as an attractive girl whom I called 'tomato face' because of her very red cheeks, but most of her friends called her 'the Zuleika Dobson of St Hugh's'. However, it was in 1940 that we really started courting.

Did you know then that she was the one for you?

Not at the beginning. She was my girl and we liked one another very much, but we didn't really think about marriage. I didn't want to make that kind of commitment at that time, partly because I thought I would probably be killed in the war. I lost five years' marriage allowance by forgoing popping the question until I got back from Italy.

There is often a kind of Anglo Saxon awkwardness which men, particularly Oxbridge men, feel with women . . .

That was never so with me. I always felt comfortable in the presence of women, and I had had girlfriends from the age of 16, though I'm bound to say I don't think I went to bed with a girl until almost the last year at Oxford. That was one of the many enormous differences between the 30s and today, that boys and girls didn't go to bed with one another; that was absolutely not the case in the 30s, and I don't think one suffered particularly because of it. I'm not against people going to bed when they want to, but I don't think the present situation is more desirable than the earlier one. And we didn't have the pill in those days. If you were wealthy and well informed you could – like Mary McCarthy – get a Dutch cap, but otherwise you relied on your male partner being prepared to wash his feet with his socks on; which not many were.

Politics is a high-risk occupation for marriages and families . . . you have been very fortunate in yours. Do you think this was good luck, or good judgement?

It was good luck that I had good judgement. [laughs] We've had a happy marriage, Edna and I, with very little upset, but we were lucky. I think it's very difficult for a politician's wife, particularly if he's in London all week and she's in the provinces, which is the case with many. An enormous number of MPs have affairs with their secretaries, and the poor wife's social life is confined to weekly visits to Sainsbury's.

What view do you take of the current interest in the private lives of politicians and what might be called their moral frailty?

I think it's grossly overdone. The French cannot understand the way we go on about this, but of course people wouldn't go on about it so much if the government didn't say it was returning to core values, and Barbara Cartland wasn't able to claim authorship of the Tory attitude to life. That, I think, is what has made them excessively exposed. But if we take specific examples, such as the astounding press coverage of the actress in the oral sex case, I can't think of anywhere in the world where that would be so except Britain. Sex is still a dirty thing to be sniggered at; what D H Lawrence called 'the dirty little secret' is still more prevalent here than in most countries.

But do you think it's reasonable to expect higher moral standards of behaviour from politicians?

Not unless they *preach* higher moral standards. A clergyman caught out in adultery or pederasty is always going to be especially vulnerable, but in this context I recall a glorious remark by Schelling, the German moral philosopher, who was discovered to be sleeping with his girl students, and when he was asked how he reconciled that with his lectures, he replied, 'Have you ever heard of a signpost walking the way that it's pointing?'

When you entered the House of Commons in 1952, it was still regarded as something of a gentleman's club . . . I imagine that was an aspect of political life which you fundamentally disapproved of . . .

To be fair, it was only the Tory side that was a gentlemen's club. When I arrived in 1952 you could tell which party an MP belonged to by looking at him. The Labour people tended to have badly cut suits or, if they were public school boys, to wear tweed jackets and scruffy trousers. Most Labour Party members were people who had worked as trade unionists in manufacturing unions. Now that's totally changed, and you cannot identify the party of an MP if you go into the central lobby. The dress and behaviour of the classes have moved together very much in the last 40 years since I came in, and the manual working class is now scarcely represented. Ernie Bevin who was, I think, the greatest British foreign secretary this century, was an illegitimate child of a girl who worked on a farm; his education stopped when he was 11 years old, and he worked with his hands until he became a trade union leader. People like him have disappeared from the House.

145

Lord Healey

Didn't Bevin fail to handle the problem of Palestine by handing it over to the UN? Michael Foot for example, regards him as being responsible for what he has called 'the Labour government's act of eternal dishonour with painful consequences for our world today'. Isn't that something you rather gloss over in your memoirs?

No, I think I deal with that very directly because I had to defend Bevin's policy in front of Golda Meir in Zurich at the socialist international meeting. History will tell us whether Zionist nationalism in the end has been a good or bad thing, but a lot of my Jewish friends after the war belonged to a small party in Poland called the Polish Jewish Bund which was very anti-Zionist, because it regarded Zionism as a form of imperialism. So I could see the argument against taking land away from the Arabs and against the ethnic cleansing which the Jews carried out in Palestine during the first war. I saw that it would create enormous problems for Britain and the United States in the Arab world, which it has, and not only the Arab world, but in much of the Third World also. So I don't feel as Michael Foot does about that; but then I don't think Michael has much sense of reality, and this is one reason why he wasn't a very useful leader of the Labour Party. The Foreign Office was almost universally hostile to the creation of a state of Israel and gave up because we came under such intolerable American pressure; but most of my friends in the Labour Party were Zionists, like Laski, Hugh Dalton, and some of the most remarkable Tories, like Winston. I had friends in the Zionist leadership in Israel – Shimon Perez is still a good friend – and a lot of them, particularly Aba Eban, who was a don at Cambridge before the war, always knew that the moral position of Israel in the Middle East would undermine its political position, as it has. Equally you have to come to terms with reality, and of course the state of Israel is a reality, though it's also done things which one can't possibly approve, such as some of the activities of Mossad, and the nuclear cooperation with South Africa, and so on.

In your autobiography you say that your first ten years in parliament were dominated by the internal divisions of the Labour Party which prevented it from mounting an effective attack on the Tories till Harold Wilson became leader. Hasn't the Labour Party continued to be dogged by internal divisions?

Once Wilson became leader there were divisions over his leadership, but they weren't fundamental policy divisions, and the same was really true of Callaghan. But I always regret that out of my nearly 50 years now as an active national politician in the Labour Party, both as an official and as an MP, we've lost two decades through internal arguments about dogma basically – the Bevanite ten years and the Bennite ten years of the 80s – and it takes a long time for a party to recover public trust. As for the Tories' struggles now, the tension between the dogmatists and the pragmatists is just like the home life of our own dear queen.

You became defence secretary in 1964 in Wilson's government, a post you held for six years. Looking back, were those the best years of your political life?

Yes. First of all, it was the first time I'd had power which is an indispensable condition of influencing policy at government level, so I enjoyed that very much. Secondly, perhaps to my surprise, I very much liked the people I worked with, and I was intimately involved in foreign policy which is my main interest. We were fighting wars in South America and Borneo, and it was the period when we had to decide, in order to cut our coat according to the cloth, to give up our role east of Suez, apart from Hong Kong which we were committed to by history. I also had a major role in trying to reconcile the German and American positions on nuclear weapons in Europe. I enjoyed it very much, and on the whole I think I did a pretty good job.

You have described Wilson as 'essentially frivolous'. In view of the recent biographies of Wilson, in which he has been largely rehabilitated, have you modified your critical view at all?

No, not really. He had very few political principles. He had no sense of direction, and he was an awful Walter Mitty. None of the people who worked for Wilson in the government – whether it was Barbara Castle or Dick Crossman – really had much good to say about him. One of his weaknesses which wasted a lot of time is that he didn't like to use his authority as prime minister to go against a majority of the Cabinet, and so to get round the problem he packed the Cabinet with yes men and yes women, just so that he'd have a majority.

Lord Healey

Your five years as chancellor from 1974 to 1979 were rather stormy – the period was marred by a sterling crisis and then intervention by the IMF. How did that period compare in terms of job satisfaction with your time as defence secretary?

It was intellectually very much more testing, and it was physically much more demanding. I never had any spare time at all, but I think it was worth doing, and I've been relieved to find that a lot of my foreign friends who are still around think I did a very good job. Controlling spending is appallingly difficult, as all governments and chancellors have found, but the real problem is that you are at the mercy of external events. We've now got a single global financial market in which a thousand billion dollars a day can cross the exchanges in search of speculative profit, so no country can control its own exchange rate and therefore its own interest rates. We've also got a single global investment market, and people now will put a new factory wherever the relevant labour is cheapest or where it's closer to the ultimate market. The power of the chancellor is terribly limited; things can come out of nowhere and hit you.

In the general election campaign of 1983 you did battle with Michael Heseltine, then defence secretary, but it was commonly believed that you despised Labour defence policy just as much as Heseltine. Isn't that the unacceptable face of politics, to advocate something you don't believe in?

Yes, but if you're going to have choice and democracy, you've got to have parties, and you have to go along with the party unless you leave it. Some of my friends left the Labour Party, but nothing came of it, and I never thought it would. You say it's unacceptable, but I'm afraid it's the real world.

You became, as it were, the Greatest Leader Labour Never Had, and your fight against Tony Benn and the Bennites is given credit for turning the Labour Party away from almost certain self-destruction. Do you acknowledge that?

Yes. If I look back on myself as a politician, I think I should have worked harder for the leadership which I never really wanted, because as I've always said, I'd rather do something than be something. Because I didn't fight harder we've had 15 years now of what I regard as very bad government. Of course once I'd lost that battle I felt I had an absolute obligation to fight Tony Benn hard for the deputy leadership, even though as the Americans say of the vice president's job, 'it's not worth a barrel of warm spit' as a job in itself. If I'd not won that battle which, because of our weird constitution, I won by a hair of my eyebrow, I think there would have been a haemorrhage of people out of the Labour Party. I always believed that if we stuck to it so that the sensible people finally had control of the National Executive we'd be all right, and I warned my friends in the Gang of Four, like Shirley Williams and David Owen, that it would take two years, and if they weren't prepared to wait two years, too bad, but outside the party they wouldn't come to anything; and they haven't.

If you had won the leadership contest you would probably have become prime minister . . . what are your feelings about that?

Well, in a way I would have liked to have been prime minister, but I've only really wanted leadership to prevent baddies getting it, whether it was in the party or in the government. The premiership was never my objective. The thing I most regret about my life is that I never had a chance to be foreign secretary at a time when we had influence in the world. We don't have influence now. Hurd can spend ten days in the Middle East and nobody knows he's been or come back.

You have been described as the Labour heavyweight who never made it. Does that description wound?

I'm not wounded by what people say about me. I've always upset people by saying that as long as my wife loves me I don't care about what the rest of the British people think. Besides, I get better treatment from the press than many people, although that's partly because I'm not competing; I'm a clapped out old fart.

One analysis of your political career is that you've been more highly regarded out of office than in office, almost like a great painter who is suddenly discovered after he is dead. Presumably you see things rather differently?

To be fair, I was very highly regarded by people interested in defence when I was defence secretary, and I still am. Views about my record as chancellor are much more mixed, but I still think I got us through the most difficult period without the tragedies we've had since '86 when everything went very badly wrong under Thatcher.

[handwritten margin note: BULLSHIT, JUST TERRIBLE SEALOUSY AND MYSOGINISM]

Charles Laurence, writing in the Daily Telegraph *in 1989, said: 'When Healey's moment to strike for the leadership came, he had too few friends left, and the Left had too many. He had spent too much time in the hinterland and not enough on the single minded pursuit of high office.' Would you agree with that assessment?*

No, I wouldn't entirely, because the reason I was quite popular with the public is that I had a hinterland and people didn't feel I was a career politician interested in nothing but his own advancement. My misfortune was that I had to run for leadership just after having to inflict misery on the party as chancellor, but if you make politics the be-all and end-all of your life you will be incredibly miserable, like Mrs Thatcher and Gorbachev.

[handwritten margin note: DEAD SEALOUS]

You are fond of Kipling's lines, 'If you can meet with triumph and disaster/And treat those two impostors just the same . . .' Is that a principle you have put into practice in your time in politics?

Yes, on the whole, although that was one of my father's favourite poems rather than my own. I prefer Kipling when he's not being so didactic but reflecting on the lessons of life, and one of my favourite passages from him is where he says: 'The dog returns to its vomit, the sow returns to her mire, and the burnt fool's bandaged finger goes wobbling back to the fire.' He was a wonderful writer, greatly underestimated, and although he was a great believer in the British role in the world, he was not a triumphalist imperialist at all.

Your wife once famously remarked that Mrs Thatcher had no 'hinterland', by which she meant, to put it bluntly, she had read very few books and had no sense of history. You suggest that the same might be true of John Major, Trollope notwithstanding, and you conclude that public life is the poorer for it . . .

Well, there is a big question mark over Major's devotion to Trollope. The point is you've got to have your real values outside the political world, so an interest in music and painting and literature is very valuable. The other important thing is – and I feel this particularly since the end of the Cold War – it's very important to know history. I did a course in economics as a mature student when I was chancellor, and I've read books of political science, which is an oxymoron like public privy, but the one thing you *can* learn from is history. Human situations recur again and again in history, and you cannot begin to understand what is happening in the Balkans or Eastern Europe, or even more Russia, without knowing a bit about the history of those countries. If you know about Nicholas II, Yeltsin is very easy to explain . . . another man who produces the first democratic elections and then dissolves the *duma* because it votes against him.

Your own interest in Virginia Woolf and Yeats and Emily Dickinson suggests that you do not think there is any sort of gulf fixed between poetry and prose. Are they just alternative uses of the imagination?

No, not entirely, because first of all poetry is very much more concentrated. The ambiguities which Empson discussed are much more complex in poetry than in prose, and in poetry the sound is also important.

When you read Virginia Woolf and Emily Dickinson, do you feel yourself in contact with something specifically feminine, or are they rather two sensitive minds among others?

I think Virginia Woolf was self-consciously feminine and up to a point she was feminist. In *A Room of One's Own*, you do feel you're in touch with a woman's mind, but a woman of extraordinary intellectual range and sensitivity. On the whole I prefer her diaries and letters to her novels. Dickinson is absolutely unique – no man can write like that – and she clearly is very conscious of being a woman in what she writes, but without being in any sense feminist. I've no time for the claptrap of that charlatan Camille Paglia suggesting she is a sadist – people will say anything for money.

I have the impression from reading My Secret Planet *that you take a*

Romantic view of literature . . . Shelley calls literature the record of the best and happiest moments, and Wordsworth believes that it might improve our moral sensitivity. Is that a view you share?

I half share it. You can only approach problems of the spirit in my view through the arts, and poetry is one of the main arts. But the greatest poet in our language was, if not gay, bisexual, and he was deeply realistic. That was why it was comic for this poor headteacher in North London to describe *Romeo and Juliet* as being infested with heterosexuality. [laughs] Shakespeare's view wasn't Romantic in the Shelley sense at all, and Wordsworth I put in a totally different group from Shelley because Shelley was an upper-class young man who wrote a typical public school Romantic leftism. But Wordsworth came from a provincial professional family; his father was a solicitor, and he felt very much out of the centre. His big experience was being excited and carried away by the French Revolution and then being terribly disillusioned by it. I admire Wordsworth enormously and I know why he's called Romantic because he happened to write in that period along with Byron and Keats and Shelley, but I would put him in a way slightly ahead of the other so called Romantics. Again, you can't conceivably call Aeschylus, Euripides and Sophocles Romantic in that sense and yet I admire them more than any of the others, including Wordsworth; and Shakespeare lived in this violent, brutal, cruel world and wrote about it totally honestly, without any spirituality. He had no feeling for that at all, just as he was very confused about sex – 'the expense of spirit in a waste of shame'; yet on almost any page you read, you find something stupefyingly good.

Modern critical views tend to be dismissive about the meanings to be found in literature, saying it is all a matter of context . . . have you any sympathy with that way of thinking?

Not really. There's a book by the Bishop of Oxford, Harris, who is rather a Tory on religion and beauty, in which he argues that religion is enormously enhanced by the arts, which I would hold; except that my view is terribly heretical in the literal sense in that I do not believe that any theology is worth the paper it's written on. You cannot use the sort of logic you use in examining the phenomenal world, or in producing the microwave or the atom bomb, to consider questions of value. Questions of value relate to the spirit or the soul which you can best explore in my view through the arts. Religious experience I believe in strongly, but I don't believe in a personal God.

You are also very interested in music and painting and photography. Does literature offer us something that the other arts do not, do you think?

Oh yes, of course it does. Music is the purest art form with no phenomenal references in the Kantian sense; poetry has to use words which are all referential, but it also uses sound, and the sound of poetry can be sweet: 'daffodils,/That come before the swallow dares, and take/The winds of March with beauty . . .' There is a music in Shakespeare's lines which you cannot relate very directly to phenomena.

In My Secret Planet *you quote Emily Dickinson saying, 'It is an honourable thought to suppose that we are immortal', but also when she says: 'They went to God's Right Hand/That hand is amputated now/And God cannot be found'. Can poetry offer us some viable alternative to what used to be called the comforts of religion?*

Yes, but it can also provide the same comforts in a way. I don't regard these as strict alternatives, because we're now talking about an area which is not susceptible to logical analysis. I was told that Jonathan Miller described it as sentimental tosh when I said that the *Heiliger Dankgesang* from Beethoven's Opus 132 in A Minor, The song of Thanksgiving to the Deity on recovery from an illness, or indeed the Cavatina from his Opus 130, that these took me to the heights, or perhaps the depths, of religious feeling; but they do.

You write in your anthology that it was T S Eliot who made you realize that it was possible for an intelligent man to be a Christian. But if you reject the theology and dogma of the Church, in what sense would you argue that an intelligent man could be Christian?

Well, it's difficult. If you belong to a church then you either have to accept one of the Protestant theologies, or the Catholic theology, yet Protestants and Catholics have actually killed one another for believing different theologies, and they're doing so today in bloody Bosnia; so I regard theology as a mistaken endeavour, as Kant did. Once you erect an institution to promote a theology you're moving in the worst political direction, because you are creating an institution which is supposed to teach a partisan view and to maintain that all other views are wrong, or even sinful.

If Donne and Vaughan, Marvel and Milton owe their power as poets to a religious conviction you can't share, how can you regard them as other than interesting museum pieces?

Because they appeal to some of the deepest instincts I have in my spirit. But I don't have to take their religion seriously, and of course Blake, whom I greatly admire, believed that Milton was of the Devil's party but didn't know it, and that the real hero of *Paradise Lost* is Satan.

In your book you raise what you call the most difficult question which confronted you at Oxford – the relationship between art and life. Have you been able to approach an answer since Oxford?

I hadn't really thought about these things very systematically until I wrote *My Secret Planet*, and I don't despair of producing a useful little contribution in this field during the second half of my life.

Like Kathleen Raine whom I interviewed last year, you are very dismissive of Iris Murdoch. Raine called her 'a mere journalist', you say she is 'unreadable'. Doesn't this smack of intellectual élitism?

No. I liked Iris very much when she was a friend of mine as a student and I introduced her to Beckett's *Murphy*, which I've always regarded as the pebble which dislodged her avalanche. But the problem is that I find her novels are basically games with characters who have characteristics you recognize but who don't make up believable people; that's my worry with her. About the only book of hers which I found compelling to read right through was *A Severed Head*, but I haven't really tried very much recently because she seems to me to be doing an up-market intellectual Alan Ayckbourn. She is a serious thinker, of course, and though I haven't read the new book she's done about morality, my impression from the reviews is that she really rather agrees with me about all that.

Throughout our cultural history poets have sought to defend poetry against the prejudices of those inexperienced in it. What are the grounds now for a defence against the philistines, those with no sense of history or literary heritage . . .?

If people can't appreciate poetry, too bad for them, but I don't feel a need to justify or defend it. There's always a risk when you get into that sort of argument that you'll end up defending bad cases. It always struck me when I was a boy and I started taking an interest in painting, that there was a scandal every year about something being rejected by the Royal Academy, because it was too modern; but actually the paintings that were rejected were never very good. In any case there's so much poor poetry at the moment. It's rather like feminism: the great writers who want a square deal for women, like George Eliot and Virginia Woolf, they speak for themselves, but if I'm asked to defend Camille Paglia or one of these pretty new feminists like Roiphe or Naomi Woolf, I'm not going to waste my time.

You have earned yourself the reputation for being something of a political thug with remarks such as 'virago intacta' about Mrs Thatcher and 'savaged by a dead sheep' with reference to Geoffrey Howe. Is the political thug tag something you regard as a badge of honour?

Not particularly. The trouble with journalists is that one of them will use a phrase and the others rather like it, so they all use it from that moment on. The remarks you quote are not thuggish; they're rather witty, which is why they've survived. The thuggery comes much more from those occasions when I have shouted at people or had to deal with those who voted against us on public spending in the House. But I'll tell you of one exchange which hasn't appeared in print before. After the '92 election the Speaker held a party for all the retiring MPs, including me and Maggie. Maggie came over to me and said, 'Oh Denis, I've just come across a phrase you used about me when we first were fighting across the floor of the House. You called me a "passionara of privilege".' I said, 'Yes, but the best remark I ever made about you was only last year, when I said you combined the economics of Arthur Daley with the diplomacy of Alf Garnett.' She looked terribly puzzled because she had never heard of either. But that's not thuggery . . .

You have always reserved large quantities of vitriol for David Owen whom you likened to the Upas tree – poisoning the ground for miles around. Have you modified your opinion at all in recent years?

David's tried to do a good job in Bosnia but he was put in when the chance of success had already disappeared. Once we'd recognized Bosnia as a state on the basis of a referendum in which the largest minority refused to take part, we were on a hiding to nothing. But I think he's worked hard. He can be very offensive, but perhaps that was the one situation in which, as he was dealing with bastards, it was a good thing that he was a bastard too.

Your wife has never forgiven you for expressing in a speech in the House of Commons a personal affection for Mrs Thatcher whom she regarded as 'lacking in common humanity'. Did you yourself come to regret what you call this moment of 'careless charity'?

No, not really, though I can add something of interest to that. Edna and I both watched the four television programmes about Thatcher – *The Downing Street Years* – in which she looked exactly like her Spitting Image puppet, and I said to Edna at the end that it was the most frightening thing I had ever seen on television; to think that we were run by a raving hag who was surrounded by ministers who were fighting one another like weasels in a sack, that we had this for 14 years and nobody did anything about it. But Edna said, 'No, I have quite a different feeling. I really felt the human and personal tragedy of this bright prefect from a grammar school in the provinces, who got to the top and then everything crumbled.'

You have sometimes said that you have lived in the most interesting time imaginable. That is the mark of a happy man . . . are there any shadows on that happiness?

The shadow is the fact that the end of the cold war has meant a return to the worst aspects of history; we're entering a period that will be as cataclysmic in its effect on the world as the period that came after the French Revolution. That was followed by the Napoleonic wars and then total uncertainty and the revolutions of '48. I think we're in for a very difficult century, but it won't be a European century; it will be dominated by the powers in the Far East.

As you grow older . . . do you ever contemplate your own death? Are you afraid?

There was a book written shortly after the war by a young Hungarian about his experiences when the Russians came in, and the title was, *I am 17 and I Do Not Want to Die.* At that sort of age, the thought of death is profoundly repellent, but I find it much less so now. As people get older they don't rage so much against the dying of the light.

PETER JAY

PETER JAY

Peter Jay was born in 1937 and educated at Winchester and Christ Church, Oxford where he took a first class honours degree in PPE. From 1967–77 he was economics editor at the *Times* and during the same period presenter of the ITV programme *Weekend World*. From 1977–79 he was ambassador to the United States. In 1980 he became chief executive of TVam and later presented *A Week in Politics* for Channel Four for three years until 1986. He was then appointed chief of staff to Robert Maxwell at Mirror Group Newspapers. Since 1990 he has been economics and business editor at the BBC.

You grew up in a political family. Did that early contact with the cut and thrust of politics turn you against embarking on a political career yourself?

I grew up in a particular kind of political family. My father was the kind of politician who was ideas-driven, not power-driven. Politics to him arose out of his studies of philosophy and economics and in his own writings there is a conviction that by managing the nation's affairs in a different way people, especially poor and unemployed people, could be enabled to live a better life. That's why he joined the Labour Party and remained in it all his life. Cut and thrust wasn't what politics was about; it was about principles, ideas, policies and the amelioration of life for people in general. To answer your question directly, I don't believe in the existence of the subconscious, but I grew up semi-consciously assuming that I would end up in politics; for no other reason than it is a natural disposition of sons to assume that they will follow the trade of their fathers. Somewhere along the road, I must have come increasingly to the feeling that it was not a life that I really wanted. I realized that deep down I would be a lousy politician and I didn't want to be one, from which moment I felt hugely relieved. There certainly were things about political life as I observed it which made me realize how disagreeable it could be for a serious minded person. My father was a deeply serious person, and probably the most fulfilling part of his life was in the war years mobilizing British industry to produce the armaments for the war effort. Then, for 13 years he was with the party in opposition. There are some politicians, and perhaps they are the truest, who revel in opposition. But if you're the person my father was, this does not appeal; it's 13 wasted years. Not because you crave office and power but because you're in the whole thing in order to implement certain policies which you believe are terribly important for the country. If all you can do is criticize the other lot, then that is frustrating and disagreeable. Another thought that increasingly came home to me was how disgustingly we treat politicians. For example, if you're a politician and you participate in any kind of public discussion on radio or television the rules more or less require that there is somebody else present to say whatever you said is rubbish and that the opposite is true. That's what's called balance or impartiality. Politics in a pluralistic society is about compromise, about teamwork, about coalitions, about groups of people agreeing together for short to medium term purposes to do things that none of them fully believe in because life can't go on on any other basis. So it's important to respect the necessity for that kind of wheeling and dealing in smoke-filled rooms. If you just hate that kind of thing, it's as

Peter Jay

well to recognize that you're no good at it and do the things that you are good at.

You did have one unsuccessful attempt to stand for election in 1970. Was that a serious foray into politics or were you just testing the water, so to speak?

It's an exaggeration to describe it as standing – I didn't even get to the stage of being a prospective candidate. But it is quite true that in 1970 I got as far as attending two meetings, one at the local furniture makers' trade union and the other at the Fabian Society. That was when I realized how much I hated it all, and anyway I didn't get beyond the absolutely pre-primary stage.

You went to America quite late in the sense that you delayed until your late 20s. Was that simple lack of opportunity or did it not attract you initially?

It wasn't strictly lack of opportunity because I could have gone in 1960 when I was selected for the traditional Oxford Union debating tour of the United States. This was a time just after I graduated when I was in a high old state of indecision about which of five or six different lines to follow. I found these decisions very difficult to make but I ended up rejecting the debating tour. Thereafter I had no money to go to the United States on my own account and anyway I was working as a civil servant, but five years later, in 1966, I was invited by the Ford Foundation to go on a three-month tour. My employer, the Treasury, kindly gave me three months off to go, and that was the beginning of a very long and continuing love affair with the United States.

What is that you find so attractive about the United States?

It's the vigour, the optimism, the confidence that problems are exciting, that they can be tackled and overcome. It is the friendliness, the hospitality, it is the sheer quality and ability of its citizens. Of course I'm speaking subjectively of the people I met and knew. It's also a paradise for children, and therefore it was a very attractive place to live for five years with my own children. Insofar as any generalization is permissible, you can find everything – the good and the bad in the rest of the world – raised to the power of *n* in the United States; if you want to look for bad things, whether social, personal, political, or environmental, you'll find them in the United States more than anywhere else. You'll find the funniest people, the most boring people, the cleverest, the stupidest, the richest, the poorest. I'm not expressing enthusiasms for the bad things about it . . . nonetheless, they have the openness, the ability, the respect for intelligence, the whole 'why not?' attitude. These are all clichés, I'm not claiming any originality at all, but it swept me off my feet. And in my opinion I was right to have the feeling. It is a marvellous place.

When you were ambassador in Washington you made the much quoted remark: 'Anyone who left here to return to Britain would be very foolish.' If it was as foolish as all that, why did you come back?

I don't remember making that remark, nor have I ever seen it quoted before. I'm not questioning your research, I just can't believe that I would have said that since it sounds like a rather unsuitable thing for a British ambassador to say. If I did say it, it would have been my personal private observation. From the point of view of scientists who've got good research opportunities, or academics, or journalists with interesting jobs, whether for British or American papers, or maybe people in money, finance and banking, it's a very exciting place to work. A young person or a young middle-aged person in those positions would have to have very strong personal reasons for wanting to give all that up. That would have been the context. In my own case there were personal reasons for returning, but in addition I became involved in the bid by the TV-AM group for the new breakfast franchise. During 1980, the year when we were bidding for it, I was commuting between Washington and London, spending probably about two thirds of a month in London, and one third with my family in the United States. And then on the 28 December of that year, a date I remember well, we won the franchise and from then on it was a full-time job. I was doing a number of interesting things in the United States, but nothing comparable, so from then on I was committed to being in Britain.

In a sense your enthusiasm for America is a bit surprising. It does not seem to fit easily into a pattern of socialism. There is a huge underclass living on

163

Peter Jay

or below the poverty line there and a marked unwillingness to act effectively.

As I said, the enthusiasm I expressed about the United States is a personal feeling; it is not an endorsement of all the things about the country which are bad. I have never felt any approval, or even tolerance, of the American social and economic system, most of all as it affects the most disadvantaged people. The disagreeable aspects that you rightly draw attention to became very much more accentuated in the Reagan period, though of course there was poverty and unemployment and inequality in very high degrees long before. But Reagan was rare, possibly unique in this century, in not only making those problems more rather than less acute, but positively setting out to do so. The Reagan era occurred after the period in which I formed these enthusiasms.

When you were appointed ambassador to Washington there was a lot of adverse comment. It was, I suppose, inevitable that the cry of nepotism should have been raised. You were not a professional diplomat and Washington must have been the plum job. Why do you think you were chosen?

I know in a very precise way why I was chosen. I should preface my answer by saying that you're quite right, Washington is *the* plum job, also the most demanding job, and in the post-war period in that job, though not in any other British ambassadorial appointment, there had been an equal number of career and non-career appointments. My appointment was controversial, not because it was non-career, but because I was a journalist and because I was related by marriage to the prime minister. The reason I was appointed was that David Owen had been searching for someone he could appoint to this position in order to overcome what he saw as a problem of there being a closed circle of career Foreign Office officials in certain key positions in the Foreign Office in London, the Washington Embassy and elsewhere. As he perceived it, these officials were conducting policies separate from, and sometimes in conflict with, their ministers, and he felt it necessary to stop this. He took the constitutional view that ministers were appointed by the Queen to run the government and civil servants were there to help, assist and advise them, not to conduct a separate policy. David Owen wanted me for the job, but there was a problem of my connection with the prime minister. Both of us were loyal,

164

and in my own case devoted to the prime minister; the last thing in the world I would have wished to do was to damage him. David had talked to him before he had approached me, and after some consideration the prime minister gave his approval, though he obviously would have preferred that such a problem had not been presented to him. Even when David suggested it to me, I more or less fell off my chair with surprise. I then insisted on talking to the prime minister myself. I said, 'We both know this is going to be politically damaging to you. On the other hand, you're the wisest politician I know, and if you tell me that you're content to ride this out, it's a very exciting challenge and I will do it. But if you have any reservations at all, let's forget it.' He answered, 'You go ahead and do it, I'll deal with the politics,' which showed the nobility and generosity of the man. He could very easily have vetoed it, and I need never have known. But he was like that; if he thought something was right he was not going to stand in the way for reasons of avoiding political trouble.

You obviously got on well with him . . .

I was extremely fond of him and remain so to this day. I admire him, I like him, and I have enormous respect for him, but I don't want to give you the impression that I thought I was a sort of chum. He was a great man, I was a boy. I had enormous respect for him, and still do, in every possible way. And my respect for him was increased by that episode because I think three politicians out of four would have said they had enough problems to deal with.

We hear a great deal from time to time, even now, about the special relationship between Britain and the United States. How evident was it in your time as ambassador? And does it exist in reality?

I will tell you what I used to say about this and what I still believe: nothing is more stupid in my opinion than for governments, British and American, but particularly British, to talk about a special relationship. Even in the Winston Churchill/Franklin Roosevelt period, the more you read about that, the more you realize how desperately difficult that relationship was up to and including the Atlantic Charter, until both sides were actually fighting. Then it got easier, but that was late in the day. The second point is that the special relationship is better practised than talked about; it is the

Peter Jay

property of the peoples of the United States and Britain, it is not the property of governments. I always used to say that the relationship between Britain and the United States was like the relationship between a man and his mistress; it required no solemnization by priests or lawyers; it was not written on a piece of paper that it would last for a thousand years or for ever; it would last just as long as the mutual affection lasted.

One of the first things that Mrs Thatcher did on coming to power was to sack you as ambassador in Washington. How did you interpret that at the time?

The factual premise is not correct. Oddly enough, the process was just the opposite. The first thing I did when the result of the election was known, was to telephone the private secretary at No. 10 and say, 'Please inform the new prime minister that my post is in her hands.' That is the proper and correct thing to do if you're a non-career appointment. I then received a message from Mrs Thatcher saying, 'You're doing a wonderful job, you çan't be replaced, please carry on for the time being,' and also a similar message from the new foreign secretary, Lord Carrington. I wasn't sure whether or not I would be able to carry on; it depended on the policies of the new government. In relation to strategic arms control and to the Rhodesian negotiations, there were lines which the new government could have taken which would have made me feel so unhappy that I wouldn't have wanted to be there. But actually they didn't take either of those two lines and so at that stage there wasn't a problem. And then about three or four weeks later I got a letter – which I still have – from Peter Carrington, written in his own hand, a frightfully strange communication to the effect that the press seemed to have built up an expectation that the government were going to make a change in Washington, so he supposed they had better do so after all. So it was not the way you describe it; far from being sacked I offered a resignation and was told to carry on, which I did until Peter Carrington's letter. I have great admiration for Peter, so this is not a criticism; I merely recite historical events as they occurred.

You are now the BBC's economics editor. Do you see this as a stopgap job, or do you regard it as a post you would be happy to remain in indefinitely?

166

Very much the latter if the BBC is happy to have me. Being a journalist, particularly an economics journalist, has been a big slice of my life. I hugely enjoy it, and in my opinion this decade is going to be an absolutely fascinating period for economic policy. It's true I feel schizophrenic about what I like doing. I never have had a career path, and things don't lead naturally from one to the next; they jump about all over the place. There's a bit of me that is basically an administrator or a manager, a leader if you like, and there is a bit of me which is a journalist, a commentator. In retrospect, in mellow middle age, I am probably happiest doing one of those things for a while, and the other for a while, but my job at present is not in your sense of the word a stopgap. One of the things I've noticed is that under the age of 40 if you do a lot of different things people say, gosh what a versatile chap. After you reach the age of 40 people say, why doesn't he make up his mind what he is? Is he a journalist, a civil servant? But frankly, what people say doesn't matter; the important thing is to fill your days with things that you find enjoyable and fulfilling.

On the subject of what people say, you have had some rather unkind things said about you by other members of the corporation – 'not wanting to muck in', 'rather arrogant' and so on. What do you think prompts such responses? Do you think you are naturally aloof in some ways?

I had no idea that these comments had been made. I find the BBC exceedingly friendly, a nice place to work. I've been received with great friendship and tremendous help and support, and I was not aware that anybody had expressed the sentiments that you describe. But the BBC is a very big place, I'm very thick-skinned, and people are perfectly free to criticize, and perhaps they're right. However, I don't think that the people in the economic and business unit, which is my particular patch, would say I was aloof; rather the contrary, I think. We have great discussions about our work and how to cover different stories, and it's all pretty egalitarian.

Now that you have had some experience at the BBC, what is it that prompts you to feel that the licence fee is not the best way to finance the corporation?

167

Peter Jay

It's a very long and complicated argument. The services which broadcasting, television and radio currently deliver are of the kind best suited to the price mechanism in its classic form; in other words where consumers buy things in relatively small packets, pay for them when they buy them, thereby exercising their right to choose what they want, what they don't want, and by so doing send market signals to the producers and suppliers. A classic piece of market economics. That works at its best in my opinion where you're selling very large numbers of very small things, in this case programmes or each individual's consumption of a programme. In the long term that is the right way for both information and entertainment publishing to be supplied. However, it is also true that you will not achieve that consumer sovereignty so long as the consumer is not actually buying the products, but is merely being given them free because the advertiser is paying for them. What's going on is that the publisher is selling audiences to the advertiser, not selling programmes to the consumer, and each act of viewing is equally valuable, because that's one viewer reached by the advertisement. Now under those conditions all the valuable and benign effects of the price mechanism break down, because the whole point of market forces is that you or I will pay more for a better pair of trousers or a better meal in a restaurant, than we will pay for another one, and the market can then respond to our demand. If, however, the makers of trousers or of meals all received the same sum from advertisers for everything they produced, irrespective of whether it was a good meal or a bad meal, a good pair of trousers or a bad pair of trousers, then there would be only a pretty low-level meal or basic pair of trousers made and delivered. In my opinion it's not for parliament or wise men or the Archbishop of Canterbury to say what quality should or shouldn't be given to the public. With books you get a range from trash to great literature, but if you're selling audiences to advertisers you don't get a range, you get homogenization round a lower standard than the public choice would actually want. So until such time as it is technically possible to charge for the act of consuming, viewing, in the same way that you charge for the telephone, so that there would be variable prices depending on what you're viewing, it is vitally important that you continue to have choice and the only way that you can preserve choice is by planning choice, as it were, and the only way you can do that is by having something like the BBC publicly financed. There are better mechanisms than the licence fee for publicly financing it. The obvious one which I've advocated for decades is simply to add a surcharge on to all sales and rentals of television sets and associated equipment, calculated in the first year to produce the same as the television licence produces. Then you get away from the poll tax aspect of the thing. Secondly you get rid of all the collection, policing and evasion problems that go with it; you simply collect the fee through the retail network.

Your career started with a bang. You were president of the Oxford Union, the youngest ambassador Britain ever sent to Washington, but since then there has not been quite the same glitter. Were you aware of things at some point starting to go wrong?

Your frame of reference in looking at it like that is perfectly natural – is it going up, is it going down, has it got glitter? But I've never thought about life like that, and I wouldn't want to. Things happen and what is important is whether you enjoy them, whether you think they are worthwhile, whether they're interesting or helpful to the people you care about, your family, your friends. I remember writing in my early 20s when I was reflecting on the nature of the classical civil service, or indeed on the middle class professional career, that there was a fundamental irrationality about the way in which the professional middle classes looked at careers. The measure of success is always related to where you were on the last day before you retired, that if you were head of the civil service, or if you were at the top of any other profession on the last day, then it was 'successful'. If on the other hand you weren't, then it was 'a failure'. This is an absolute contradiction of everything that commonsense and economic analysis suggest; if you are going to make an investment, the return you look at is not the return on the last day, it's the sum of the returns over the whole period. And secondly, because of time preference, the return tomorrow is more important pound for pound, than the return the day after or a year later or ten years later or forty years later, so the closer the thing is the greater weight you give it, the further away it is the less weight you give it. The right way to think about this is not to see a career as 'successful' or 'unsuccessful' depending on where it is on the last day, but to think of it as a working life; the worth of which to you is the sum of all of the days. That is much the more sensible and humane way of looking at life, and I am constantly amazed that mine has worked out so much better than I expected or had any right to expect.

Yes, but your contemporaries all acknowledged your brilliance, you had the 'right' background, you married the prime minister's daughter, you had all the trappings of fame and distinction, and your career showed such early promise. Then something went wrong. What was it?

If people thought that I was engaged in some kind of *cursus honoris* to great eminence and distinction, then they were wrong. It is true that there were a number of episodes in my early life which would have perhaps fitted that model, but that wasn't how I thought about it. I could painstakingly take you through, item by item, how it happened that I did the Oxford Union; how it happened that I did the civil service exam. It was my father who wanted me to be a civil servant, and I thought the simplest way to deal with this since I didn't have the courage to say to him frankly that I did not want to join the civil service was to take the exam which I expected to fail. I didn't fail, so that plan went wrong. I didn't marry the prime minister's daughter; I married somebody whom I fell in love with as a student, whose father later became the prime minister. He was an opposition spokesman on colonial affairs at the time I married her. Life, certainly my life, consists of a series of absolute accidents. It is true that the early accidents were rather high profile, but I've always described my life, not only ironically, as a long pursuit of anonymity. This seems to be an ever receding goal, but nonetheless, that's how I think of it.

Have you enjoyed your encounters with power?

Let me answer your question very specifically, because this is something I formed a clear opinion on very early in my life when I was the private secretary to the permanent secretary of the Treasury, hobnobbing with chancellors and prime ministers and so on. There is no power in British society. Power means the ability arbitrarily to command this or that, just because you want it to happen. Now it may be that there are people like Saddam Hussein who exercise power, but in highly developed, mature, pluralistic societies of no great world influence like Britain, there is no power because power is infinitely diffused. If you actually watch at first hand the inner centres of government conducting the business of the government, these are not men who are saying, 'Off with his head!' or 'Give him a million pounds!' These are men desperately trying to find ways out of absolutely insoluble and intolerable dilemmas, and the so-called solutions all have terrible disadvantages attached to them. So this is an exercise in dodging brickbats; it's very high profile, yes, and if it is done honourably, it leads to great distinction, but it is not an exercise of power in the sense that any sensible man would understand it. There may be some businesses where there is a very strong dominant leader who is exercising power and saying, fire him, hire him, like some medieval potentate, but that is unusual and often such people come unstuck after a while. This has always been my opinion from that early observation; it is a complete will-of-the-wisp invented by tabloid newspapers and writers of very inferior novels to make the story sound more exciting and more simple than it really is. It is not true, in my opinion, that I have ever exercised power, or indeed that anybody else has.

The TV-AM enterprise did not work out as you had hoped. I know that you were hoping early on that you could introduce a more substantial sort of journalism to the world of TV. With the experience of TV-AM behind you, do you think that is still possible?

I think it's absolutely possible; I also think it was perfectly possible in the case you mention. What happened in the TV-AM story, or my early part of it, is that after winning the franchise and building the company, getting the studios created on time and on budget, we did not actually deliver on air in the first month the programmes we'd talked about. I don't want to go into the painful reasons for that, but it was nothing to do with the five presenters who were absolutely magnificent and held the thing together on air despite a lot of chaos behind the scenes. We made some quick changes and by March the ratings which collapsed in February were recovering and were on track to be in April what they needed to be in order to satisfy our advertising goals. What then happened was that there was a good old fashioned coup d'état. Jonathan Aitken wanted to be king. All is fair in love and war and business, and he made a threat that if he didn't become king he would call an extraordinary general meeting and the company's financial advisers advised that if that happened, even though he would lose (I had about 65 per cent of the votes, he only had 35), some of the financial backing for the company might be withdrawn. I took the view, rightly or wrongly, that it was ridiculous to hazard the whole life of the company for the sake of a personal scrap between me and Jonathan as to who should sit on the throne. I'd had all the fun and excitement and success of winning the franchise and setting it up, so I thought, well, if Jonathan wants to be king, let him. After I'd gone, the IBA – idiotically in my opinion – refused to allow Jonathan to remain in that position even if he gave up his seat in

Peter Jay

parliament which I think he would have done. That led to his cousin being appointed, after which the affairs of the company collapsed. Unlike me and Jonathan he did not know anything about the business and he also had a number of crazy attitudes, not least towards women, which were disastrous and caused the ratings to collapse again. The whole spring advertising wave was lost, the cash flow went to hell, the company had to be given away. The other crazy thing that the IBA did was, having thus caused the collapse, they then panicked and totally unnecessarily abandoned the central principle of their own franchise. It was they who had invented this franchise, it was they who had invented its defining terms – graven on my heart – 'primarily but not exclusively news information and current affairs'. Since TV-AM was not fulfilling the franchise, all they had to do was to give it to somebody else who could fulfil it. It would have been fulfilled, as indeed the BBC very successfully fulfils it now. I therefore blame the incompetence of the IBA for failing to understand what was going on, failing to have the courage to stick to their own principles, for causing the crisis by refusing to allow Jonathan to sit on the throne, and thus for the fact that their original conception was not fulfilled.

The presenters were widely perceived as prima donnas . . .

Precisely the opposite was true. The five presenters were very well known and distinguished, but their professionalism, their hard work in that first month when they were not receiving the support from behind the scenes which they should have received, held it all together. They were the very opposite of prima donnas: they were loyal, they were disciplined, they were professional and they never made any trouble of any kind; they could not have behaved better.

Jonathan Aitken described you as 'the best example of impeccable behaviour from a departing chief executive I have ever seen'. Was there a lot of swallowing of pride and effort of will involved, or was it down to native good manners and good breeding on your part.

You invite me to be very arrogant. I was clearly confronted in the marbled parlours of Barclay's Merchant Bank in Gracechurch Street with Jonathan's formal statement: he would move for an extraordinary general

172

meeting to throw me out and install him. It was like Solomon and the babies, because this was passionately my baby. I was faced with the choice: either you fight, in which case your baby will be killed, or you go gracefully, and the baby will survive, though it will have a foster mother, as it were. Manifestly you don't have to be some kind of saint to see that the right course in that situation is to say, well, I've had two or three very exciting years; if Jonathan wants that much to be king, let him be king, and let the company survive.

In a way you have had quite a lot of ill-luck with women in your life, though I expect others might put it differently. How far have these theoretically private matters impinged on your public career?

They've not impinged on my public career at all. They are, as you say, private matters.

Nora Ephron's book (and subsequent film) and the controversy surrounding the birth of your son Nicholas must have been traumatic. You have always said that being in the public eye teaches you to build up a layer of resilience under this sort of pressure, but surely it must take its toll?

I'm very proud of Nicholas. I see him regularly, he's a lovely boy. I'm fighting great battles at the moment with the local education authority and indeed the Department of Education to get them to give him the support and help he needs with his learning difficulties. In the early stages I wasn't sure whether or not I was his father, and that's why I insisted on having scientific evidence, because I thought he was entitled to know, and I was entitled to know. Once I was sure I was very proud and fond of him. He's a good son. I've said in the past that I think in some ways Nora is the single most evil woman I've personally ever encountered, the only person I've ever known who would sacrifice her own children as well as other people's to her own personal promotional and career gain. That's all I have to say about her.

Do you think it's reasonable that the press should exploit such situations when public figures are involved? They would certainly argue that the public interest is best served by revelation, but what view do you take?

Peter Jay

I take two completely different views, depending on whether I'm the journalist or I am the subject. If I'm the journalist, I have always had an absolute rule – and Richard Ingrams can confirm that this goes right back to the discussions we had as undergraduates – that morality applies to what you do to other people without their consent; it doesn't apply to what you do alone or with other people with their consent. That is a definition of what ethics is about according to J S Mill, and according to me. As a journalist I never would, I never have, considered it legitimate to write about the private domain; as a subject I would never ever complain, I never have, I never will. I believe in Enoch Powell's statement that men in public life who complain about the media are like ships' captains who complain about the sea. They chose the wrong line of work. As a subject you must expect it, you must regard it as normal, you must not be bothered by it, and you must always be polite and courteous to other journalists who, as they see it, have a job to do, even if their interpretation of the job is not one that I would as a journalist ever adopt. That has always been my position very strongly and I adhere to it to this day.

You once said: 'The happiest things in life are the sharing and the building of a family or a relationship . . . and to do that successfully you can't keep stopping and starting from scratch again with one relationship after another.' Is that a view you still take?

Yes, absolutely. In my opinion a family relationship is something which is built over a long period of time; half of the stuff of the relationship today is made up of the memories of things that you all did together in the past. Sometimes you're forced to start again because somebody dies or something goes hopelessly wrong or whatever, and therefore it's not an argument that you should then retire to a monastery if that happens, but it is an argument that the very strong and obstinate and determinedly pursued aim should be to build this one great thing. I think if you do find that you have to start again, you should start again in that self-same spirit.

What puzzled a lot of people at the time of your going to work for Maxwell is that after a glittering career, you would opt to work for someone who already had a tarnished reputation – he was certainly known to be a bully. It seemed a bizarre appointment in a way. Did

174

you have no sense of selling your soul, or your dignity?

Perhaps I take myself less seriously or less pompously than other people do. At that time, in 1986, nobody else was offering me a job that would be demanding and fulfilling in that sort of way. I was on the edge of boredom, and boredom in middle life is a very dangerous thing; not only does it corrode the mind and the character, it is also unpleasant in itself. As to the question, was there a problem about going to work for Robert Maxwell, a controversial figure? Firstly I took very careful and specific soundings in exactly the way that one does these things. I asked the Foreign Office and the Bank of England if there were any reasons why I shouldn't take the job. Of course I didn't expect them to give me reasons, I just wanted to know from certain very senior people whether they would give me a nudge and a wink not to go and do that kind of work. But I got a complete OK from both. Secondly I consulted all the people I most respected, including very senior ex-Labour Cabinet ministers who had known Maxwell politically over a long period, and they encouraged me to go ahead. Thirdly there was the question of whether I should be bothered about the famous 1970 report. In my opinion that was a discredited document for three main reasons: one, that they themselves had acknowledged a serious error in their first report, and produced a second report which withdrew some but not all of the findings of the first report; two, that the Department of Trade had in effect admitted that Maxwell had been denied natural justice, in that if you accuse somebody of a very serious misdeed you should, in accordance with basic principles, tell him what he is accused of so that he has the opportunity to defend himself; and three, that it was all getting on for 20 years ago. So there seemed to me to be absolutely no reason not to take this job on. There were also many good things about Robert Maxwell which I liked, including the fact that he enabled the *Daily Mirror* to survive and publish a little bit of party political balance in our national press. At the same time I said to myself, if he ever asks me to do something or I become aware of him doing something which isn't right I can always walk away. So I think I would have had to have taken myself much more seriously, been much more pompous than I hope I am, to have been deterred by the kind of consideration implied in your question.

You described Maxwell as 'a heroic and romantic figure whose courage and generosity I admire'. Is that how it struck you at the time?

Absolutely, and I mean it now. There is not the slightest doubt in my mind that he had those qualities that I described. He could also behave disgracefully to people, and sometimes he did. There were lots of disagreeable sides to him, but he was undoubtedly a heroic figure, a romantic figure; he dreamed dreams, extraordinary futuristic dreams, and he did some great things. If the newspaper reports are right as to what he was up to in 1991, and one has to assume that they're not completely invented, then during that period he behaved in business terms in an absolutely disgraceful way; but I never saw any sign that he was doing any of those things.

But was the experience with Maxwell worthwhile? Did you learn anything from him?

I don't think I learned anything from him. It was exhilarating, it was exhausting, it was extraordinary, and there was a great sense of camaraderie amongst colleagues. But that was all.

What exactly did you do for Maxwell?

Administration. It's hard to describe. Maxwell didn't have the foggiest idea about modern business organization; his personal headquarters were in extreme administrative chaos. Like any minister in a department he needed a private office and a sort of permanent secretary, so that information flowed upwards, decisions flowed downwards. He needed somebody to bring order to all that chaos, while he got on with his next dream or business plan or whatever it might be. I was excited by that challenge . . . after all I'd been a private secretary in Whitehall, and though it's hard to make this sound credible, I love administration, it gives me a real aesthetic pleasure. Gradually I came to realize that it was impossible, because he was incapable of accommodating himself to the disciplines of administrative order. The thing I learned in Whitehall is that the hinge between the minister and the department is crucial; if that fractures then the whole machine breaks down. To begin with I thought that I could explain those very elementary procedures to Maxwell but I then realized that he was somehow temperamentally incapable of accepting them, and that he was actively hostile to any form of organization as such. This was symptomatic of the romantic hero in him – his natural style was to be at the head of a band of horsemen who were galloping across the Asian Steppe, capturing a city here and a city there and moving on; insofar as there was any 'organizational structure' in such a band of horsemen it was that every now and then they would stop and have a huddle and then the leader would say, right this is what we do next, and off they would gallop again. Maxwell could scarcely bring himself to read anything that was more than about two or three lines on a piece of paper, and then only for some mysterious reason if it was received through a fax machine rather than in any other way. Most of it was farce; it wasn't some great giant conspiracy or plot, it was just straight, low farce, of absolute and continuing chaos.

When you look back on your life, do you have any regrets at all?

I have a few. I would have been wiser to have left Washington immediately I left the embassy, though I had strong private reasons for not doing so. Another very specific and intense regret centres on the day of the great TV-AM melodrama, 17 March 1983, after the encounter in the Barclay's Merchant Bank that I described to you. I passionately wish I could have the second half of that day back again and do what I omitted to do. I remembered to call my children and tell them what was going on so that they were not stunned by newspaper headlines, but what I failed, fatally failed to do, was to tell Anna Ford and Angela Rippon and the others that evening, or that afternoon, what had happened. Strictly speaking I had signed a most solemn legal undertaking not to tell anybody, but I do wish I could have told them because it would have saved them from the very noble but by then ineffective gesture they made the next morning. Anna and Angela in particular took a very brave and defiant stand about what was going on when in fact the die was irrevocably cast by then. I bitterly regret that I didn't think of telling them. I think that Anna at least has always felt that I let her down and it is very natural that she should feel that; it's one of life's awful accidents and I regret it bitterly. These are my public regrets; I shan't go into my private ones, but they are not very large.

DR GRAHAM LEONARD

DR GRAHAM LEONARD

Graham Leonard was born in London in 1921 and educated at Balliol College, Oxford of which he became an honorary fellow in 1986. He was appointed bishop of Willesden in 1964 and bishop of Truro in 1973. He opposed the Anglican-Methodist unity scheme in the 1970s, and as bishop of London (1981–91) he became the focus of theological opposition to the ordination of women to the priesthood. In 1994 Dr Leonard was received into the Roman Catholic Church and conditionally ordained as a priest by Cardinal Hume.

This may seem a rather blunt opening question but can you distinguish for me between religion and superstition? I mean, what counts as one rather than the other?

Religion must be based on how things are, on what the world is, on what Charles Williams would have called 'the is-ness of things'. Religion must be based on reality, and supremely on God Himself from whom all that's real has its origin. Superstition is based on what we would like things to be, even if they are not; in other words it is based on unreality.

But reality is something you normally feel and experience, and there are certain aspects of religion which don't fall into this realm . . .

I think I'd question that. It may be a reality we do not totally comprehend, but I would certainly not want to reduce religion to being concerned simply with how things actually are. The reality which we experience in religion is greater than our limited minds can comprehend, and this is the distinction I'm trying to make. There is a fundamental difference between our inability to comprehend God and aspects of our universe which transcend understanding, and our desire to base our life, our attitudes, on that which has no basis in reality.

When a private person leaves the Anglican Church and moves to Rome, that is a matter simply for the person himself . . . but you were a bishop and had the fullness of the priesthood. Did you not feel a fundamental obligation to those you had led for all those years?

Yes, I did, but if it proves impossible to continue to exercise that fullness of the priesthood, you have an obligation to ask where you can do so. God was not withdrawing my vocation, but He was saying to me, you must exercise it somewhere else. I said that I would come to Rome 'as a supplicant without presumption' – that was my phrase – but I did lay down one condition, and that was that I could not be asked to deny my former ministry, however regarded. And that was made very clear, not only by the fact that I was ordained conditionally, but also because in the course of the service it was recognized that ministries outside the Catholic Church could be vehicles of grace. Obviously I gave a lot of thought to those whom I was, as it were, leaving behind, but given the situation in the

Dr Graham Leonard

Church of England, it seemed to me that one way forward was to accept the Roman claims and to seek to be received into the Roman Church; and it has been understood in this way by a number of people.

It must have been very distressing for many of your parishioners, however. Were you conscious of that, did you take full account of that in your decision to leave the Anglican Church?

I've had a good deal of criticism from those who don't agree with me, but I've also heard from many Anglicans who have told me they are now considering the possibility of doing what I have done. I really can't think of more than perhaps one or two letters which have taken the line that I have abandoned my parishioners or let them down.

I suppose it must irritate you that so many people concentrate on your objection to women being ordained when there are other reasons for your decision to move to Rome. Before we get on to women priests, can you tell me something of those other reasons?

They were set out very clearly, surprisingly enough, by the Church of England House of Bishops, who then didn't attempt to deal with them, mainly because of the pressures of secular thought. But at the time they said that the issue affected our understanding of the nature of God, of the way He created the world, and it raised the whole question of the authority of the Church. Having set these issues out, they then didn't take any notice of them. And so one of my great sadnesses was what I would call the theological levity of the Church of England in not being prepared to face these fundamental issues.

There are two popular views about the Anglican Church: one which sees its doctrines being modified to accommodate changed cultural circumstances; the other which thinks of it as being determined to be all things to all men (and now to all women as well), and that it really has no firm principles at all. Do you incline to either view?

Not exactly. If you look at what happened in the Reformation in this country, it was above all an act of state. Henry VIII proclaimed himself

182

Dr Graham Leonard

Head of the Church and broke with Rome. The position of the Church of England emerged as a kind of response to what had been forced upon it by the state. It was never based upon a coherent theology of its own; it was rather an accumulation of responses which took three forms. First there were those who maintained that the Church of England was still Catholic, and that in spite of not being under Rome, it could still claim to be Catholic since some formulae of the Church of England were in fact designed to preserve certain Catholic elements. At the same time there was the Protestant element which came from the Continent and found a footing here, and the Protestants played a great part in modifying the various liturgies and service books produced at the time. And thirdly there were those whose commitment one might say was predominantly rationalist, though they didn't really come to have such a profound effect until the 18th century. So there were these three streams coming through in the Church of England, and they were never really related. One hears a lot about the comprehensiveness of the Church of England but it's been a comprehensiveness of plurality, not of understanding. Way back in the late 60s and early 70s when the Anglican Methodists' scheme for union was in debate, I pleaded for those in each strain to admit what was wrong and to take what was good in their understanding into a more cohesive whole. That's never happened, and what is now clear to me is that the secular pressures are so great that this kind of approach just won't stand the strain.

You have said that the Church of England cannot now claim to be anything other than a sect. Are you conscious of the fact that the view will be regarded as offensive to a great many people?

With all due respect, I don't think that was my quote, but John Gummer's. I have fallen over backwards to try not to be offensive to the Church of England.

But is it a view you share . . .?

Whether I would use the word sect is another matter, but I would say this: the Church of England in the past has claimed, in the words of Archbishop Fisher, to have no faith of its own; it has only the Catholic faith enshrined in the Catholic creed which is held without addition or diminution. It can't say that any more. What has happened is that the Church of England

183

Dr Graham Leonard

to a large extent has become a communion in which it is required that you accept something which is quite explicitly rejected by the vast majority of Christendom. Before the vote was taken, both the Pope and the ecumenical patriarch for the Orthodox Church made it clear that this was not acceptable to them, they did not believe it to be part of the Catholic faith, and that if we pursued it and it went forward in this way it would cause great difficulties; but it still went ahead on its own and decided that in a matter of this gravity it could make its own decision. Now, whether you call it a sect or not, the Church of England has now claimed in a sense to be autonomous. It has claimed that it can define by itself what is integral to the Catholic faith, and in that sense I believe it has isolated itself.

Many people will understand the arguments from tradition about the ordination of women, but is there a theological argument separable from the argument from tradition?

I believe there is, and it's very profound. In the first place Our Lord actually allowed women to be witnesses of the Resurrection at a time when the witness of a woman was not accepted by the Jewish people at the time. He talked to a woman at the well alone, and in many ways overturned the common practice of the time, but when it came to choosing his disciples and then apostles he chose only men. Of course it is commonly said that if Our Lord were alive today He would, because of our culture, do things differently. First of all, I don't accept He isn't alive today, but the fact remains that the culture in which God chose to become man was the culture He chose; it wasn't an accident. And I believe that the whole of Scripture compels us to say that that particular culture, being the deliberate and free choice of God, has a significance for us which we cannot ignore. We can't amend, we can't alter the Christian gospel to suit each successive culture; that would be building on sand. Certainly the culture in which God became man was patriarchal, but I believe that was a fact of God's choice ... Our Lord came, as Scripture says, in the fullness of time, after a time of preparation. This for me is a very profoundly theological reason. There is also the question of representation. It is sometimes argued that in order for humanity to be truly represented in the priesthood, you need men and women, and you can't have a true representation without both. But one thing that cannot be denied is that God was incarnate as a male person only. But if you say that you need both men and women to represent humanity, you are in fact saying that the representation of humanity in Our Lord is inadequate. To my thinking humanity is represented in both men and women who live in a relationship of complementarity, each bringing his or her own particular qualifications and characteristics and contributions in order that the whole of humanity shall operate in a healthy and proper way. To say that man alone cannot represent humanity is to raise some very fundamental questions about the very basic fact of the Christian gospel.

Is God male?

To me God has no gender but He is the source of gender which He gave to His creation; in all His dealings with us He takes account of the fact that we are men and women. In so doing He tells us, for example, to address Him as Our Father, and in Scripture we are taught to think of the Church as the Bride of Christ. There is the complementarity, and I cannot as a Christian think it is wrong to address God as Father because that is the way God has revealed Himself. This may sound very impertinent of me, but God doesn't do things without reason, and yet this is always difficult for people to grasp. It is no surprise to me that when God became incarnate He was incarnate as a male person, and it is perfectly proper to say that although God is without gender in His Own Being, nevertheless, in the way He tells us to talk about Him, to think about Him, He tells us to use gender, because it's part of the way He made us.

Does dogma or conscience have priority in church? Would you regard it as a Christian duty to believe what has been revealed by Scripture?

Well, I promised to do that when I was received as a Catholic, but I have always attributed immense importance to the matter of conscience. I do not believe you can ask somebody to act against his own conscience; you must respect it. At the same time, and this is largely forgotten, it is a fundamental maxim of moral theology that our conscience is always in need of correction. It never points absolutely true to the north, it has to be corrected, and that happens when we live, as it were, under the judgement of dogma. When I look at the New Catechism, it is far greater than I can wholly encompass in my own limited mind, but I happen to live under its judgement. Dogma is given to us in order that our consciences may be cleansed, may be corrected, but meanwhile we have to act according to what our consciences are, and I don't believe that it is incompatible to live in this way while accepting the truths of revelation.

But which has precedence – dogma or conscience?

In the last resort, as Newman would say, it must be conscience, but you may have to accept the consequences of that. What I find so difficult is the people who say that their conscience tells them to take a line which is in fact quite contrary to the teaching of the Church but think that they can still go on as faithful members of the Church. In my view, if your conscience actually tells you that you believe something which is quite contrary to what the clear teaching of the Church is, then it seems to me you have a proper course of action, which is to leave. What you can't do is to tell the Church it's got to alter its beliefs to suit your particular conscience at a given time.

How powerful in your mind is the thought that the ordination of women to the priesthood in the Anglican Church will separate it from the universal Church as presented by Rome and the Orthodox?

I think it has separated us in a very sad way in the attempt to be autonomous and the extent to which what I would call secular thought has been allowed to dominate what should be theological decisions. A lot of feminists, for example, not only advocate a liberal view within the Christian Church, but claim that the Christian gospel as traditionally presented is not compatible with feminism.

In the early Church, however, women are recorded as teaching the faith and it seems to have been perfectly accepted. Was the early Church wrong to allow this to happen?

No. Women were given a proper part to play in the early Church, no doubt about that, and in fact I have pressed at times very strongly for women, who have particular gifts, to be allowed to develop in spiritual directions. But as far as exercising the sacramental role of the priesthood, the Church has been quite consistent in this from the earliest times; and where that has happened it has been condemned.

You have argued that if God had wanted women to be priests He would have made at least one apostle a woman, but isn't it presumptuous to say what God would or would not have done? And isn't it anyway a rather crude version of the argument, 'if God had wanted us to fly He would have given us wings' . . .?

I see what you mean. Well, it may be presumptuous to say what God would or would not have done, but what is important is to say what God did, and I can't get away from that.

Yes, but if we accept your argument, then shouldn't we perhaps take account of the Jewishness of the apostles? The Church ordains males who are not Jews, but Jesus didn't . . . why concentrate on one aspect and not the other?

Because for me the distinction between male and female is fundamental to all humanity; it is not simply a characteristic like Jewishness. I wouldn't want to say that nationality is a second order issue, but I don't put it on the same level as gender.

You said that women are not able to represent the maleness of Jesus in the celebration of mass. But isn't there a case for saying that what matters is not Christ's maleness but His humanity?

I know that argument has been put, but if you say that humanity can be represented only by both sexes, you are saying something fundamentally destructive of the incarnation, because God was incarnate only as a male person. The Church is sometimes accused of denigrating women, and while that may at certain times in the past have been true, you only have to think of the position which has always been given in the Catholic Church to Our Lady to see that a woman has been extolled beyond measure.

But do you think feminism unduly influenced the decision on the ordination of women priests?

Oh, it certainly did in some places, particularly in America, but also to a considerable extent in this country. A good deal of feminist literature which I've read sees the ordination of women as one of their aims in securing the acceptance of what I would call extreme feminist views.

You have sometimes said that women would take things too personally, would be too emotional to be effective, and so on. But would you not allow that this might also apply to some male priests, their maleness notwithstanding?

I don't remember saying that, though I wouldn't deny it. I think there is a fundamental difference between men and women in the way they deal with problems. That isn't to say that some women don't have a more masculine approach, and some men may well have a more feminine approach, but it is vital that the basic distinction is recognized and not blurred.

It's only comparatively recently that women have been allowed to vote, or indeed go to university. Do you think you might also have opposed these changes at the time?

I don't think I would. Looking back over my life, I have consistently tried to distinguish between what I would call fundamentals, basic truths, whether a revelation or something else, and other things which might be subject to change. The idea, for example, that my highly intelligent wife couldn't vote would be most offensive to me.

Even though you don't see them as being analogous issues, don't you think that in the fullness of time – as is happening now in the Anglican Church – they will be seen as comparable, and women will come to be accepted in the priesthood, even in the Roman Catholic Church?

I don't think so. The last apostolic letter of the Pope makes it quite clear that it is not on the agenda in the Catholic Church. Until recent years the Church of England said it maintained the Catholic faith, not by exercising an authority of magisterium but by the contributions of worship and teaching, from which the truth would emerge. Well, it may be possible for scholars and holy men to do that, but that won't happen with the ordinary person in the street who does not have the facility for doing that kind of assessment of the truth. I mean, I use my word processor but I don't pretend to understand for a moment how it works, but it doesn't prevent me from using it, and to some extent that applies to theological thought. What is very worrying in the Church of England is the fact that when synodical government was introduced, nobody realized what was actually happening. There is a most extraordinary provision which gives the General Synod power to make doctrinal changes. The clause says something like this: that the General Synod shall not pass anything which is contrary to the doctrine of the Church of England or indicative of a departure therefrom. That sounds all right, but the next sentence goes on to say, but if the Synod shall pass anything that shall conclusively determine that it has not done anything which is contrary to the doctrine of the Church of England or indicative of a departure therefrom . . . in other words the Synod can do exactly what it likes, and the formularies of the Church of England no longer have any authority. This confirmed what I had always feared, that the General Synod could change the formularies, it could change the creed if it wanted to, it can do anything.

Since the Roman Catholic Church has held out against married priests, and you yourself are married, does this not mean that in effect you are undermining the authority of the Roman Church on this question?

That is a very fair question, but I would say first of all that the celibacy of the clergy is of course a matter of discipline, not of doctrine. After all St Peter was married, and in the Orthodox Church you either have to be married before ordination or be a monk. I did of course discuss this issue with Cardinal Hume, and there has never been any suggestion that because some of us have now been accepted as married priests, that this is altering the discipline. Any ex-Anglican, for example, who seeks to be ordained *de novo* will have to accept the celibacy role. What applied to me was an *ad hoc* decision for a particular group of people at a particular time, and it has been made very clear both by the Cardinal and by Rome that it doesn't alter the overall position of the Church.

Do you think the Roman Catholic Church has gone far enough to accommodate Anglicans like yourself?

All I can say is that the welcome I received has been overwhelming. I

189

thought that I would be given a period of what I would call decent reticence, but it hasn't worked like that, and I'm being asked to go round and talk everywhere.

Do you think that the Roman Catholic Church is right in not allowing priests to marry?

I think there is a great deal to be said for it. I don't yet feel that I know enough about the internal life of the Roman Church to be able to make a judgement, but we are living in an increasingly secular society, and the pressures of that society are becoming greater upon us. It is very hard to think that it's right to bring a wife into the kind of pressures under which a priest now has to live. I would think it is probably wiser in the present situation as it looks like being for some time ahead for priests not to be married. Also when I was in the Church of England and dealing with married candidates for ordination, it was very difficult to discern whether the wives or the fiancées were really going to be able to live in that public relationship to an ordained man in the future, especially if they were relatively young. How are they going to respond when their husband is having to stand out for things which they personally find difficult to accept? This puts an enormous strain on the marriage, and this makes me feel the present discipline of celibacy is the wisest thing.

You have strong views on the indissolubility of marriage. No one would underestimate the problems arising from broken marriages, but given that they are a fact of modern life, which not even the royal family is exempt from, how best can the Church respond?

In this matter I believe the Catholic Church actually behaves very wisely. On the one hand, it stands foursquare for the indissolubility of marriage, and on the other it is as understanding and flexible as possible in concrete incidences.

But a lot of people accuse the Catholic Church of being flexible only when it comes to the rich and famous . . .

Well, I wonder if this is true. I have heard that said but my experience, limited as it is now, is that if the rich and famous get some nullity or invalidation, it does of course hit the headlines. A lot of simple good pastoral care is given to individuals who wouldn't come into this category, but their cases do not attract publicity.

You yourself have been married for 50 years, and your wife is known to share your views. But your wife was content to give up her career to look after you and the children, to take a role secondary to yours. Would you have been happy if the positions had been reversed?

I'm not sure that I would agree with your description of it as a secondary role. What I constantly realize, looking back, is the extent to which she supplemented my role. That sounds a rather condescending way of putting it, but I'm very conscious of how many people speak of what they owe to her for the friendship she gave, for the fact that the house was always open for people. What she has been able to do, particularly as a hostess, has been very significant and it certainly has satisfied her.

You are quoted as saying that sexual experience is not essential for a full life. How did you arrive at that view? Isn't sex at the very basis of humanity, an experience of great beauty and joy, and indeed a gift from God?

I would agree with all that. My remark was made in the context of those who were saying that it was wrong to seek to control sexual experience. Also, if you say that sexual experience is an absolute necessity for a full human life you are in fact saying that Our Lord did not live a full human life. There is no evidence that Our Lord had sexual experience, it has never been assumed that He did, so to me it hits the incarnation fundamentally. Besides, some of the most saintly people I've met in my life have not been married and they are such people that it is inconceivable that they would have had any sexual experience, and yet they have been able to direct and canalize their extraordinary gifts in a most remarkable way.

What are your views on homosexual priests? Should the Church show them compassion?

My line on that has been quite consistent. I make a distinction between being homosexual by disposition and indulging in homosexual genital acts. I cannot accept that the latter are right and good, but at the same time I have always taken the line, particularly when I was Bishop of London, that you cannot assume, just because two men are living in the same house, that they are indulging in homosexual genital acts. People used to write to me and ask, what are you going to do about so and so? And my answer was always, what reason is there for me to do anything, what evidence do you have that they are in fact living in a physical relationship, and of course they could never produce this. On the other hand, if a priest said to me, I am living in a physical homosexual relationship, I would say, that is sinful and you must give it up.

Are there still core doctrines, without adherence to which you cannot legitimately call yourself a Christian?

That's not an easy question to answer at the moment. I see the Catholic faith as a whole, but nevertheless if you press me on that point I would say that the cardinal doctrine is that of the incarnation, that Our Lord is truly God and man both. And I would want to go further and put the Resurrection in the same category. But I prefer not to isolate doctrines and give them degrees of importance.

The Church of England seems now to be irrevocably divided. What future do you see for it?

I don't know. I try not to speculate about the Church of England or give advice to it. Some indication will be given by the debate which is going to take place soon on lay celebration of the mass. If that is given a fair wind I think it will be a clear indication that the Church of England is irrevocably committing itself to being at one with the Protestant bodies, because it would be so subversive to the Catholic structure of the Church. In other respects it's difficult at the moment; I don't think anybody really appreciates the significance of what the Church of England has done.

To outside observers it can seem a little strange that on the one hand there is a mood to encourage the ecumenical approach, yet on the other hand there are more and more obstacles put in its way. Why has this come about?

That's a very interesting question, but it doesn't have an easy answer. Even in my lifetime I can remember the Anglican Methodist proposals for a union, or the times of the covenanting proposals as they were called a bit later on, and the great cry then was, we must do nothing to prejudice unity. It was also said that we must do nothing apart that we can't do together. All the emphasis was on unity, but that's gone now. As one bishop said at the Lambeth Conference in '88, no price is too high to pay for the ordination of women – it doesn't matter what divisions it causes. So there's been an extraordinary sea change here, and the prospects of any kind of organic union between the Church of England and the Church of Rome are just not on the agenda.

Politicians are keen to confine clerics within a moral enclosure where they can do no harm – even the Pope is keen not to have his clergy engaged in political action. How can the Church mediate effectively between God and Mammon?

Again there's no easy answer to that. I myself have been fairly intensively involved in political issues of one kind or another, but while the Church must involve itself with politics because it is concerned with human beings, those who hold official positions in the Church of England should make it quite clear that Christian commitment forbids them from giving total allegiance to one particular party interpretation, something which politicians find hard to understand. They must first and foremost be Christians and exercise judgement according to the issue.

Is it possible that in the future Christians may have to be content with a version of ecumenism which is more like a confederation, a group loosely allied by subscription to a central doctrine whose sense is not too closely defined . . . in other words a bit like the Church of England in fact?

I think there is a certain amount of truth in that. People forget what an extraordinary change of attitude has taken place, even in my lifetime. When I was first ordained in 1948 churches had very little to do with each other. I can remember how we were told by the Catholic Church that we couldn't even say the Lord's Prayer together. Now the relationships have totally changed without any question of visible unity arising, and I think you're probably right: for Christians divided as they are, for them to live together in harmony, to listen to one another, without compromising what they see as their essential beliefs, that is the future for the foreseeable period.

A very small proportion of the country's population, something like 6 per cent or 7 per cent, now regularly attend Christian worship. Do you think it will be possible to re-engage the nation spiritually?

It should be, and I think that is something one simply must work for. The only way it is going to come about is by the recovery of a genuine spirituality among the present worshippers, so that those who do worship draw others to themselves. I certainly can't see this happening by any dramatic moves or legislation. It may happen of course, such is the way of human history, by the situation within the Church becoming much more difficult. It's one of these ironies of history that the blood of the martyrs is the seed of the Church.

Can you explain exactly how you felt when the General Synod voted in favour of the ordination of women priests? What was the predominant emotion . . . anger, betrayal?

Neither. It was relief. I just felt, well, thank God the issue is resolved now, because I had already come to see the way things were going in the Church of England. I felt relieved that I wouldn't have to go on with this battle any longer.

Your protest against the move to ordain women priests caused a great deal of embarrassment to the former Archbishop of Canterbury . . . do you regret this?

I regret that it was necessary. I did try and make my opposition as far as possible principled rather than personal, but I do regret that I had to stand out in the way I did.

You have also been critical of the present Archbishop, Dr Carey. Do you think he abandoned Anglicans like yourself?

I don't really want to comment on the present Archbishop of Canterbury. I would simply say this: I think he seriously misjudged the position of those who share my views, and I do find it quite extraordinary that he should imply that neither the Catholic Church nor the Orthodox Church has the mind of Christ.

There are those who claim that you would like to have been Archbishop of Canterbury yourself and that you feel disappointed that you were passed over. Is there any truth in that?

No, there's not. I didn't expect to be, and I was even surprised to become Bishop of London. Looking back, it would have been extraordinarily difficult for me to have done that job, since I would question the theological basis of the Church of England anyway. Let me put it this way – I don't really see how I could have coped as Archbishop of Canterbury while obeying my conscience.

You have upset quite a lot of people in the Church of England and perhaps because of that you have sometimes been described as a man with delusions of grandeur . . . how do you react to that?

I just laugh at it because I honestly don't think I am. I know that phrase. What people never can understand is that you can be totally devoid of delusions of grandeur but at the same time hold very firm opinions.

You have now retired, but if you had been a younger man, would your position in the Roman Catholic Church not have been very unsatisfactory? It seems unlikely that you would have been recognized as a bishop . . .

I don't know, that's an open question. Rome made a decision about my priesthood, and I was ordained conditionally, but I made it well known publicly and privately that at the age of 73 I did not want to exercise

195

Dr Graham Leonard

episcopal functions. But I am able to exercise all that I wish in terms of my priesthood: I can say mass, I can hear confessions, I can preach, I can minister to the sick, and that is more than enough for any man. And I feel no bitterness towards the church I left; only sorrow.

196

SIR RONALD MILLAR

SIR RONALD MILLAR

Ronald Miller was born in 1919 and educated as Charterhouse and King's College, Cambridge. Before his career as a playwright he began in the theatre as an actor, and later (1948–54) he worked as a Hollywood screenwriter. He wrote a number of successful plays, notably *The Affair* and *The Masters*, both dramatized from the C P Snow novels. For over twenty years he has written political speeches for three prime ministers – Edward Heath, Margaret Thatcher and John Major. He was knighted in 1980 in recognition of his contribution to Mrs Thatcher's speeches, which included the now famous phrase, 'The lady's not for turning'. His autobiography, *A view from the Wings*, was published in 1992.

Your father was killed in an accident when you were only 18 months old so you knew him only from photographs, but your mother kept him alive for you with stories which you could never hear often enough. Did this turn him into an impossibly romantic and glamorous figure in your mind?

Not really. Later on in my life many other people talked about my parents as the ideal couple, two people who were really made for each other. They lived on the river in the days when the river was a very romantic place to live. It seemed to have been an ideal relationship, but that didn't make me regard my father as a saint or anything of that nature. I never knew more than the photographs, but he didn't become an icon.

Were you conscious that your family circumstances were not like those of other boys?

I never noticed it really. I never knew what it was to have two people who had charge of one's life. My mother was a very remarkable woman, and she acted as mother, father and everything else.

Psychologists are fairly certain that the first few years of childhood set the pattern for life. Is this very evident in your case, would you say?

There is some truth in it, but my mother was very conscious of the fact that a boy alone with his mother could become very tied to the apron strings, so she was extremely careful not to let this come about. I went off to boarding school in Bexhill at the age of about 5 and a half, which of course is far too young in normal circumstances, but as she was an actress and touring all around, she didn't want me to get involved in the theatre in any way. It was no life for earning a really good living; more than half the profession is always out of work and so she was always very careful to keep me a little bit at a distance. Enormous waves of affection broke through of course, and we were very close in spite of it all.

But did you suffer, even momentarily, any sort of rejection when she sent you away to school?

I didn't understand it for about half an hour or so, but kids adjust with the speed of lightning, and I soon settled down with the other prep school boys. It could have been a rather neurotic childhood, but it wasn't. She was a very astute woman.

Would you have been happy to send a child of yours to boarding school?

As a matter of fact I wouldn't, but she had very good reasons. Her determination not to let me become a kind of symbol, a replica of my father, was what was in her mind, and I think she was probably right. I learned to be independent very young and that, as life turned out, was invaluable.

In those days it was not thought entirely proper for a woman, let alone one's mother, to be on the stage. Did you experience embarrassment on account of this?

No, I loved it. The theatre was wildly exciting, an escape route for a young boy, and I was spoiled rotten by the stagehands. It was all very stimulating and new, and other kids didn't have this experience. I would go backstage and stand in the wings watching my mother acting, and the stagehand would take me up into the flies above the theatre, showing me how the curtain went up and down, how the lights came on and changed colour. This was a romantic experience which of course imbued me with a love of the theatre that has gone on all my life.

Did you feel a sense of pride to see your mother being acclaimed on the stage?

Oh, I thought she was the cat's whiskers, yes. But I thought that anyway. I didn't know what it was all about, but it seemed to be a sort of wonderland, an everlasting pantomime, and of course it had an enormous effect on me and has done to this day.

On the whole you seem rather to have enjoyed school life at Charterhouse. Do you think in some way it was a substitute for the family life which had been denied to you because you didn't have a father?

200

No. I felt it was a stepping stone, a means to an end, an education. My mother was absolutely determined that I should have a solid, safe grounding in education so that I would have a solid, safe job, and not get involved with things like the arts, or the theatre, or God forbid, the movies. She wanted me to have an intellectual background.

You describe your eagerness to serve in the war as having nothing to do with heroism and everything to do with sentiment and a certain romanticism. Did the reality of war finally hit home, or were you able to keep it at bay until you were invalided out?

It always remained to me a kind of unreality. In a way it was another kind of stage show going on. I had been brought up in this way and had been involved in arts theatre projects, and the Footlights at Cambridge, and somehow or other the war seemed a by-product of this slightly unreal world. It never really occurred to me that I would be killed . . . until afterwards; then I thought, my God, I might have been. I was not without fear because I was so brave, I was without fear because I was a bit of a damned fool; I had never really taken on board the fact that at any minute I could have been wiped out.

After leaving the navy you decided not to return to Cambridge. Was that because you felt fundamentally changed by war and unable to get back on the previous road?

I felt I had grown up in the war, that it was a quite different world that I came back to, but I also felt I had been changed by it. I didn't any longer feel I could go back to more exams, getting a degree and all that. I had done a lot of exams – life had consisted in 'Don't write on both sides of the paper' – and after I had been in the war, I thought, my goodness, that's schoolboy stuff.

The theatre was in your blood. But did it also seem like an escape route from the horrors of war?

No, not a bit. The horrors of war were still going on. The blitz was still on in London, and in the provinces where we toured – Plymouth and

Sir Ronald Millar

Coventry and Liverpool – there was still bombing. The war was perhaps
more real to me on land than it had been at sea.

What prompted the transition from acting to writing?

Accident. I called my book *A View from the Wings*, but I nearly called it
An Accidental Life, because time and time again things happened in my life
as if something was guiding me this way or that. With great impertinence I
often used to change my lines as an actor. I was generally encouraged to do
it, though if anyone had done it later in a play of mine I would have killed
him. Finally someone suggested that if I could alter lines so well I should
have a go at writing a whole play. That's how I became a playwright.

*You had a close alliance with C P Snow, adapting several of his novels for
the stage. Were you attracted chiefly to the moral issues which are exposed
by Snow?*

Partly, but not entirely. I found that his books had a great core of drama,
and very interesting characters, but the essence of drama in them was
smothered by a novelist's style of writing that he came to call rest passages,
though I'd never heard that expression. The plays that I made out of his
books came to be known as 'Snow without tears'. I don't know if he ever
knew that, but it was widely said.

What did he think of your adaptations?

He was very pleased because it made him a lot of extra money. The first
one I did was based on his novel *The Affair* which I had warned him might
have only a limited appeal, and my God, it ran a year in the enormous
Strand Theatre. Naturally we were both encouraged by this and he wanted
me to do *The Masters* which dealt with many of the same characters, but I
refused on the grounds that people would regard it as a rehash. I wanted to
do *The New Men*, which was all about the making of the first atom bomb,
but people didn't want to go and see a play about nuclear fission. We were
living under a threat of the bomb, and I hadn't spotted the fact that this
might not be entertainment for young honeymoon couples, or ladies up
from Harrogate. So that only ran three months. After that I did try *The*

Masters which he and a lot of people thought was the best of the three, and that had another long run, about nine to ten months.

Some of your plays in the old tradition came to be seen as unfashionable and often provoked the critics to vituperative reviews. Did this worry you or upset you?

No, no; criticism up to a point can be helpful if you listen carefully. James Agate was the doyen of the dramatic critics in my early days and was responsible for my first play coming into the West End. If he liked what I'd done, that was OK with me. I had my audience, which was not the audience of what ultimately came to be the Royal Court, but there was room for both.

Bernard Levin described your play The More the Merrier *as 'the kind of horse leech of a play which needs to be picked off the body of the English theatre before it bleeds the patient to death'. What was your reaction to that kind of criticism?*

I thought he was an idiot. He's an entertaining writer and journalist, a man obviously of considerable intellectual capacity, but my plays would never be the kind he would like. Well-constructed plays which didn't use four letter words weren't intended for him. He supported the idea, and he probably was right, that it was time to move on from what came to be known as the kitchen sink plays, because the class consciousness of Coward and Rattigan had been prevalent in the theatre for donkey's years. But no, Mr Levin didn't worry me. A lot of people admired him and a lot of people execrated him, and I was somewhere between the two. I admired his writing but not his judgement.

Were you ever tempted to return to acting?

I thought originally that my whole life would be as an actor. It was marvellous to go to the theatre every night and act. I suppose it was a kind of escapism. But once I had really become involved as a playwright I began to realize that I didn't have to go every night. I had to go to rehearsals, I had to re-write, but once I had written the damned thing I could go and see

Sir Ronald Millar

other plays or go on the river, or take a holiday. So I wasn't tempted to go back.

Your involvement with prime ministers came about accidentally when you were invited to write Mr Heath's final election broadcast in 1970. How did you feel about being asked – were you flattered, intrigued, curious...?

I wasn't flattered. I was certainly intrigued and curious. I thought Mr Heath had lost the ways and means of communicating and I wanted to help him restore them. That led on to other opportunities, to Mrs Thatcher, and ultimately to Mr Major, though I must stress that I was not the only one who wrote for these prime ministers. I happen to have written for three which is unusual, but there was a kind of team around and I always worked with one or other of them. I happen to have been the longest and best-known permanent speech writer, first of all for Mr Heath, and then for Mrs Thatcher, who inherited me, and then for John Major who inherited me from Mrs Thatcher, but believe me there are other very good writers around.

How well did you get on with Mr Heath? Were you ever close to him as a person?

No. I don't think many people were in the political world. He was a shy man who seemed at times to be rude, but he was not. He was simply withdrawn and reserved, and this gave rise to a feeling that he was rather off-putting and not a friendly man. I think he missed out a great deal in life, and it came about through his innate shyness which perhaps stemmed from his social origins. He lacked outer warmth and also humour, although he could be very jolly at times. He wasn't an easy man to know, but he was a man worth knowing.

Your professional relationship with Mrs Thatcher lasted 16 years during which time you became extremely close to her and came to admire her very much. You have said that you understood her. Did you also understand why other people took a different view of her?

Perhaps it was because they weren't constantly with her as I was. With

Margaret it was a very different story from working with Ted. She was outwardly warmer as a personality, and I think because I didn't have an official job she found it very easy to get on with me. She couldn't actually tell me what to do, nor did I have any fear – as others might have had – of being fired. I was a kind of maverick, and our relationship developed and became a very close one. She became of very great importance in my life.

People who criticize her say that she perhaps became too theatrical for her own good in the end, that it was Margaret Thatcher the actress bereft of any real feeling towards her audience.

That's nonsense. She had great feeling. She wasn't by nature a good orator, nor was she her own best friend. Again her whole approach was governed by her origins, by her humble background in Grantham, a rather stiff and starchy upbringing by a very powerful father, a man who believed deeply in Methodism. It was therefore very difficult for her to break into the much more sophisticated world of politics. She lacked sophistication, and there remained with her a certain naïvety right to this day in the ordinary give and take of the outside world. I don't think she became theatrical in the sense you mean. Of course with an audience of five thousand people at Blackpool, or Brighton, or Bournemouth, where we used to go for the party conferences every year, she had to become theatrical to some extent. She wasn't a natural speaker ever, but she could be on a good day very effective, and always at the end of the party conference she roused the faithful as no one else I have ever heard.

Mrs Thatcher was like your leading lady and you wrote and taught her how to deliver the best lines. Did you ever feel uneasy about your role in any respect?

No. I don't say all the speeches were good. I brought my own experience to bear on the situation, and like anybody else I was right only sometimes, but you have to be right more often than you're wrong, otherwise you wouldn't continue to hold down the job; neither would the person you're waiting for.

Your phrase 'The lady's not for turning' more than any other has stayed in people's minds, perhaps because it was seen to capture the essence of Mrs Thatcher's character. It shows that she was strong and resolute and unwavering, but on a different analysis, that she was intransigent, uncompromising, unyielding to advice of others. Which was it do you think – a strength or a weakness?

She became associated with that phrase, and any other wavering politician suffered in consequence, but she was privately much more able to compromise than was known at the time. Historians will find that she was much more amenable to other people's views than has ever been known. Her iron will was seen as an asset because in those days there was a clichéd view of the weak woman who wouldn't have the strength of a man, but my God, she was like Elizabeth I, who said: 'I know I have the body of a weak and feeble woman but I have the heart and stomach of a king'. But she wasn't that tough. I found a different side of her all the time. She was very emotional and sentimental, and when terrible things happened she was really stricken, and if anyone was in distress she was at their side in a flash. She was deeply upset over Airey Neave's murder – who wouldn't be – but she was tremendously moved and overcome. There's a good deal more to Margaret Thatcher than the 'lady's not for turning' woman.

I have the impression from your book that your view of prime ministers is that they are people in need of a great deal of help, that they must be properly groomed for office and taught basic skills of communication. Are the days of natural leaders over, do you think?

No, I don't think they're over at all. It just so happened that I have come into contact with three of them who were not natural orators. Iain Macleod certainly was a natural, and he wrote all his own speeches and delivered them brilliantly. There are such people around. Enoch Powell is another example – the best prime minister the Tories never had. I just dealt with the material that was handed to me, and if by any fluke it had been Iain Macleod or Enoch Powell, I would have said, 'you don't need me, they've got it all'.

One also has the impression that speechwriting as you describe it can be a very haphazard business, that ideas and ways of expressing them are often hatched on the eleventh hour. Does this not suggest a certain lack of substance and direction . . .?

Speeches will always change at the last minute because politics is a never ending business of change; it's constantly on the move, hour by hour, almost minute by minute across the world. When you start to write a speech a fortnight beforehand, the central item in the news will almost certainly have changed by the time you come to deliver it. That does not imply that you're making policy up on the hoof. Policy is worked out in depth with a lot of help from civil servants, and things don't happen by accident, though they still go wrong.

But when things go wrong is it then expedient to change course totally? The government has changed course so many times now that whatever Mr Major says, nobody believes it.

You exaggerate a little, if I may say so. Mr Major is under sustained bombardment from every branch of the media in a way that exceeds even what Mrs Thatcher went through. Who or what is responsible for Major's difficulties at the moment is a very long and contentious story. It's clear to me that the attack is as sustained and organized as I have ever known it, and although I can't prove who is responsible, I have a rough idea. All this has produced the effect of a man who is perceived to be dithering and changing his mind, but that is wide of the mark. Recently I went to a dinner at a male club with an audience of about a hundred where what is said, it is understood, will never be repeated outside. John Major spoke to them off the cuff and it was absolutely stunningly brilliant. He amazed that audience, which was not pro-Tory or pro-Major at all, but an audience which had been brainwashed by the incessant attacks on this man and his administration. There is far more to John Major than sugar and spice and all things nice. He's as tough as old boots, and provided he comes through the very worst of it, as indeed Margaret did – though this is worse than what Margaret went through, even in 1981 – then I think you may find that we have a very remarkable prime minister indeed. That is my unemotional objective opinion of what there is in this man.

But who is orchestrating this onslaught, and why?

Sir Ronald Millar

I can't tell you who is doing it; all I can tell you is that there is no such thing any more as the Tory Press, though you must know this better than I do. The attack is spread right across the tabloids and the quality papers. None of them really expected him to win, and they are keen to establish their own power. Newspapers have discovered a power which they did not have before, and in a curious way they have become united. There is no groundswell for John Smith, nor particularly for any other leader of the Tory Party that I know of. There are very able people about, like Ken Clarke and Michael Howard, and Heseltine before he was taken ill, but there is no great move for change. One comes back to the feeling that the media sense they can control things, albeit in a negative sense – in other words destroy rather than build. I don't think Margaret is behind it in any shape or form. John Major is the outstanding man of his generation, and I don't think there is any member of his Cabinet who would deny that.

Why do you think Margaret Thatcher is so hostile to him? After all she chose him . . .

I think perhaps she wanted something in the nature of an echo, an understudy, and thought she'd got it; she wanted someone to carry out politically exactly what she would have done, and in the way she would have done it. Well, there ain't such an animal; she was unique.

You describe Mrs Thatcher as 'something of a stranger to the ordinary pleasures of human experience'. That sounds as if you rather pitied her in some way.

My goodness, I don't think she needs pity. There was a kind of innocence, a lack of sophistication about her. She never had any hobbies in my experience; she wasn't particularly interested in the arts, in the theatre, in paintings. She was a politician to her fingertips 24 hours a day.

You never accepted payment for speechwriting and regarded it more as a privilege. Did this sense of 'privilege' not wear a bit thin after 20 years?

No, it still remains with me, funnily enough. I'm not easily impressed, nor do I easily take a subservient role in anything I do, but in this case I did. I

208

had a kind of romantic concept of this kind of service. I had other means of income – my plays – and I continued to write them from time to time. Working unpaid gave me a certain independence of thought which those who have wives or families to think about and have no other source of income find difficult.

By not taking money, did it make you feel more powerful?

I felt like the Health Service, that whatever I did was free at the point of delivery. And I was quite happy for it to be so.

Some may find your explanations in the book somewhat implausible in the sense that you said you did not want to be paid because you wanted to be free to go at any time if you ever felt out of sympathy with Mrs Thatcher. But as time went on it must have been clear that you were very much in tune and that you were never going to feel out of sympathy . . .

The reasons I gave in the book are correct. There's nothing secret about it, and I'm not a saint . . . for heaven's sake, I like money as much as the next man. It may not sound plausible, but I can only tell you those were the reasons.

Your knighthood in 1980 was presumably in recognition of your contribution and a favour from Mrs Thatcher. Were you happy to regard it as such?

Yes, I'd been with her since a week after she became leader in 1975, so I went through all the years in opposition and worked very hard with her then. I helped to teach her how to make speeches, I wrote some of them for her, and worked extremely hard on her television appearances which were crucial in the election. So yes, I think it was gratitude for what I had done for her, and I thought it was very nice. I was very touched and indeed honoured, and I still am.

You have always said that you have no political allegiance, but surely your loyalties must have been to the Conservatives for you to have worked so closely with the team.

Sir Ronald Millar

I can't say that I was dedicated to the Conservative Party as such, but the idea of conservatism appeals rather than the idea of socialism. In a way I'm a kind of independent animal by nature, and I could never become chairman of the Conservative Party or anything of that sort. I'm not saying this is a good idea for anybody else or that politics can possibly work that way; you have to have party members, you have to have party allegiances, and in the sense that I would help in a very small way to bring about a Conservative victory yes, I am a supporter, but I'm not a passionate label man. I just was not the other thing; I was not a socialist.

You said that your political innocence vanished on November 13th 1990, the day when Geoffrey Howe committed what you call 'that single act of brilliantly executed matricide'. Were your thoughts on that occasion chiefly with the personal impact they would have on the woman you had come to admire so much?

I certainly thought that the impact would be immense. Geoffrey Howe went beyond what was normal in any resignation speech that I'd ever heard. He said what he had done and why he resigned but he then invited his colleagues to take the same view. In other words, he who had been deputy prime minister was inviting them to get rid of the Prime Minister. It was most brilliantly written and performed, even by the very nature of its quietness. It was stunning and it became the catalyst for everything. I sensed it at once, and I'm sure Margaret did too.

You have described Mrs Thatcher's downfall as a Greek tragedy, and your allusions are often theatrical. Do you believe that politics has essentially the same elements as good theatre, including the ability to ennoble, to elevate, to offer catharsis . . .?

Yes, I certainly believe all those things. If I express them in terms of drama, it is because the theatre has been my life. There is no greater drama than being at the centre of political power. Nothing is more fascinating than that.

You are said to be hurt by Mrs Thatcher's recent coolness and 'unmistakable resentment' towards you. But surely she is bound to view your working for John Major as an act of disloyalty, however irrational that might be.

It was totally irrational, but the coolness is over now. It lasted about three months, and then we had a very nice dinner together at her house. She thanked me for the book, which is not always favourable to her, and I gave her an inscribed copy. Don't forget, Mr Major was the man she had chosen, so her reaction could not have been more irrational. It was a very female reaction. I understood it, and I haven't said anything very violent about it; but I was temporarily, yes, a bit miffed, no more than that.

You have said you felt keenly for Mrs Thatcher in the bereavement of her exile. Do you think she has behaved well since?

We have to define the period. For about a year afterwards she was shattered. The effect upon her was enormous. A prime minister's diary is filled for about a year, sometimes even longer, and suddenly overnight it was wiped clean. To many other people this would not have been so shattering, because they have other interests. She had no other interests. Politics was her profession; it was also her hobby. I knew the vacuum that had been created, and I was very concerned for her. It seemed to me that she was a woman in psychic pain, with no idea of what to do with her life. If one had any imagination at all, one could not but be deeply concerned and sorry for her. Even her political enemies had some feeling for her. Obviously she has created problems for John Major since, but not as many as she would have done if she had stayed in the Commons like Ted Heath. She gets attention from the media because they will do anything that will give them yet another weapon with which to beat John Major about the head.

Do you think that John Major can ever be divorced from his Spitting Image persona of Grey Man?

He is not, believe me, a grey man in that sense at all. The man who talked for 40 minutes at the meeting I mentioned would be a revelation to anybody. His use of language was particularly astonishing, because I didn't think he had that command on his own; and he does. He was really roused and I will never forget it. Perhaps he should never have a speech written, perhaps he should just talk, but of course the press would hate it because they always want the text in advance. But if we said, to hell with speechwriters, let the man talk, we would discover how very difficult it would be to destroy the man I saw that night.

Of the three prime ministers you have worked for you say that John Major is by far the most naturally courteous and warmly human. Do you think that in politics this is perhaps a weakness?

No, I don't think it is a weakness in any man in any profession. He happens to be a nice guy. It is only a weakness if people think that's all he is.

Your true love is the theatre, and perhaps in that light politics might be described as your mistress. Are you at all regretful that it is your mistress that has brought you more into the public eye?

No. I'm always in favour of having any number of mistresses [laughs] and I don't mind which one brings me into the public eye. In fact – and this may sound a strange thing to say for someone who was an actor – I've never particularly sought the public eye in the sense that some people do. If I had never become known at all, it would not have bothered me. And anyway, I'm not a household name, for goodness sake, I am known only to people in politics and in the theatre. I daresay farmers don't wake up in the morning and think, well, what is Sir Ronald up to today?

You have never married, although you say you have come close several times. What do you think has held you back from the brink?

I suppose having so much of my life divided between two different professions. Originally it was the war that prevented me from marrying. I had a girlfriend to whom I was devoted but held back because I thought it would be selfish to marry if I were going to be killed. Perhaps I was over cautious but I didn't much like the idea of a widow and a child and no father. After the war life suddenly moved into top gear with plays and then films, and I found I was having a hell of a good time with various girlfriends without committing myself.

Freudians might say that no woman ever measured up to your mother . . . is there anything in that, do you think?

No . . . that's too easy, that's too simple. Absolutely not. She cut the apron strings, and they were never joined up again by me. I have several very close women friends, and I wouldn't like to live without them. In the theatre you meet a lot of homosexual people, and I have friends amongst them too, but that is not in my own nature at all. Women are a joy and a delight. Not marrying has never been a problem for me, except that I feel sometimes I would love to have had children.

Presumably you have always been so busy that you have never had time to feel lonely . . . do you ever fear loneliness in old age?

No. I have an enormous number of friends from different walks of life and many of them younger than I. I would expect them to be around to give me a decent funeral.

You called your book A View from the Wings. *In your heart, have you missed being centre stage?*

No, otherwise I wouldn't have called it *A View from the Wings*. I'm very happy to be around, just to be there. Shakespeare has King Henry V say in his famous Agincourt speech: 'And gentlemen in England, now a-bed/Shall think themselves accurs'd they were not here,/And hold their manhoods cheap whiles any speaks/That fought with us upon Saint Crispin's day.' At quite a number of key moments for this country during my lifetime, I was there. That's enough for any one man.

SIR DAVID NAPLEY

SIR DAVID NAPLEY

David Napley was a senior partner in Kingsley Napley Solicitors. He was born in 1915 and educated at Burlington College. He served with the Queen's Royal regiment and the Indian Army, being invalided out in 1945 with the rank of captain. He contested the general elections of 1951 and 1955. He was a founder of the London Solicitors Association of which he was president from 1960–63. He was chairman of the Law Society's Standing Committee on Criminal Law between 1963 and 1975. He is the author of several books on the criminal law, and his memoirs, *Not Without Prejudice*, were published in 1982. Sir David Napley died in September 1994 shortly after this interview was conducted.

People often regard members of the legal profession with a good deal of suspicion. Do you think this is wholly unwarranted?

Yes, because I suspect that this suspicion is based on a failure to understand what are the functions and duties of the legal profession. People always say that lawyers make their money out of other people's misfortunes. There's an element of truth in that, but the real function of the lawyer is to help people either avoid or solve their problems, not to foment them. I have certainly spent a large part of my time trying to persuade people not to litigate on the basis of principle, which is the worst thing to do.

The legal profession has in recent years been involved in a rather public argument, with one group trying to preserve its privileges and the other trying to trespass on them. Do you think this internal squabbling has brought about improvements to the system?

We're talking here of rights of audience in the higher courts, and I was one of the great proponents of that change. It's too early to say that it's had any effect because it's hardly taken place, but in the long term it's bound to be beneficial for the simple reason that in the early days the Bar was largely drawn from the public school, and over the last two decades that situation has radically altered. Lawyers in both branches of the profession are now being drawn from the same educational and intellectual pool. Besides, if you do not give both branches of the profession the opportunity to practise every aspect of the law, the public suffers, because there are an enormous number of solicitors who could adequately deal with the advocacy just as there are barristers who might be better doing the work of a solicitor.

Your autobiography seems to express a regret that you did not go to the Bar . . . have you stopped regretting that?

I try not to regret it. I would have enjoyed very much having had a wider field to operate in, but I don't believe in life that you can ever jog backwards. I've also been moderately successful as a solicitor and – who knows – I might not have been successful at the Bar.

Most solicitors seem to agree that your greatest achievements are as a reformer. Are you happy with that assessment or would you prefer to be recognized chiefly for other things?

In many of the cases in which I have been instructed it would have gladdened my heart to have been an outstanding advocate, but being denied that I'm perfectly happy with what little I've done. What tends to happen in law reform is that you project an idea then you sit back and see somebody else put it into effect, but you just have to accept that it doesn't matter who gets the credit as long as it comes about.

There is some suggestion that your campaigning on behalf of solicitors has caused some embarrassment in the ranks, and that most solicitors take the view that it is wise to have QC and counsel in court . . . in other words they are happy with the status quo. What do you say to that?

I'm sure that there are a significant number of solicitors who are satisfied with the status quo, but for my part over the years I have not been entirely happy with the way many members of my own profession operate, and the ones about whom I would be most critical are those who pass the buck to QCs. Lloyd George used to say, if you want to understand a subject, promise to speak on it, and there's a great deal of truth in that. If you know that you might be doing the advocacy you will put much more care and preparation into the case.

One solicitor was quoted as saying: 'Sir David, I think, takes the view that he is more competent than lots of junior counsel. This has not made him the most popular figure at the Bar.' Does that worry you?

Certainly not. I believe that I am more competent than some junior counsel, but I also recognize that I am probably less competent than a good many other members of the Bar – it's relative. But the majority of clients who come to a solicitor pay for his skill and knowledge, and I personally abhor the idea that what they're getting is the skill and knowledge of a member of the Bar.

In your memoirs you say: 'It seems to me wrong to exclude solicitors who by and large probably have a much better understanding of and closer

*connection with the behaviour and frailties of ordinary people than the
slightly more remote life provided at the Bar.' Is there not a case for saying
perhaps that both barristers and solicitors are hopelessly removed from the
life of an average criminal . . .?*

Yes, both barristers and solicitors must of necessity understand the
problems of those people at second hand. All I was saying is that it is the
solicitor who talks to the client, listens to his story, gives him sympathy,
whereas the barrister gets the case laid out and interviews the man for only
a short period against the very long time that a solicitor spends with him.

*Outside your profession you are best known as the lawyer who attracts
notorious cases and big names. How important and rewarding has that
aspect of your career been?*

It's always good and satisfying and gratifying, ego being what ego is, to be
involved in notable cases but I think I can say with all honesty that some of
the most absorbing and fascinating problems I've had to deal with have
been much smaller cases with no public interest at all. It doesn't follow
that these big cases are necessarily the most interesting.

*One of your most famous cases was the Jeremy Thorpe case. Exceptionally,
you appeared in court for him instead of briefing a barrister, something
which attracted criticism at the time. What was your reasoning?*

I have always taken an enormous part in the preliminary hearings of the
cases in which I appear. Throughout the whole of my life, it has been my
uniform practice when I've been instructed that I do the preliminary
enquiry, the committal proceedings, and then pass it over to the Bar
because I have had no right of audience in the higher court. If however the
client had wished it, I would have gone on with the case. When it came to
the Jeremy Thorpe case I took the view that I shouldn't conduct it any
differently from the way in which I had with some success conducted cases
in the past. It was discussed at great length with Jeremy Thorpe as to
whether we should bring in a barrister or whether I should do it, and we
agreed that I should do it. What upset the Bar was the fact that in those
days the committal proceedings – as a result of a measure which Roy
Jenkins introduced – were restricted from publication in the press unless

someone asked for the proceedings to be open to the press. Prior to the hearing it was agreed that we would not open the proceedings to the public. However, the advocate who represented the fourth defendant did not attend this meeting. When we all went down to Minehead this fourth fellow, who is now a member of the House of Lords, got up and without telling us in advance opened the proceedings to the public. The whole thing then became front page news, and that's what upset the Bar. A number of them thought that I opened the proceedings to the public, which I didn't.

You and your wife mixed socially with the Thorpes. Was this not rather unusual and perhaps rather unwise, given the circumstances?

In point of fact, I didn't know Jeremy Thorpe until the case started. The case was to be heard at Minehead magistrates' court. There was an enormous amount of work to be done in the evenings for the purposes of these proceedings, and it was very difficult to get a hotel room because they were all taken up by the press. Jeremy Thorpe had a small cottage at the side of his house, and rather than get myself involved on a daily basis with the press, and have Jeremy come to see me at a hotel, it seemed more convenient for me to be there. It worked very well, and I don't think it in any way embarrassed me or him, nor was it in any way undesirable or improper.

Have you minded upsetting the barristers of your profession by speaking in court?

No, because the more sensible members of the profession at the Bar have recognized the spirit in which it's been done. I've given an enormous amount of work to the Bar, and I hope that while I'm spared I will continue to do so. I think the Bar has a valuable part to play and there's a great deal of merit in having true specialists to whom the general rank and file of the profession can have access. But what I'm against is the idea that a young man goes up to university, he reads law, he then qualifies as a barrister, people imagine he'll be able to solve any problem instantaneously, when in point of fact he knows very little practical law and has very little practical experience.

Your profession is an extremely hierarchical one, and there are those who would say that you should have accepted the strictures of the role of solicitor and not tried to tread on other people's toes . . .

People are entitled to say that if they wish. It isn't a question of getting work; happily I've not been short of work. It's more a question of what the client wants. When a case has to go into court, I would always want to discuss with the client the advantages and disadvantages of having a barrister or having a leading counsel, what it would cost, what influence it would have on the court, and so on. These are issues for the client to decide, and it's not a question of whether I want to serve the function of a barrister or whether I want to tread on his toes.

In the early days of your career you were known to be diligent rather than charismatic. What do you regard as the turning point in your career?

I'm not really sure that there was a turning point in my career. I think that my career was a progression from the bottom of the ladder. Because of my love of advocacy I was doing cases and preliminary hearings which other solicitors, certainly in those days, tended not to do. I was almost unique. The result was that when a case was reported my name was in the newspaper, and over a period of years I therefore became known to the public to a greater extent than other solicitors.

In 1955 you stood for parliament and fought Gloucester, nearly winning the seat. Have you ever reflected on how different your life might have been if you had gone into politics all those years ago?

I have indeed. At that time I was imbued with the political spirit, and very much wanted to get into parliament. I was so enthused that when I used to visit the House of Commons and stand in the lobby, I almost felt an electric tingle going through my body. But in retrospect I think that God was looking over me and that I was very lucky not to go into parliament. It would have made my life much less interesting, much more perilous, and when I look at politics today I feel that I was well protected in being kept out.

You were not approached to stand again, and felt rather hurt by Eden's attitude. Did that make you disillusioned with politics?

Yes. After I fought Gloucester I began to realize what an enormous amount of time and effort I was putting into politics without making very much headway. My wife was very influential in bringing me to the conclusion that I could occupy my time to better advantage. Looking around the political scene today fills me with despair. The standard of politics has declined so much over the years. It used to be that you could go into the House of Commons and hear people who had both the knowledge and practical experience of the subject under discussion. That was an enormous virtue in a democratic society. We now have people whose whole existence and experience is within the field of politics; they are now in it to earn a living as politicians and that has inevitably diminished the stature and quality of the House.

You once said: 'The invasion of privacy which is motivated by greed or the desire for financial gain is indefensible.' Do you think the private life of people in the public eye should always remain private?

No, but I think that there should be a genuine test of public interest. Motivation is also an important factor. If an editor with his hand on his heart honestly believes that some information which he has about a public figure is something which the public ought to be told, then he should be allowed to do it; but not if he's doing it merely to increase circulation and make more money.

Newspapers would say they are defending the public's right to know. If the public interest is to be served, presumably privacy has to be invaded sometimes . . .

You have to start from the premise that the public does not have a right to know. I do not accept that there is any right in our constitution, or any other constitution, including America, where there is a right to know. There are some things which in the public interest you ought to know, but that's not the same as having a right to know.

Sir David Napley

There has never been a whiff of scandal about your own private life. Does that make you more or less sympathetic to those who have not led blameless lives?

It is difficult to think of many people who are wholly bad. One also recognizes that a lot of people are victims of circumstances, and who am I to say what I would have done if I had been in the same position? So one has to approach these cases with a degree of tolerance, and I don't think the fact that I've been fortunate enough not to be involved in anything that the newspapers could have a field day with to my detriment colours my view about the position of others.

Presumably you would not dispute that large numbers of people are denied justice on the grounds that they are not rich enough, or poor enough to qualify for legal aid. Do you think you might have done more to help change this aspect of the system?

I entirely agree with you. Far too many people are denied access to justice by reason of lack of money, and the rising cost of litigation is making it more difficult by the day. It's very difficult to know what steps you can take to make the courts more easily available to the public. It's easy to be critical, and I am critical, but when you sit down and try to resolve it, it's not all that easy. One of the things I would like to see and I've tried to bring about in my time, is a simplification of procedures. I personally think that the public would be happier with a day in court where their grievances would be aired and adjudicated upon by reasonably competent and informed people. It would be better to do it in a much more truncated way, rather than to preserve the English system which aims at excellence.

But don't you think the legal profession tends to overcharge?

There are some people who overcharge. The cost of employing fashionable barristers today has become prohibitive, and that needs to be reduced because the expenses which a member of the Bar carries are very small compared with the expenses of a solicitor. The vast majority of solicitors who practise in this country earn a very modest income, and a considerable number of them, particularly today, are very hard pressed to make ends meet. The vast majority at the Bar also have pretty modest incomes, but

223

Sir David Napley

the relatively few high fliers who make enormous sums are the ones who are written about in the press.

You have sometimes been sensitive on the issue of the large fees which some solicitors, including yourself, command. Are you completely opposed to there being any controls on the fees charged?

The only professional people in this country whose fees are subject to control, with the possible exception of taxi drivers, are solicitors and barristers, because anyone can go to the court and ask for fees to be taxed, and the court's job when they're taxed is to decide what is a reasonable fee. The court can of course set the fee at X thousand pounds, but if the client has chosen to go to a leading silk, it's no good saying that somebody ought to control the fees; he is the author of his own misfortune.

But sometimes you might feel you have no alternative if you want to stand the best chance of winning . . .

Some people feel they have no alternative but to have a Rolls-Royce, though they'd probably get there just as well in a Peugeot. If you choose to have the best in order to have what you think is a better chance of success, good luck to you, but I don't think you can blame that on the system.

Would you agree that our adversarial system sometimes suppresses the truth since victory in a case is sometimes the result of successful rhetoric?

I would agree with that, but I think the alternative is worse. The adversarial system is based upon the idea that each side will be fairly and equally represented and put its case to its own best advantage, and an independent informed person at the centre will make a judgement as a result of the arguments and the evidence. That's the theory and that's the ideal. Where you're dealing with human beings you deal with human imperfections and fallibility; and sometimes you will get a better man on one side than on the other. But the alternatives would produce far more injustice. The inquisitorial system is so disliked on the continent that they are now looking at England with a view to introducing the adversarial system. The only man who seems to think it's a good thing is Ludo

Kennedy, and he's never practised it. The inquisitorial system has a lot of defects and the principal defect is this: whereas the adversarial system is no better, as you quite rightly say, than the quality of the advocates on either side, at least each is trying to do his best. In the inquisitorial system quality is no better than the quality of the inquisitor, and the result is that if he hasn't routed out the right evidence or doesn't deal with it in the right way there will be far more injustice.

You have always had a special interest in advocacy. What percentage of cases would you say are won or lost according to the quality of the advocacy?

The quality of advocacy is not primarily or even principally a reflection of the rhetoric or the presentation in court. The most important thing in advocacy is the preparation, investigation, research and the command of the case. And if a case is properly prepared it will be much more likely won by a poor advocate than a badly prepared case will be won by an outstanding advocate. And so whilst it would be stupid to contend that the quality of the advocacy doesn't play a part and cannot win cases, the majority of them are won because the case itself is a good case.

Do you think perhaps that as times change society is going to expect the solicitor to play a different role, that of conciliator and problem solver, rather than someone who engages in battle with another solicitor?

That is already the role of over 90 per cent of solicitors. I spend most of my time dissuading people from going into litigation, and most of my colleagues do the same. One of the curious things about this is that if you're looking at it from the commercial point of view, a case lost is very often a client lost. So it isn't really in the interests of any sensible solicitor to force a man into court if he can compromise.

You would like to do away with the House of Lords as a court of final appeal, preferring to leave it to the Court of Appeal. Why is that?

The underlying philosophy of the House of Lords is that you choose a limited number of great brains and you put them into the highest court in

Sir David Napley

the land. In theory that is quite all right, but quite frankly, the great brains in the House of Lords are not materially different from some of the great brains in the Court of Appeal.

The 1974 Act opened jury service to anyone over 18 and removed the qualification of owning property. Some years later you commented, 'To say that people who have a house are more responsible than people who don't may be politically unacceptable, but in my experience it is right.' Do you still stand by that statement today?

Yes. I think that when a person owns a house and has a family he develops a certain degree of stability which almost by definition isn't present in people who have not reached that stage. The fact that your name is on the electoral register doesn't signify that you are the best person to sit on a jury. The jury system needs looking at because some people on juries are not mentally equipped for the job; they can be trying fraud cases and yet be illiterate and innumerate.

Lord Goodman whom you admire once said: 'There is almost no case that a jury, given proper advice and instruction, cannot deal with better than a judge alone.' How do you react to that?

I don't agree with it. In general terms it would be right, but in the modern world it isn't true. You will remember that in some of the recent city cases involving high finance at least one judge said that he found it difficult to understand what was happening himself. Now that may indicate some support for what is being said by Lord Goodman in the sense that the judge himself was having difficulty, but if the judge had difficulty it would almost certainly be more difficult for the jury. A common example in the courts is that you will have a case which depends upon some technical, scientific or medical problem. Each side calls an expert who gives his opinion of high complexity based upon a lifetime's research and knowledge, and in theory the jury then has to decide which of those two experts is right. It's utter nonsense.

Lord Goodman also said that there is something about a jury which inspires confidence; they will arrive at perverse verdicts but never at insane

226

verdicts. Don't you think there is something in that?

I think there is something in that but it wouldn't be much consolation for me that the jury were not insane but perverse if I myself had been wrongly convicted.

When Lord Longford published his report on pornography in 1972 you described it as 'fresh as an egg but a little cracked in parts'. What did you mean by that?

It's a long while ago and I can't honestly say that I've carried in my mind since then what was in his book. But one of the things I do remember about it was that he was saying in effect how dreadful pornography was, and then – presumably in order to sell the book – they put on a most pornographic cover. [laughs] People were persuaded they were buying a dirty book.

Over the years you have developed quite a reputation for liberal causes – not really the hallmark of your profession. Why do you think this is? Do you have a more highly developed social conscience than your colleagues, do you think?

To some extent that is unfair to my colleagues. There are an enormous number of people in my profession who are liberal in that way – I don't think I'm in any way exceptional. I happen to have an innate desire to see justice done, and I abhor injustice, but that is true of most of my colleagues.

Do you think your profession would benefit from the presence of more women?

No, I don't. At the moment the profession has more women than I've ever seen in my life. I'm all in favour of men or women getting jobs according to their ability, and I'm not in the business of excluding women, but I don't think there is a need for any more.

Sir David Napley

Helena Kennedy QC has argued persuasively that the criminal justice system is not sensitive to the reality of women's lives. She doesn't suggest that there is a conspiracy against women, more that the legal world is dominated by men and that myths about women are maintained and perpetuated by the system. Are you sympathetic to her arguments?

There are an enormous number of women who think they're dominated by men and if you saw them in their own home environment you would find that the men are generally dominated by the women. I have in my practice a number of very able women, and I admire their abilities and qualities, but I wouldn't be prepared to say that as a general proposition women are as effective as advocates as men. I'm not saying there aren't exceptions but I wouldn't say that women speaking in public are as adequate as men. When did you ever hear, save on rare occasions, a woman make a superb after dinner speech? It isn't really in their nature. To hear women advocates addressing a court, you can admire their ability, you can admire their analysis of the issues, and they can be exceptionally good, but I think at the end of the day there is something in the timbre of their voices which differs in quality from that of their male counterparts.

Kennedy points out in her book, Eve was Framed, *that in the case of Sarah Tisdall whom you defended, she was portrayed by both the prosecution and the defence as a sort of 'silly little girl' who didn't know what she was doing, rather than as an adult who had acted on principle. How do you respond to that?*

It is awfully difficult for me to comment on a case with which I was concerned, and it's such a long while ago that I would want to look at the papers again if I were going to comment. All I will say is that Helena Kennedy's comment is not one which revives immediately some note of recognition in my mind. If she's saying we don't take people like Sarah Tisdall seriously, I find that a little difficult to accept because if we didn't take them seriously they wouldn't have been prosecuted. I should also be sorry to think that Helena Kennedy or any other advocate would consider it expedient in every case in which a woman was involved to say that she acted on a matter of principle, or she did it because she believed what she was doing was right. Whether that would better serve the client's purpose than arguing that the probability was that she didn't realize the enormity of what she was doing is very much in doubt. At the end of the day the object of the exercise was to try to stop Sarah Tisdall going to prison.

Do you always need to believe your client in order to defend him or her?

It is not a question of believing or disbelieving. If my client tells me a story, civilly or criminally, and he doesn't tell me that he's lying, it's my duty to put that case before the court fairly and honestly and to its best advantage. It isn't for me to form a judgement as to whether he's telling the truth or not, and if I think he is lying but he won't admit he's lying I still have to put the case forward. Now, as to what effect that has upon me, I may think he's ill advised and I may tell him so, but it is no more difficult to do that than to take out a man's appendix when you think he's a basically unpleasant man.

Do you sometimes have to suspend moral judgement when defending a client?

Yes. I have defended people who have said they are innocent, but who were probably guilty, and in some cases because of the enormity of the crime I have been very worried that they might get off. Unhappily you have to train yourself not to allow that to influence you, because the system would break down if you didn't.

Do you believe your reputation suffered as a result of being involved in the Guinness trial?

The short answer to that is no. Is there implicit in your question the suggestion that in some way I might have behaved improperly?

Well, during the trial you were accused of lying by Oliver Roux ... was that a testing time for you?

It wasn't in any way a testing time. Oliver disagreed with what I said but I'm not sure he ever used the word *lying*. I think what happened was that Roux gave one account of what happened at an interview, and I gave a different account. It was never suggested at any time as far as I know in the course of the proceedings that I was lying. The fact that two people did give a different account of the interview is as maybe, and this happens frequently in litigation, but I've certainly never heard it suggested before that it adversely affected my reputation.

You have said that the war against crime requires draconian measures . . . what would these measures amount to?

The war against crime needs to be fought on two fronts. We have long since moved into a situation where personal safety ought to become more important than personal wealth. One of the peculiarities of the English law historically has been that we've always placed more value on wealth than we have on injury; that's changed but it's got to change still further. Secondly, we have to recognize, whatever it costs, that the only means we have of curbing people who are prone to violence is to lock them up, and that means that they have to be locked up until they mature or till the public can be reasonably certain that they are safe. Throughout the history of the penal system we've tried all kinds of things – hard labour, flogging, long periods of imprisonment, short sharp shocks, and unhappily none of them has worked and none of them is likely to work. All this political talk about stringent measures which will kill crime is all my eye and Betty Martin. What we have in this country is an inadequacy of discipline in education, and that begins in the home. The other thing which is extremely disturbing is that the popular press are prepared to serve the prurient interests of the public in order to increase their circulation, and the result is that you get a constant diet of violence, sexual deviation, misbehaviour, and people become conditioned by it.

You haven't had any time for religion in your life – have you ever found that to be a disadvantage in your career?

No, I haven't. I'm really an agnostic, I suppose. When I look at a garden or a view I find it difficult to believe that the way nature presents itself is the result of some scientific accident. There is a beauty and a grandeur which I'm not able to explain in scientific terms. On the other hand, I don't believe that there's a benign gentleman sitting up on a cloud above me looking over the world. But happily my absence of religion has not made it any more difficult for me to know the difference between right and wrong.

Most people need some sort of spiritual dimension in their lives . . . what is yours?

I am disadvantaged in that respect. I've never had experience of a spiritual dimension, and I'm probably the loser for it. Unfortunately, I'm a very pragmatic sort of person.

STELLA RICHMAN

Stella Richman was born in the East End of London in 1922. After early theatre experience she began her career in television at ATV where she was in charge of the script department. She then moved to Rediffusion, becoming head of series there in 1967. In 1970 she was appointed controller of programmes at London Weekend Television thereby becoming the first woman to sit on the board of a television company. In partnership with David Frost she formed the first independent TV company, Stella Richman Productions, creating series like *Jennie, Clayhanger* and *Bill Brand*. For nearly thirty years she was chairman and owner of the famous White Elephant Club and author of the popular *White Elephant Cookbooks*.

You were born in 1922, the year the first war ended. As a child, were you aware of the aftermath of grief and horror resulting from the war, or were you completely sheltered from it?

I was only aware of the fact that everybody around me was poor, but since I lived in the East End of London and the country was in a state of such poverty, it seemed to me a natural thing that people begged at street corners. I would sometimes see a man with one leg selling matches, and I would ask my mother why he only had one leg and she would reply, 'Well, that was the war, dear.'

How do you remember family life? Was it a happy time for you?

It was both happy and unhappy. My family were Polish Jews, living originally right in the heart of the East End of London. Gradually they moved a little way along, just off the Mile End Road, into Drogheda Square which has now become so fashionable. We never went without but it was a struggle to earn a living. The reason for my unhappiness was that Jews who had emigrated from Poland, Lithuania and Russia had created, without knowing it, a little ghetto around themselves, and once I started going to school and mixing with everybody, I always had a feeling that I wanted to go over the wall. I thought there must be something more than the street in which we lived. But I wasn't beaten, I wasn't starved, and within the limited experience of my parents, I was treated very well.

Did you experience anti-semitism during those days?

We did a little at school. I went to an ordinary state school round the corner and there were some girls who would say, 'You're only a bloody Jew, what do you know about anything?', but I can't say it plagued me night and day. There were also a couple of teachers who would use any reason to get the word 'Jewish' into a sentence – that wasn't so much open anti-semitism as implied. But by today's standards it didn't amount to much. Within my own family I think anti-semitism was *created* to some extent. For example, if ever I brought a girlfriend home for tea my father always wanted to know if she was Jewish. 'I don't want anybody non-Jewish coming into the house,' he would say. Similarly if anyone had done anything wrong my father would always put it down to being anti-semitic.

Stella Richman

It was something he had learned from his parents, something he said automatically, but luckily I managed to stop myself being brainwashed.

Do you believe that all the keys to behaviour in later life are to be found in childhood – in other words, that early experience sets the pattern for life?

It takes all of one's life to get out of the repetition of early experience. One inherits certain things without knowing it from one's parents and one's surroundings, until one day one realizes that something isn't right. Your past should be put through a sieve; the good things should be allowed to drop down, and the things that are only repeated because they were done before 71 should be left to rot. It's taken all my seventy one years to arrive at this way of thinking.

But would you say that the principles by which you came to live your life were learned in childhood, or did you work them out for yourself later?

A lot of things my mother taught me have stuck, but I had to acquire knowledge as I went along. I picked up from anybody and everybody but I had a very good way of rejecting other people's influence if it wasn't right for me. I never thought it would be possible to have an open mind at this advanced age, but I have. It helps me a great deal with my children and grandchildren.

I believe you always had aspirations to be on the stage . . . was this something that was encouraged or disapproved of at home?

My mother approved of anything I did, my father disapproved of everything. At the beginning of the war, I trained at a marvellous school called the London Art Theatre, and then I ended up in Scotland in repertory, which I loved. I toured the whole of Scotland and Ireland, and acted quite happily on and off. But once I had my daughter, Cookie, I felt it was awful to sit by a phone waiting for people to say they wanted me to work, so I turned my hand to other things.

You married the actor Alec Clunes during the war. Was there something

236

special about marrying in wartime? Was it a way of saying there would be a future, a time of peace again?

That didn't apply to us because Alec was a registered conscientious objector. He ran the theatre in Great Newport Street, which is where I met him, and we just assumed we would go on for ever. People in uniform thought differently; they felt being married established a bridge for the future. But Alec and I had lived together for ages, and when he suddenly asked me to marry him, it took me totally by surprise.

The marriage didn't last very long . . .

No, but we'd been together for about seven years beforehand and we did a great deal together. We were the first English company to be sponsored by the British Council to tour nine countries, starting in Prague, so we were the conquering heroes in a city which had just been liberated. We performed *Hamlet* and the whole house just cheered and cheered, not so much for the quality of the production but because there we were, Churchill's people. We went all over Europe doing that, it was lovely.

Why do you think the marriage failed?

Because I had changed and he hadn't. I had always been in a subservient role as his girlfriend and his one time secretary, and when we got married he thought that I would stop work and suddenly overnight turn into a housewife. Nowadays the fashion is to talk out these things, but we never did. When Alec married me he thought I would give up running theatres and sit at home, waiting for him with the supper. I never thought that way, so it came as a great shock to my system that I was suddenly expected to be a different person. It was as simple as that.

In 1953 you married Victor Brusa, with whom you had your two children. Did motherhood suit you?

Yes. My daughter had the benefit of me being at home for four years. By the time my son was born I was already at ATV – I had signed the contract without knowing that I was pregnant. I wore men's shirts, thinking rather stupidly that these people didn't know me at all, so they wouldn't care whether I was pregnant or fat, but in the end I knew I had to tell them. Lew Grade said, 'God in Heaven, what are we going to say to the governor?' I had my baby and went back to work in two weeks, so my son got the au pair girls. But in retrospect I think I was quite a good mother.

Would you say the relationship you have with your children is better than the one you had with your own parents?

I would say yes, but they might say, who is she kidding? There was a terrible generation gap between my parents and their children, but I think for people like me who have been in the entertainment business, there's been a necessity to know what youngsters are doing. We have made a greater effort to understand what it is that makes children tick. Now I rely on my grandchildren to keep me informed.

You started your career proper at ATV and before long you had created the highly acclaimed 'Love Story' in 1963. Was that the first real success for you?

Yes. I had moved from the script department to production and the first thing I did was to think up this idea for an anthology series, even though anthology is a dirty word in television. I called it 'Our Romance', because I knew that they'd never pass anything called 'Love Story' – there's a difference in sophistication. It was so wonderful in those days because once Lew Grade had said, 'Don't drive me mad, go away and do it', I just went away and did it. I was incredibly fortunate because all the writers I used then – Richard Harris, Freddie Raphael, Edna O'Brien, Doris Lessing – they all wanted to write a love story. I could not believe this was happening – it was beginner's luck.

How was your relationship with Lew Grade?

Unbelievably happy. It's just a great pity that the possibility for such relationships has died with the present way of running things. At first when I knew him it was very much Mr Grade and Miss Richman, but when I came back as the controller it was Stella and Lew. He was always absolutely marvellous to me, and it's sad that youngsters starting out today don't have a boss figure who just lets them alone. From what I hear today, both at ITV and BBC, it's like those Russian dolls: every boss you take out has another one inside. There are always at least six people telling you what you have to say and do, and that is an impossible way of working. You only have to look at the screen to see the results of that system. Whenever Lew did want his own way, it was usually about money. I remember when we employed Doris Lessing, she'd never written a play before, and I paid her £400 instead of the £350 everybody else was getting. Lew rang me up one day and said, 'Miss Richman, who is this Doris Thing you're paying £400?' I had to do him a little précis of what Doris Lessing had done, and then everything was all right. One of the things Lew taught me was that you never say no irrevocably; you must always leave a little space for manoeuvre.

Did you always have a special interest in romantic stories? Was love a guiding force in your life?

It was an important force in my own life, and when I fell in love I fell in love good and hard. In television I liked doing stories about personal relationships, as long as they were sophisticated and real. I was never into the Barbara Cartland market.

In 1965 your husband died tragically in an accident. You were only 43. How did you cope with the grief of it all?

I can only say that it's friends who get you through. I was cushioned by an incredible number of people from television and also by the staff at the White Elephant. The difficulty, or perhaps the blessing, is that when something like that happens you have to deal with the children first, and because you have to deal with them, you don't deal with yourself. I went on working for a bit and then suddenly I couldn't. We went away, the children and I. And when I came back I was a bit thinner and sadder. That grief has stayed with me 29 years.

After your husband's death you became the owner of the White Elephant, the club in Curzon Street. How important a part of your life did that become?

Stella Richman

More important than anything. At one point I was employing 95 people. There was a very strong Italian element and I was in love with all of them, and they were in love with me. It lasted for 28 years till 1988 – I got out just in time before the recession was officially announced.

Was your heart in the restaurant business or did your heart belong to television?

That's a difficult question. When I was doing television my heart was very much there. I never liked doing anything unless I believed in it, unless I loved it. It's always had to be something that was mine – I couldn't really enjoy doing other people's ideas. So I was split down the middle, which is probably one of my problems.

In 1967 you went to work for LWT and within three years you had become controller of programmes, the first woman ever to sit on the board. Did you feel you'd arrived?

[laughs] Oh, I don't know. It's a very difficult thing when you find there are 34 men at your first meeting, and you feel you've gone into the wrong room. It's rather like Kafka. The crunch came when I desperately wanted to go to the loo. I was listening to all these men without understanding a word, and eventually the chairman asked if there was something wrong. When I told him he said, 'Have my key. It's on the eighth floor.' All the heads turned to watch me trip out, and everybody waited till I came back. It was unbelievable. I didn't feel I'd arrived at all – in fact I thought it was a bit of a joke. I thought we were going to be discussing the programme content, not finances. Nowadays we all know that the bottom line is finance, but then it was very subtly done so you had to get through a whole wadge of rubbish before it became clear that you were there to price programmes. It was an interesting year, which I wouldn't have missed for anything, but it isn't a life for a woman. In my experience women don't like sitting for long meetings. I shall probably be criticized for this, but some things need saying: I think certain kinds of men in big business and in television love being able to say to their wives, or mistresses, 'Unless somebody dies, there's no way you can reach me, because I'm at the IBA board meeting.' The whole of the morning is spent rustling papers, scribbling, then there's lunch, and there's more scribbling in the afternoon;

240

and I never remember during that time anybody receiving a phone call. It's a way of escaping the real world, I'm sure.

In 1972, you formed Stella Richman Productions with David Frost and there followed some productive years. Was that a good period for you?

That was probably the best period of all. David was the most perfect chairman. Nobody wanted to know about independence but until we got things up and running David saw to it there was enough money, and I was allowed to develop about 12 different projects. It was an extremely happy time.

Your planned series on Clementine Churchill was axed by Nigel Ryan of Thames TV. Was it simply a cost cutting measure, or were there other reasons in your view?

Entirely other reasons. Thames was a very rich company then, as it is now. It was actually internecine warfare between the managing director, Brian Cargill, and the controller of programmes, Nigel Ryan. *Clemmie* just happened to be convenient cannon fodder. I know this to be true, I'm not making it up. It was a great story, yet it was axed after they'd spent three quarters of a million pounds of real money. And all to massage somebody's ego. That's an expensive massage, isn't it?

Was that typical of your experience?

There are always clashes in any big enterprise, but if people are well mannered they manage to keep them under wraps. This incident was different because it was open warfare. There were two men at each other's throats; they sat in their offices and refused to see each other. And to write off three quarters of a million pounds was really extraordinary.

Was it disillusionment at the dropping of the Churchill programme which led to your leaving television, the thought of all that work counting for nothing?

241

Very much so. It was a bitter disillusionment, not to mention a year's work – I have the notes and the documentation to prove it. It was almost like having a miscarriage, that's the only way I can describe it, and I was left with the sorrow of it all.

You once remarked that people who intentionally crossed you in your career always got their comeuppance. Did you regard this as some curious law of nature?

[laughs] That was not my remark, but one made by my lawyers. At the time when I was divorcing my ex- and now late husband, the lawyer said to him, 'Don't be silly, because you know whoever crosses Stella always gets their comeuppance.' I would never have said it myself. And I wouldn't waste time wishing anybody ill in that way.

For example, Nigel Ryan, who axed the Churchill programme, lost his own job soon afterwards . . . it must have been difficult not to feel some degree of satisfaction . . .

[laughs] I know, I had to laugh. With him it was different. And I also felt satisfaction before he got fired when I made him do an unheard of thing. I felt he owed something to the people at Thames who were working on the programme, so I made him invite them all to the boardroom to hear his explanation of why he had axed it. There were about 30 of us in the room, all sitting round a very long table, and it was very interesting to watch him squirm.

Was he good at wriggling out of it?

For an ex-guards officer who had been head of ITN, no, he was very bad.

Your marriage to Alec Hyams ended in divorce in 1977. Were you able to regard that marriage as a happy period?

Nine years were very happy, the tenth year was very grotty. My children both thought we had some wonderful times together, and my daughter in particular said she could remember only the good things that happened, which is lovely.

What went wrong?

I think having two White Elephants wasn't enough for him. Alec was restless by nature and he wanted something which was created entirely on his own. It was that and the other women. I'm not the sort of woman who could sit by and not mind; you either have a marriage or you don't.

Did you manage to avoid bitterness in divorce?

Bitterness is not part of my nature, thank goodness, but I was intermittently bitter, mainly because I was deceived, and nobody likes being deceived. But it didn't last very long, which I'm very glad about. Like jealousy, it's self-destructive.

By that stage in your life, when you had the divorce, you had been married three times. Were you beginning to think that area of your life was ill-fated?

Yes, absolutely. It was my fault in that I was used to ordering people around and running things, and it was very difficult to switch off at 6 o'clock and go back to being Stella the housewife. I'm autocratic by nature, to my own detriment. My better relationships in terms of romance and love have been out of marriage, or between marriages, because I haven't expected anything from them or they from me and they were much freer as a result.

Do you think that it is generally more difficult to sustain a stable marriage when the woman is also highly successful, perhaps even more successful than the man, and therefore perceived to be in competition? Was that a factor in your marriages?

Not so much in mine, but I think it is generally a very difficult problem. Men swear it isn't, and women swear it isn't, but if you've got two high achievers in the same family a competitive element does enter into it. It is extremely difficult to get the right balance. It is terrible to generalize but a lot of men who consider themselves to be modern and want their wives to be equal in every way, really feel in their hearts that they're taking second place. They may be very proud of their wives – they'll tell you she's pulled off some amazing deal – but there is still an ambivalence. My first husband was half Italian and a very proud man. When I started earning money at ATV, and I wanted a new frock or a new suit or something, I would actually go through the motions of saying, 'Oh darling, I'd love a new suit', so that he could come with me and pay for it. He felt insulted if I paid for it myself because he was of a generation of Italians who had to feel they were supporting their wives financially. So I had to be very careful. It was a ridiculous game to play if you think about it, but it was worth it because it saved him from being unnecessarily upset and hurt.

You were undoubtedly one of the most successful women in television, but your success was not achieved without a lot of hard work and the ability to stay perhaps one or two steps ahead of the men in the business. I imagine that you weren't altogether sympathetic to the feminist view that women had an automatic right to be in the top professional jobs . . .

I always thought that was a monstrous idea. On my very first day as controller of programmes at London Weekend, two very senior women staff came to me, and the opening remark was, 'Now that we've got a woman in charge we can get our ideas accepted.' I told them that it would depend on the ideas. In the event they were absolutely terrible, just not worth thinking about, but I decided to pay them the courtesy of explaining why I couldn't accept them. They became frostier and frostier and assumed that I was turning them down because I didn't want other women doing anything, which goes to show you can't win anyway. I was very against militant feminism and the idea that women should be given more consideration than men. What the Labour Party has just done is absurd. By all means let us have more women, but only if women with brains are available. Pretty dresses are not enough.

Do you believe that women are still discriminated against?

I certainly read and hear that they are, but I cannot say that was my own experience. For 20 years I have been asked the same question: 'What does it feel like to be a woman in a man's world?' Well, there's only one answer to that – it feels marvellous, thank you. But I disappointed those women who expected me to say that I had the most terrible time getting to the top. I remember arriving in America at the time of the burning of the bra. Fashionable writers were writing anti-male pieces and women's lib was everywhere. I went to a meeting of 7000 women in broadcasting and they wanted me to talk about bodies strewn around, the corpses I had walked over to reach the top. But I could not claim that men had stood in my way at every turn, and because I didn't conform, my audience became very fed up with me. I think this eternal war between men and women is stupid. The final issue must be that all individuals, men or women, have to make the best of themselves and what they have to offer. It's no good to say, oh I didn't get on because I'm Jewish, or I didn't get on because I'm a woman; you've got to have enough confidence in yourself to overcome all these negatives.

You are the living proof that there is nothing to stop women reaching the top in television, but presumably you paid the price for success. How would you analyse the price, and was it worth it?

It was worth it then. These days I would not want to rise to the top in television because I think the top is ugly. There are no human faces there; it's simply business, business, business. You're not your own boss any more, you're at the beck and call of the money markets. Television very much reflects the state of the nation; the country's in a muddle, and television is in a muddle. I should hate it now, because I don't see there's anything but a business empire to go to the top of. The days would be spent talking about the cost effectiveness of everything.

You have always had a consuming interest in the lives of other people – you even list 'reading biographies' as your recreation in Who's Who . . . *why has it mattered so much to you to know and to understand other people's lives?*

I think it was A J P Taylor who said that without history man knows nothing about himself. I think that's it really. Without history you don't know about the present, and biographies give one an insight into history.

245

Reading about other people helps you to understand a lot more about what is happening, how everything repeats itself. Sometimes you find a spark which runs parallel to something in you and helps you understand yourself better. I get very disappointed with a biography which is not up to standard. For example, I recently read Daphne du Maurier's which everybody's raving about, but I found it the dullest thing because she is such a selfish, dull woman.

You have now passed the famous three score years and ten. Are you reluctant to grow old?

Not reluctant to grow old, but reluctant to accept the fact that in this country once you reach the age of 50, you're over the hill. I don't want to believe that because I'm 71 I must become a cabbage and that my mind doesn't work properly, and that I can't walk properly . . . because it's all rubbish.

Were you never tempted to marry again?

No. Definitely not. There are some people who don't have the talent for it, and I'm one. If you have the ideal companionship in life, it is much to be envied, but there is no point in putting up with somebody just because you happen to be together, or have been married a long time. I used to feel lonely but I don't any more. I have stopped feeling sorry for myself, because I realized it was absurd.

Has the physical desire disappeared?

No, of course not. It's not like one used to have, but one still has the desire to have a cuddle, let's say. It's not just a question of age; with some people, let's face it, sexual desire has gone at age 21 because they've never known the joys, poor things. But now at my age, instead of behaving badly, I think, phew, come along Stella, you're a grandmother . . .

WILFRED THESIGER

WILFRED THESIGER

Wilfred Thesiger was born in 1910 and educated at Eton and Magdalen College, Oxford. At the age of twenty-three he made his first expedition in the Danakil country of Abyssinia and two years later he joined the Sudan Political service where he explored the mountains of Tibesti in the Libyan Desert. During the war he served in the Ethiopian, Syrian and Western Desert campaigns with the rank of major. His widely acclaimed travel books *Arabian Sands* and *The Marsh Arabs* tell of his two famous sojourns in the Empty Quarter and the Marshes of southern Iraq. In 1994 he published *My Kenya Days* which describes the country in which he has lived for the past thirty years with the pastoral Samburu tribe.

Your life has been defined in terms of travelling . . . where do you now regard as home?

I suppose Maralal, in Kenya. I've been in Kenya on and off for over 30 years, and now that I'm older and have stopped travelling seriously, I've based myself there.

Presumably you still feel English. How important is your Englishness to you?

All important. I wouldn't want for a moment to be anything but English and I have a profound admiration for the English. I will also never entertain any running down of the British Empire. When people – whether they be English, or Americans or foreigners – criticize the Empire, they are quite unable to give one instance of brutality or oppression, apart from Amritsar which was General Dyer's personal error of judgement. That aside, there were no other examples of real oppression, which is an extraordinary tribute to the British.

Probably you feel as at home in Kenya as it is possible for a non-Kenyan to feel. Do you think this dimension of 'otherness', so to speak, of the outsider looking in, has made it possible for you to value their way of life in a quite unique way?

I am less involved in Kenya than I was with the Bedu from the Rashid in Southern Arabia, for example, or indeed with the Marsh Arabs. I'm happy in Kenya, I like being with the people, but I have not studied them or done any anthropological work among them. I just live with them.

Your autobiography is called The Life of My Choice. *Do you consider it to have been a very privileged life?*

I haven't thought of it in those terms. It's been exactly what I wanted to do all my life, and if something went wrong at any time, it invariably led on to something better. I don't think it's been privileged, because when I travelled with the Bedu in Southern Arabia, in and around the Empty Quarter, it was probably as hard a life as any human beings lived, including even the bushmen. I was determined when I went there that I wanted no concessions; I wanted to live on equal terms with them, face the challenge of the desert as they did. If ever they tried to ease things for me, I tended to react rather badly, and this earned me their respect and their loyalty.

But are you very conscious of the fact that if you hadn't had private resources this way of life would not have been possible for you?

I never had anything in the way of private resources. My uncle paid for me at Oxford and we were a poorish family until my grandmother died. Then my four brothers and I got about £300 a year. When I joined the Sudan Defence Force they paid me another £400, and since there was nothing to spend it on it accumulated. But it's never been wealth.

You were born in Abyssinia and your early experiences in Addis Ababa seem to hold the key to your adventures in later life. In your ambition to travel and explore, were you never deflected by the years of traditional public schooling at Eton and then at Oxford?

No. From the start, it was what I was determined to do. The event which had the most profound influence on me was when the Shoan army came back after the big battle of Segale. I still remember in detail the triumphal re-entry of the army into the town: the embroidered hats of the drummers; a man falling off his horse as he charged by; a small boy lifted high on shoulders – he had killed two men, but seemed little older than myself. At that time there was nothing Western or European about Africa; it was at its most barbaric and most colourful, and that made a great impression. In 1917 we spent my father's leave in India where my uncle, Lord Chelmsford, was viceroy. On our way we stopped off in Aden where the British were fighting the Turks not very far away. We stayed with General Stewart for two or three days, and he took my father and myself – I was perhaps 7 at the time – right down to where the fighting was, and I remember we stood watching the shells bursting over the Turkish lines. That was another memorable experience for a young boy. Then in India there was all the pomp and ceremony of the viceregal court. We stayed with maharajahs, we were taken on a tiger shoot, and so when I came to school in England I rather longed to get back to the adventurous life. Later, in the summer of 1924, Haile Selassie, at that time the Regent Ras Tafari, visited England. He'd been very close to my father who'd helped him a lot during the revolution, and he asked my mother and myself to meet him. We had tea and spoke in French, and he expressed sorrow at my father's death. As I left the room, I turned to him and told him how I longed to return to his country. He gave me that very sweet, gentle smile of his and said, 'You will always be very welcome. One day you shall come as my guest.' Four years later at Oxford, I received a personal invitation from Haile Selassie to attend his coronation. I was to be attached to the royal party, the Duke of Gloucester's, and that had a profound effect on me. I was the only person who got a private invitation. Haile Selassie had remembered the 14 year old boy and that touched me greatly.

It was always important for you to be more than a spectator in your travels, something which set you apart from other explorers. Was this because you wanted to live the life of the natives as much as possible rather than simply record and observe?

Yes, indeed. When I travelled with the Rashid they had never met a European, they'd never seen a car. For five years I journeyed barefooted because I wanted to be exactly like them. Again, when I was with the Marsh Arabs I wanted to get as near as I could to living as they did. Even in Kenya today, although I don't take it quite to the same extent, I do live a very primitive life.

How did you manage to bridge the divide, to avoid the master and servant relationship?

There was never any question of that with the Rashid; they would never have accepted it. It was I who was trying to live up to their standards, not only their physical standards, but their pattern of behaviour, something I found much more difficult. Their patience, their endurance, their courage, all these things were extremely hard to aspire to.

Did you come across the colonial attitude in your compatriots, or anything which smacked of superiority?

251

Wilfred Thesiger

I was extremely lucky because when I was in the Sudan I was under a very remarkable district commissioner who had travelled and lived with the Arabs there. His overriding consideration, and that of his men, was the welfare of the people they were ruling. There were no British businesses, there were no settlers, just the governing administration. It would have been different in Kenya where the colonists had settled.

Between 1930 and 1940 you did a great deal of hunting big game before there was any threat of extinction. You believed then that men have an inborn desire to hunt and kill – do you still believe that?

Yes, I do. I think it goes even to the extent of killing other men. It's well submerged in our civilization but if there is a war then it emerges at once. During the time I was in the Sudan, I suppose I shot far more lion than almost anybody has ever shot – 70 in four years. I never shot a lion with a bait, or out of a car; they were all on foot or ridden down on a horse. I was charged 16 times and knocked down once, and all the time I wondered whether I'd get away with it again. I believed they would kill me in the end, but I had the same sort of urge as those people who ride in the Grand National – they feel they'll break their necks sooner or later but they can't stop doing it.

But why did you kill these poor lions?

Poor lions! You wait till you've been charged by a lion as I was! Also lion were very numerous and were regarded as vermin by the Sudan government. You were allowed to shoot as many as you liked – there were no restrictions. Besides, if a lion came and raided the encampment and killed one of your cows, it was a matter of honour that you collected the men and together you went out in the morning on horses and rode the lion down. The lion was brought to bay in a patch of thick bush and after making sure it was going to stay, the men went in shoulder to shoulder. They had no shields, just their spears, and inevitably they were charged. Generally while the lion was killing one of them, they killed the lion, but I remember one time when they went out on their own they had seven casualties, four of them fatal.

252

Wilfred Thesiger

Do you ever have any moral doubts about your hunting days now?

No, not in that setting. I don't regret the fact that I hunted. I enjoyed it enormously and I felt it was completely justified. Thank God when I started my hunting there was no question of having a white hunter looking after me with chairs and tents and tables and all that sort of thing. Of course I'm a complete conservationist today, since so many animals are endangered, but that wasn't the case when I hunted. The last time I ever wanted to kill anything was in the marshes in Iraq where there were a lot of wild pig. I shot a lot of them because they ruined crops and attacked people who were cutting reeds to feed their buffalo. I was always stitching them up.

Your travels in the Empty Quarter with a handful of Bedu companions were amongst the most dangerous you undertook, and yet you regard this period as the supreme years of your life. What made them so wonderful?

Being with the Bedu, observing their qualities. The Bedu were the only society to which I could apply the term 'noble'. They had a nobility which was almost universal among them. Of course you can say that some of the British were noble – Auchinleck for instance – but you wouldn't call the British a noble race, at least I certainly wouldn't. The ordinary man you meet in the street has no nobility about him at all. But the Bedu were different; they were always anxious to excel, to be known as more generous, braver than anybody else.

You say you would have remained with the Bedu indefinitely had political circumstances allowed, and that you came to adopt their attitudes as your own. One such attitude was the absence of veneration for human life. How on earth was someone of your background and breeding able to assimilate?

I can't say I have this veneration for human life. If somebody had killed the two lads who were with me, and to whom I was particularly attached since they gave me everything they had to give in the way of loyalty and endurance, I would have joined at once in the hunt to find the killer. And I should have been hoping that it was I who killed him.

In your autobiography you write: 'I have no belief in the sanctity of human life.' But isn't that at the basis of what we might call civilized values?

It probably is. But then I don't think that I have what one might call civilized values.

You have always held Haile Selassie in very great regard, and indeed you helped restore him to power after the Italian occupation of Abyssinia. Was your admiration based largely on your personal knowledge of him?

Yes. He was a man for whom I had an enormous respect. Ever since he was a boy his one aim in life was to assist his country, to look after his countrymen, to improve their lot. On top of that he was a man who had no interest in money – I never heard anybody accuse him of avarice.

Ryszard Kapuscinski, highly regarded as an investigative reporter on social conditions in Africa, portrays Haile Selassie in his book The Emperor *as an autocrat who ruled by terror and insisted on absolute loyalty . . .*

That's absolute balls. This is something I would challenge very strongly. Back in 1932, for instance, there had been an attempted coup by Ras Hailu, the hereditary ruler of Gojjam, who was jealous of Haile Selassie and wanted to reinstate his son-in-law Lij Yasu as Emperor. The plot failed and Ras Hailu was arrested. Any other ruler would have confirmed the sentence of death passed on him for treason by the high court, but Haile Selassie merely fined him and imprisoned him. Later when Italy invaded Abyssinia Ras Hailu collaborated with the Italians and plotted time and again against Haile Selassie. In every other country in Europe collaborators were imprisoned or executed by their countrymen, many for offences less grave than Ras Hailu's. But Haile Selassie proclaimed that past offences must be forgiven, and merely sentenced him to house arrest. This is just one example of his humanity. He would do anything to avoid signing a death warrant, and in my opinion there was no question of his wielding power by threats.

Kapuscinski also suggests that the result of his corrupt policies was intolerable privation and misery for his people. Was there any truth in that, do you think?

Let's get this straight. His government and the people who were working with him were undoubtedly corrupt, as all Africans are, but there's never been any suggestion of corruption on Haile Selassie's part. You can check this with the Foreign Office. His dominant passion was the welfare of his country.

I was struck by the extreme dislike you expressed towards Evelyn Waugh who wrote about Haile Selassie's coronation. Why did he arouse such intense feelings in you?

I'm not quite sure. It was to do with his holding a court of his own and trying to make himself out to be very important. He got very angry with Sir Sidney Barton, the British minister, who hadn't invited him to lunch. Well, he was only a journalist for the *Graphic*, why should he have been asked to lunch? I disliked him on sight – the grey suede shoes, the floppy bow tie, the excessive width of trousers.

The situation in Ethiopia must now be a source of great sadness to you, and the reign of Haile Selassie must seem like a Golden Age to many of the inhabitants, perhaps even some of those who plotted against him . . .

Yes, I'm sure that's true. After what they had to put up with under Mengistu, with his utter disregard for human suffering, many must now remember their Emperor with the appreciation he deserved.

Do you think most of the current difficulties there are man-made, as opposed to natural disasters like drought?

I believe the droughts themselves are man-made. In the past there were no droughts on the scale that they've come now. We hadn't had them in Kenya, they didn't have them in the Sudan, and I think they are the result of the mass numbers of cars and factories and modern technology which are causing changes in the climate.

Wilfred Thesiger

Looking round the parts of the world you explored, it must seem as if you made your travels just in time before the countries were changed out of all recognition, whether it was by revolution or the discovery of oil. Looking back, is your feeling principally one of privilege and pleasure at having been able to do what you did, or is it blighted by regret at the disappearance of various cultures?

Looking back I feel nothing but happiness, but I am distressed by the disappearance of cultures. One of the biggest misfortunes in human history was the invention of the combustion engine, which has led to aeroplanes and tourism on a massive scale. I've always hated cars and aeroplanes, and even as a boy I felt that they were going to diminish our world and rob it of all diversity. It was much better when the fastest you could go was on a galloping horse.

How would you advise any young man nowadays with the same ambition and aspirations as you had all those years ago?

I'm constantly meeting people who say they would give anything to be able to do what I did. There are so few places left, but I think that in north-western China there is still some exploring to be done.

You are known to dislike America's interference in the affairs of other countries. Is interference ever justified, do you think?

Very rarely, and I believe that this is what has caused all the troubles in Africa today. If you take Kenya, for example, independence from British rule was achieved peacefully in 1963 under Jomo Kenyatta. Even when he died the transfer of power was peaceful. Why did the Americans and British not leave well alone? Despite the advice they were getting from two high commissioners who were dead against it, they wanted to impose multi-party government, which could only mean one thing: a return to the worst forms of tribalism. Up to that moment there had hardly been any trouble at all in Kenya; we'd had 30 years of uninterrupted peace, rare in Africa.

How does American influence differ from, say, former British imperialism?

256

The British interference was well informed. They had a profound knowledge and understanding of Africa, as did the governors in Kenya and elsewhere. I don't say it wasn't imperial; it was to some extent, but it varied. Generally speaking, however, if you don't know what you're talking about it is better to stay out.

A propos the UN's censure of human rights in the Middle East, you are reported to have said: 'Who the hell are they to judge how other countries should behave? Why should America be able to impose its values on the rest of the world?' Setting aside the obvious fact that different countries have different cultures, shouldn't there be basic standards of humanity in all societies?

I don't think you can impose them. For instance, it seems to me that the people the Chinese arrested after Tiananmen Square were threatening the country, and any government would have done the same. The fact that they were detained seems to me perfectly justifiable, provided they weren't brutally treated or tortured. What would the Americans have said 60 years ago if the British had threatened to break off relations unless the blacks were given the vote? The Americans would have answered – as Moy in Kenya answered – that is an internal affair, and it has nothing to do with you.

But if something is morally wrong, shouldn't it be morally wrong for all people in all places?

I don't think you can apply it like that. If other people in other countries do not have our moral standards, I don't see that you can impose them. Just as it is no good trying to force Christian ethics on a lot of pagans.

You have said you are 'reconciled' to the modern world. Is it not more resignation you feel in the face of something unstoppable?

I suppose it is. I deplore all the material manifestations of our civilization. Radio and television are extremely pernicious. I remember the moment when I heard the Americans were walking about on the moon, I had a

Wilfred Thesiger

feeling of desecration and despair; despair at the deadly technical ingenuity of man.

But as an explorer, wouldn't you like to know what is beyond our planet?

No. It's right out of my world. One of the things I liked to think when I went to live with Rashid and others was that nothing in their lives would be altered by my coming. Even though they benefited from maps which I made, I did not want to change these people. When I travelled among the Danokil, they were killing each other and castrating each other, but as far as I was concerned they were perfectly entitled to do so. I shot lion, they killed other human beings, and I didn't feel, by God, it's about time somebody took these people over and civilized them. I don't want to civilize people.

Isn't it a fact, however regrettable, that many of the African tribes do not want to remain immune to western civilization?

I think that's true. The most disruptive thing in the way of destruction of their culture is modern education. In Kenya, for example, a boy is supposed to go to prep school for eight years and then for another four years if he can make it to the secondary school. But even if he spends only three or four years in the school, the last thing he wants to do after that is to go off and herd animals. When I first went to northern Dafur, it was a closed area and nobody was allowed in without a special permit. There were virtually no cars and very few roads. The DC had a car and there were one or two others, but you could travel for two or three months and never see a vehicle. Consequently the world was restricted to the area in which people could walk. Then along came mass education and the facility of getting anywhere you liked in motor cars. In Maralal where I live we have what we call the 'plastic boys', who have been to school and don't want to go back and live with their families. They cluster round the town, trying to sell things to tourists, and their one aim is ultimately to get off to Nairobi. When the British were in Kenya – I admit the population was very much smaller – but there was no unemployment and there were no slums in the towns. With the mass influx to the towns, there are slums everywhere.

When you talk about the disappearance of the nomadic tribes of Africa and the loss of their culture and way of life, how are we to raise our response to a level above and beyond that of nostalgia? Is it available to us on any other level?

No, I don't think so. Change is inevitable, and although it's for the worse there's nothing we can do about it.

Tell me about the family you live with in Kenya.

I first met Lawi when he was about 7 years old, during my early days in Kenya. I used to visit a small town called Baragoi where there was a school. The boys used to cluster round the car and talk to me, and there was one in particular I noticed and thought quite remarkable. This was Lawi, and when he was 10 he said that he'd had enough of school and that he wanted to leave and stay with me. That was over 20 years ago and he is as dear to me as my own son. Later we were joined by another two boys and I have built them all houses.

And they regard you as their father?

Yes, in Africa it's much easier to become part of the family and to feel you belong. In England, however close you are to a family you'll never be regarded as part of it unless you really are part of it. I might be called 'Uncle Wilfred' or something, but I would still be separate. But here I do belong. And if somebody killed Lawi, for instance, my blood feud feelings would return, and I would certainly feel an urge to kill the man who'd killed him.

At the end of your autobiography you say that you have felt the need for human company all your life, and wherever possible have avoided solitude. Why do you think you have found the deepest friendships in races other than your own?

Possibly as a result of my childhood. A psychiatrist would say it because I was rejected by my contemporaries when I was a boy. When I went to my prep school I was pitchforked into an alien environment with an extraordinary life already behind me. I had no idea of the conventions that were so rigorously observed by small boys in England, and when they asked me about myself I started telling them about tiger shoots or travelling with camels. I found myself ostracized as the most appalling little liar. I was driven in on myself, and I longed to get back to Abyssinia.

Even now you live a very simple life, rejecting many of the comforts which most people desire or expect. Do you think most people would be happier if they were less materialistic?

Yes, I think possessions are a burden. When I left Kenya the other day I put everything I own into a kitbag and brought it back here. I've had no urge for possessions. All the time I was in the desert with the Bedu, I had none at all. The single thing I valued was my camera.

Have you ever regretted not marrying?

No. I've had some very close women friends, but I have had very little sexual interest.

Even when you were a young man?

Even then. I did meet a girl when I was about 19 or 20 and I felt that I really could have become very attached to that girl, but then I thought, if I do it will wreck my life. My whole life has been with men and boys – of course I'm not talking sexually now. When I was travelling I didn't often see a woman. Perhaps if we arrived at a camp there would be some women there, but then we'd be off again into the desert leading an entirely masculine life. Marriage would have crippled me. If I had been married there would have been children whom I would have had to educate at Eton or wherever, and there would have been no money left for me. Also, I spend only three months a year in this country – no wife would have tolerated it.

Do you prefer the company of men?

Yes, because my mind works in their terms. I do have some close women friends, Lady Pamela Egremont for instance, but when it comes to the point, I don't want to go on safari with them.

I'm sorry to labour the point, but can you imagine yourself being seduced by a woman?

No, I can't. I would resist it.

You haven't had much time for orthodox religion. Has there been a religious dimension to your life?

No. I find it very difficult to believe in a God or in an after life. I can't see why we're any more important than ants. I think man has created God in his own image.

When you die you say you want Lawi to pop you into a hole in the garden without any nonsense. Do you hate the idea of grieving and bereavement?

It isn't that. I just don't want a priest mumbling a lot of stuff which I don't believe over my body. Once I'm dead I'm dead, and I have no regard at all as to what happens to my body. They can put me in the garden and plant a bougainvillaea over me.

I couldn't help noticing that in your autobiography of 450 pages the death of your father is accorded only three lines and your brother's death in the war gets only one line. Is this the Englishman's stiff upper lip, or is there more to it?

When my father died I was just 9 years old, and although I was devoted to him, a 9-year-old doesn't really feel grief in the way one does at a later age. But of course I was desperately upset.

You have been variously described as 'the greatest of all explorers', 'the last of the great explorers', and so on. Does this recognition give you a great deal of satisfaction and sense of achievement, or is it unimportant in the larger scheme of things?

I think it's balls. I've done what I wanted to do: I've lived with the Bedu; I've lived with the Marsh Arabs; I've travelled in the mountains of the Hindu Kush and Karakorams; in Afghanistan in the uplands west of Kabul I have seen Pathans in their black tents and Hazaras in their villages, a people whose Mongol ancestors had probably been established there by Genghis Khan. I feel very lucky to have done all that, and especially lucky that in the course of these journeys the people who went with me didn't suffer. But all this business about 'the greatest of all explorers' is not justified. It's absolute nonsense.

HIS HONOUR JUDGE TUMIM

HIS HONOUR JUDGE TUMIM

Stephen Tumim was born in 1930 and educated at Worcester College, Oxford where he read history. He was called to the Bar, Middle Temple in 1955 and has been a circuit judge since 1978. In 1987 he was appointed HM Chief Inspector of Prisons for England and Wales by the then home secretary Douglas Hurd. He was asked to serve a further term by Kenneth Clarke. He is author of *Great Legal Disasters* and *Great Legal Fiascos*.

In 1987 you were appointed as Her Majesty's Inspector of Prisons. How exactly did this come about?

Having had a retired ambassador as chief inspector, the home secretary of the day, Douglas Hurd, thought it would be interesting to have a judge. He wanted somebody who would be objective and bring out what was actually happening in the prisons, not a civil servant, and not anybody connected with prisons. When he asked for a judge, the Lord Chancellor's office sent along a number of criminal judges from the Old Bailey, but they were found to be too established in their views, and so he asked for a judge who did civil work, and the poor chap got me.

Before then you had been a circuit judge. Looking back, does that now seem to have been an unexciting time in comparison?

No. I've thoroughly enjoyed all the jobs I've done, including being what was in effect a county court judge, and it was also a very good training for my present job. I'd been working in North London mostly with poor people, and then I moved in the mid-1980s to become president of the mental health tribunal where I dealt with whether or not people should be discharged from secure mental hospitals like Broadmoor. All that was a very useful background to looking at prisons which contain another category of unhappy people. Of course this job is undoubtedly much more interesting – it would be nonsense to say otherwise.

And more powerful . . .

Actually I have no power at all. I may have influence, but I don't have power. My job is simply to advise ministers on English and Welsh prisons. I also advise the Northern Irish secretary on his prisons, and the Foreign Office ministers on British Caribbean and Bermudan prisons, but if they don't like my advice they don't have to take it.

As someone who has worked in civil law, your knowledge of criminals and prisons must have been severely limited. Did you come to see this as a strength rather than a weakness?

265

I think it is a strength. I don't entirely go along with the awful English cult of the amateur, which suggests it's best not to know about any problem you're dealing with, so that you have classical scholars looking at finances, and so on. That doesn't really work, but I do think it's an advantage to have somebody who can ask basic questions, which is what I do in my job. I'm the only inspectorate which is not led by somebody who has worked in the field: the Chief Inspector of Constabularies is a policeman; the Chief Inspector of Social Services has worked in social services; the Chief Inspector of Probation is a probation officer. The problem with that is the obvious one – that you've known Charley for 30 years and you make allowances. That sounds awful but it's inevitable to some extent, and also you don't ask the fundamental questions because you don't think about them so much. What is important in a lay inspectorate such as mine is that you have professional advisers who include very experienced prison governors and civil servants.

In an article in the Political Quarterly *you said that your two main qualifications for the job were your layman's status and your independence. You were independent in the sense that you were not inspecting former colleagues, but some people might question whether a member of the judiciary can be fully independent . . .*

I don't think that anybody has ever really challenged my independence. Being a judge is a great psychological help in this matter; people still accept in this country that a judge is independent.

Were you a complete ingénu, as it were, about prison conditions . . . was it something you had ever turned your mind to before it became your brief?

No, never. I'd only once been in a prison, a visit to Wormwood Scrubs arranged by a friend of mine when I was first appointed a judge.

Effectively you were given a licence to criticize. Did this appeal to you?

Yes. It would be very boring to be a cosmetic type of inspector in which you simply told everyone they were doing a jolly good job. The home secretary specifically made it a basis of my job that I should be prepared to make public criticism if there was something that merited it. And this also applied to public praise. It seems to me they go together.

After your first two visits to Pentonville and Liverpool you said you could not understand why doctors and probation officers and chaplains were not making what you called 'furious complaint' about the degrading and punitive conditions. Did you ever discover why they hadn't made furious complaint?

When I first went round those places I came back and told the then permanent secretary that it was quite extraordinary that there were no lavatories or sanitation or washing facilities except very obscurely and then for only part of the day. I told him I didn't understand it. He thought it was lack of imagination and I think perhaps there was a certain truth in that. If you're used to something, if you work every day as a chaplain, or a doctor, or a dentist, you don't notice the stains on the wallpaper so much. You become blinkered. There was also a feeling that nothing could be changed; it had gone on beyond human memory. My approach to this job, like all jobs, is fairly pragmatic, so I said I wanted a plumber and an architect and a researcher to look into the question of sanitation. Within a year we produced a plan whereby there were five different methods of getting lavatories and drains into prisons. The cost of doing it was quite moderate, about £40 million for the whole of England.

But what were the main feelings prompted by your findings? Outrage, shock, a sense of shame perhaps?

It was the first time that prisons had received public attention in this sort of way. Ten years ago television court drama always involved a barrister in a wig cross-examining somebody . . . nowadays it's all porridge and prisons and the clank of gates. I'm exaggerating of course, but essentially I think that public interest has grown. My reports attract press interest in a way they didn't when I started. There's a change of mood, and people are much more concerned about prison life.

But did it ever occur to you that perhaps your reaction was an over-

*emotional one . . . if not, why hadn't other professionals reacted in the
same way as you did?*

It's never over-emotional to get angered by dirt and squalor; in fact it's
highly desirable. The reason the other professionals didn't was that they'd
lived with it too long.

But what about your predecessor?

He was a very distinguished man who wrote extremely elegant and well
argued reports. He didn't bring them to public attention so much. He was
establishing a new institution of public inspectorate and he took the view,
which I'm sure was right, that you have to get credibility within the system
before you can usefully go public.

*Is your philosophy regarding prison reform ideological, or is it more
pragmatic and utilitarian?*

Goodness me, what a question. I suppose it's much more pragmatic and
utilitarian, though that may be in itself ideological. I have always taken
the view that we have to ask a very fundamental question: what are prisons
for? To me their purpose is to reduce the rate of crime. I'm not interested in
making florid declarations; I'm more interested in cutting down the
numbers of burglaries. The next question you have to ask is what sort of
people go to prison, and it is clear that the numbers of terrorists, rapists,
mass murderers are very few. The great majority of prisoners are young
men between 18 and 30 who have both failed at school and failed with
families; they are not in a real sense educated – a surprising number of them
are more or less illiterate. They're the young men from the estate who
haven't got a job because they're tiresome and ill-educated and there aren't
jobs for them, and the offences they've committed are essentially involved
with drink, drugs and motor cars. The way we deal with them seems to me
to be perfectly clear, if perhaps a little boring: we have to train them, give
them social education, encourage them to talk to their families. The
prison's statement of purpose is firstly to hold them safely and securely,
secondly to treat them with humanity, and thirdly to help them to lead law
abiding and useful lives. The purpose is not to punish them – that's for the
judges.

But anyone advocating improvements in prison care will come up against the deeply ingrained attitude in our society of punishment and revenge. The appalling conditions in some of our prisons are seen by a great many people as fitting conditions for criminals to serve their term. How do you get beyond this attitude?

You have to apply education to the public here. Because an attitude is ingrained, it's not necessarily irremovable. Of course if you read the leaders of certain newspapers, they say bang them up, but that is not a universal attitude. There are other moods, and I've always found when I've addressed audiences of all political persuasions, a great deal of sympathy and understanding of the approach I advocate, which is let us try and reduce crime.

Is it simply a matter of education, do you think, or is there something more deeply entrenched in the British approach which it would be very difficult to remove? After all it is only a few years since Lord Whitelaw was talking about the 'short sharp shock' treatment and there is still a great deal of evidence in the present government of a punitive approach . . .

I think it is largely a matter of education in the sense of getting people to understand the problems. If you lock somebody up for 22 hours a day in a cell – something which is still happening occasionally – he's going to come out a complete mess and he's going to commit more crime. The bad prison is the one in which the prisoner is lying on his bed in the middle of the day; the good prison is one where the emphasis is on activity. I'm not interested in the nice or the nasty prison – those seem to me to be sentimental words which we shouldn't play around with. The prison should be neither a holiday camp nor a medieval dungeon. The ideal role model is one which is as near an industrial works as possible. Prisoners should work in good workshops for eight hours a day, earning roughly the industrial wage which would be paid, not by the taxpayer, but by the company who wants the goods. They could then pay tax, they could pay rent for their cells and their food, they could support their families which would reduce the social security round, and they could learn how to work which is something of which many of them have no experience. I've looked at some German prisons recently where this happens and it's very effective, and I would welcome that sort of approach here. To say, oh let's just lock them up and throw away the key is an argument of despair and sentimentality in my view.

This government, perhaps more than any other in recent times, has been seen to target the victims in society, the most vulnerable – unmarried mothers, single parents, and so on. Is the political climate conducive to implementing the kind of reforms you are advocating?

One's got to remember this government has been in power for a great many years. At the moment there are certainly people in the government who feel that things have gone too far one way and it's time the pendulum swung back a bit. But having said that, I think it's a perfectly valid time to push and press for the active prison. If I were suggesting that prisons should be nice cosy soft places, the government would be quite right in refusing to pay me any attention. But I don't notice any conflict of a serious nature between myself and the people I advise.

You have dismissed criticism of an excessively lenient approach to prisoners by saying that your first concern is that they should be prepared, after serving their sentence, to take a proper and useful place in society. But doesn't that give the message to the criminal that the consequences of crime are really not very serious, at least for the criminal?

I don't think it does at all. Firstly, nobody except the occasional madman thinks that prison is an attractive proposition. I've never met a prisoner who committed his crime thinking, well, it will be rather nice to get into prison. Prisoners absolutely hate being deprived of contact with their communities, their families, their girlfriends, so that the idea of prison as a nice place or not is simply a long way from reality.

Professor Eysenck, the distinguished psychologist, has argued very persuasively that punishment is an extremely powerful deterrent, and that those who argue otherwise have never really studied the evidence or are at the mercy of their prejudices. How do you respond to that?

Punishment is a very important part of the battle against crime, but it's a part that's played by the courts and not by the prisons. It's the job of a judge to take into account the need for punishment when he deprives a prisoner of his liberty, and it's a perfectly proper and necessary part of it, so I'm in no way against it. I'm in no way against the existence of prisons either. But does punishment deter? That's a very difficult question and Eysenck is very much in the minority among academics on this issue. Of course it might deter you or me from nicking a piece of jewellery if we thought we were going to be locked up in Wormwood Scrubs, but the evidence suggests that it is not a very satisfactory general deterrent. Deterrence is one of the weakest parts of a justification of punishment. If you look at the period of English history with the greatest rise in crime, it was the period of the Younger Pitt, who vastly increased punishment. He created something like 200 new capital offences, but the crime rate continued to rise. I believe that prison is for cutting the rate of crime, and that prisoners on the whole are ignorant and rather lost foolish young men who need to be taught how to behave. I am continually coming across prisoners who say things to me that show they've really got no idea at all of the difference between right and wrong or what they ought to do, and I suspect nobody has ever told them. We're facing a long term failure in our education system and I have a great deal of sympathy for the prison service which has all the time to act as guardians, as teachers, as parents in a way.

Eysenck also says that we have precisely the wrong psychological approach to the problem of crime, in that when a youngster commits a crime we caution him and tell him in effect that if he does it again he will be in real trouble. When he does it again he is told that the next time he really will be punished, and so on. Eysenck argues that this is a way of conditioning criminals to believe that crime actually does pay. What would you say to that?

I would say that modern research completely disproves it. We know that on the cautioning system used by the police in the last few years, 80 per cent of those cautioned do not reoffend. We also know that something like 80 per cent of boys in their teens who are sent to young offenders' institutions are committing the same sort of crimes and being caught within two years. The young offenders' institutions cost infinitely more and in my view are infinitely less effective with the majority of boys. There's always going to be a minority who are very difficult, but Eysenck is simply wrong on the facts as found in our society at the moment. Cautioning has been an enormous success, and there has also been a fall-off in crime by young offenders. The increase in crime is fairly specialized and relates to older criminals.

Do you believe there is a correlation between the crime rate and what might be called social deprivation – unemployment, bad housing, and so on?

It seems to me that it's quite impossible to say otherwise. The great majority of prisoners come from the inner cities, from poor deprived areas. They don't come from South Kensington.

How do you account for the fact that during the Depression and before the welfare state when people were seriously undernourished and there was real hardship, there was very little crime? BECAUSE THEY WERE PUNISHED HARD LABOUR BIRCH

I think we glorify that period unduly. Firstly you've got to tie it in with the efficiency of the police in catching people. With modern methods it is rather higher than in the 30s. Secondly I think you've got to look at the changes in behaviour, not just in England but in the western world. Also we must never minimize the significance of drugs which have had an enormous effect on crime. I recently looked at a prison where 65 per cent of the young men admitted that they were habitually on drugs, hard or soft, and there must have been many more who were actually on drugs but didn't want to say so. It is an enormous problem.

In your idea of the model prison each cell would have a toilet and a television set and there would be properly paid work and education and so on. How do you answer people who say that conditions for prisoners would then be better than for a great many law-abiding people in society?

If you're going to reduce the crime rate it may be that you have to put more resources into dealing with some tiresome young man than you would into somebody who isn't tiresome. On the face of it it isn't wholly fair, but on the other hand if it stops old women being raped and houses being broken into, it seems to be valuable and worthwhile. A great deal of what the present home secretary is proposing is based on the idea of carrots and

non-carrots – privileges if they behave well and non-privileges if they
don't. There is a lot to be said for this approach if you're running a prison.

*But unless you improve the quality of people's lives on the outside, which
is after all such a long term business, you cannot be surprised at least that
many will point to the injustice and inequity of raising the standards of our
prisons . . .*

You're not going to improve the living standards of people outside unless
you reduce crime. Short of executing all offenders, what do you do with
these young yobby criminals unless you educate them and teach them how
to behave? We all know people who have been mugged in central London,
just walking about their ordinary proper business, and it's that situation I
want to stop. I don't know any way of doing it except by taking the
offender in hand and training him in some way so that he won't do it
again.

After the publication of your report on Dartmoor in 1992 the Daily
Telegraph *leader criticized it: 'The trend towards table lamps for rapists
commands little or no support outside the ranks of professional prison
reformers.' I suspect you might label that kind of remark as a cheap gibe
based on ignorance . . . would you?*

I'm not a professional prison reformer. It's not my job to reform the
prisons; my job is essentially to advise ministers on what's going on. I also
advise them on what can be done about it, but I'm not in the position of a
prison reform trust or one of these organizations that exists to change
things for the sake of change. I have very frequently disagreed both publicly
and privately with those organizations who take an extreme view saying,
for example, that we oughtn't to have prisons at all. My report on
Dartmoor was very critical because I thought the government was wasting
huge sums of money in rebuilding a prison in the middle of Devon where
everybody is actually very law abiding. I would have abandoned
Dartmoor, and the only reason I didn't recommend abandonment very
strongly in that report was that we had spent something like £30 million
before I went there. Besides, if you followed the line which the *Daily
Telegraph* appeared to be taking, I think you would get more crime, and
this seems to me to be undesirable. A great many people take the view

that prisoners should have everything made nasty for them, one way or another, but it is philosophically wrong to imagine it will deter criminals. It may be that in Saudi Arabia you can reduce the rate of pilfering by cutting off the thief's hands, but if you simply make it insanitary, dull and solitary, then you will increase the crime rate and not reduce it.

Do you think capital punishment is a deterrent? OF COURSE ASK A RELATIVE OF VICTIM

I don't know. My objection to capital punishment is that there is this frightful risk of executing the wrong person. A murder is a very one off sort of offence, and those who commit murders are usually in such an emotional state that they're not thinking in terms of what's going to happen to them afterwards.

Your inspection of Dartmoor was carried out in June 1991 and the report was complete in October 1991. Why then did the Home Office delay publication for eight months?

I'm a profound believer in incompetence rather than conspiracy – probably they hadn't got enough people doing the right job, something of that sort. I have no reason to think my report was held back through a desire to conceal.

Some people have suggested that the report on Dartmoor was a bit of a fudge in that if you had had your way it would have been closed down completely, but that would have invalidated the government's investment in a refurbishment programme. Was there any truth in that?

There's a great deal of truth in that. I don't accept it was a fudge, but I have to look at things pragmatically and realistically. They'd spent a huge sum of money on improving this rather sad damp prison and common sense made it very difficult to recommend closure after £30 million of taxpayers' money. I think they were entirely wrong to spend the money, but again it was probably an act of incompetence rather than conspiracy. those who authorized the money at that stage were not the same people who were looking overall at what the prison service needed.

Would you not agree that your reports have been very demoralizing for the prison staff who have to cope with conditions as they are, conditions that they did not create themselves?

No. On the whole the prison service has given me a great deal of support and they see my reports as an opportunity to give a wide currency to issues they want raised. We tend to work together rather than hostilely. Obviously there are times when I criticize prison staff, but I would do so only as a good judge after putting the case to them and hearing their explanation.

Do you think Douglas Hurd had any idea when he appointed you of how sweeping you would be in your criticisms?

Douglas Hurd would have welcomed it. Indeed I have spoken to him informally more recently and he regards my appointment to have been a thoroughly good thing.

Were you perhaps surprised to be reappointed?

I've always had a very good working relationship with ministers. Incarceration is a rather grey area, and to have an objective and independent person is of great use to ministers. Also when I recommend, for example, 10,000 lavatories, it enables the home secretary to go to the chief secretary of the Treasury and say that he wouldn't suggest spending money on this sort of nonsense himself, but the chief inspector is calling for it.

Would you consider yourself to be something of a thorn in the government's flesh?

Not in the least. I see myself as a critic of sloppiness wherever it may be, but in my report on the Brixton escapes, for example, I specifically said that they resulted from local errors and that ministers should not be blamed.

His Honour Judge Tumim

Obviously you have to strike a balance between criticism and encouragement, but some would argue that you have not always got this balance right. For example, a few days before the Strangeways riot your report was published congratulating the staff on the improvements they had made. Was that not terribly embarrassing?

[laughs] No, I don't think it was. I have a theory which is rather like the French Revolution: just when things are going along quite nicely you get a riot. Once you start improving conditions, that is the moment you have to watch for disturbance. The governor of Strangeways at the time was busy dividing the prison up into smaller groups, and I think I was right to congratulate him, though I must admit I did look rather silly when a few weeks later there was this colossal disturbance.

It has been suggested that you were unhappy with the government's response to the Strangeways riot, and although you accepted the decision to appoint Lord Justice Woolf, you did not think he should have been allowed to conduct such an extensive enquiry into prison reform which you regarded as your job. Is there any truth in that?

No, there's no truth in it. I told the then home secretary who asked me to conduct the enquiry that it would not be proper for me to do so immediately after my report. At that stage Lord Justice Woolf was perfectly correctly brought in. He wanted to widen the enquiry and asked me to join him so that it was in effect a report by both of us. We had various advisers, but we were the two principals, and I would accept him as the more principal of the two because he was senior in the legal world and he also had the advantage of being an outsider.

You seem anxious not to be linked with any of the prison pressure groups. Why is that? Aren't your aims and ideas similar?

No, they're not. The job of the Howard League, the Prison Reform Trust and many other admirable organizations is to improve the living conditions of prisoners and to reduce the use of prisons. Those are entirely different objectives from mine. My job is pragmatic; theirs is much more based on dogma.

How do you avoid being perceived as 'do-gooder' – perhaps in the Lord Longford tradition?

[laughs] Devoted as I am to Lord Longford personally, I don't share all his views. I do think it's better to be a do-gooder than a do-badder on the whole, but I don't see myself as a doer at all; I'm an adviser, and my job is to form a judgement of what I see. Each of my reports is as subjective as I can make it – it's the sort of thing one might do if one were conducting an enquiry as a judge, which indeed I am.

It was reported in the Independent *in 1991 that a leading figure in prison reform had broken ranks to say: 'The problem with Stephen Tumim is that he does not listen to prisoners. He would not make them citizens by giving them rights which could be enforced through the courts. Instead every change he would like to see would be imposed from above.' How do you respond to that?*

I think it's complete nonsense. I do in fact always listen to groups of prisoners without anybody else present and I take very seriously what they have to say. I also have a large correspondence with prisoners, I listen to their complaints and follow them up.

We apparently lock up more people than any other country in Europe but this does not seem to stop the crime rate rising. Isn't this perhaps too difficult a problem to leave to the politicians?

But who else is going to look at it? It is a difficult problem, and I suspect we do have a culture which means that the length of imprisonment in England is probably too long. There have been some very interesting experiments in Germany where they've reduced the length of incarceration without increasing the crime rate. ABSOLUTE NONSENSE

You once allegedly got into trouble for saying that three quarters of the men in prison should be freed and the rest should never be released. That remark may have been incautious but was it based on an honest opinion?

The weakness of that remark is that it's a bit of a cocktail party remark, it's a bit epigrammatic, and epigrams are never very sensible. It's obviously not wholly true but it has an element of sense about it. There are a few desperate criminals who are on determinate sentences and have to be released at some stage, and who could indeed be a menace. On the other hand, I suspect there are a great many people in prison who could be safely let out.

Your work by its very nature is controversial, your reports provocative. Is this an aspect you enjoy?

I hope they are controversial. If they did not prompt discussion there would be no action, but I hope I never slant a report to make a sensation. I'm not worried by controversy if it's inevitable. And I do enjoy my job. It would be quite intolerable to do something one didn't enjoy.

But do you never long for the comparative calm of the divorce courts?

[laughs] I think divorce courts are far more stressful than prisons.

You have something of a reputation as a bon vivant – you're a member of the Garrick Club, and so on. Isn't there a fundamental irony, some might even say an indelicacy, that a man like yourself should be reporting on people who for the most part are at the other end of the social spectrum?

I think it's a very happy and fortunate balance. If I spent my entire life lurking around the grey world of the landings, it would not be of value and my work would suffer. It's very important that you should lead a life outside your specific work.

Our legal system is currently in crisis and the reputation of British justice has suffered heavily as a result of terrible mistakes. Do you still defend the system which you were once part of?

I'm still part of it in the sense that I'm still a judge; I'm paid as a judge, and I will in due course get a judge's pension. There are obviously a lot of weaknesses in the legal system, and as the years go by I get further and further away from the real darts and arrows of the legal system and therefore less able to produce useful judgements. But in my view all institutions are rather conscious of their weaknesses . . .

But what about the Guildford Four, the Birmingham Six? How could such appalling miscarriages of justice happen within our legal system?

WHAT ABOUT THE RENAULT 5 !

Miscarriages of justice are in a category by themselves. I think it's very proper that the Royal Commission on criminal justice has said that there really must be some external body, rather like the inspectorate of prisons, because without that even the most honourable can get into trouble. I have no axe to grind, but I do believe we have the best lot of senior judges we've ever had, certainly during my career. As for those who came before, it is impossible in an individual case to form any judgement if you haven't read the papers properly and don't know the facts.

But it was proven that there were miscarriages of justice.

Yes, but it doesn't necessarily prove that the judge did anything wrong. There were expert witnesses who were criticized, police officers who were criticized, counsel who were criticized.

Judges and their sentencing policy attract a great deal of criticism . . . are you one of the critics?

No, I'm not. I'm not saying they're all correct, I'm just not one of the critics. If I were the chief inspector of judges I would go and sit in court and watch and listen and look at the papers. If you don't do that I think it's very unfair to form judgements.

Your previous work experience, apart from the courts, has been largely for charitable and literary organizations. Was it a bit of a culture shock to move to prison inspection?

Yes, it was. Also a bit of a smell. But I've managed to join up some of my interests. For example, I'm chairman of the Arthur Koestler trust for the exhibition of art by prisoners, I'm involved with several other trusts dealing with art produced by mental patients, and so on.

Looking back on your life, what would you say were the triumphs and disappointments?

I don't know that I could claim a triumph on anything, but the things I'm most proud of have been in the prisons, particularly the progress of sanitation. I'm also proud of the fact that I have inspired and got going the removal and replacement of three prisons in the British Caribbean. In other words, it's not so much ideas as bricks and mortar. Regarding the second part of the question, I've had a life without very great disappointments. There have been the obvious battles of life, the greatest of which has been having children who were born deaf. That has been a problem which my wife has mastered much more than I have; I haven't done nearly enough for them, and I feel sad that I didn't make a bigger contribution to them when they were young. But they turned into perfectly admirable people.

Everyone in Prison is a Volum

vs ...d em! who cares!

Worry about the victims, the bereaved, the mutilated or the maimed in mind + body.